IN ANOTHER LIGHT

Gemino H. Abad

In Another Light

Poems and Essays

University of the Philippines Press
Quezon City, Philippines
1976

ISBN 0-8248-0471-6

Distributed outside the Philippines
by the University Press of Hawaii

Printed in the Philippines
by the University of the Philippines Press

To Mercy
be the mind's speech as green

Letter to a Poet
Who Knows and Understands
The Name and Nature of Poetry

Friday 7 May 1976

Dear Gémino H. Abad:

There is an English-speaking world

Thank you for letting me see the typescript of your latest book.

A poetry from the last landscape

The poems are fine—as ever; they are among the finest now being written in the English language: *Baby, Cradle and All*—I don't remember ever having read a poem published here or abroad in recent times that has moved me as much.

A poetica from the first poetics

The essays constitute a poetica—our first and, until Jose Garcia Villa publishes his own, our only. It is our first: what could be more natural than that it should be drawn from the first poetics ever, the original? It is our only—but how wonderful to realize that it is applicable not only to our poetry in English but also to all the poetry that Filipinos have ever composed, to all poetry in whatever language!

Poetry is the making of fine distinctions;
Philosophy, the making of most just.

What a fine thing this book is going to be! And it can only confirm what I have always thought about you: yours is a mind capable of making the finest and most just distinctions.

Faithfully yours,

Francisco Arcellana

Room 1074
U.P. Faculty Center

[vii]

Preface

For some time now, I have been fascinated with Wallace Stevens as a poet and with Elder Olson as a critic. They seem to me quite different in sensibility; yet, Stevens was a critic too, and Olson is also a poet. What fascinates me with Stevens is his idea of poetry as a gaiety of language, as the finest form of the joy of living, as the finest form also of the art of perception. What fascinates me with Olson is his approach to poetry, his attempt to see, as critic, the poem (any literary work) by its own light. Stevens says: The Snow Man beholds nothing that is not there and the nothing that is. Olson says: If anything is worth thought, thought must be worthy of it. Both are concerned with the same discipline of the mind.

I found then that poems and essays in criticism are not incompatible. The poems came that made up *Fugitive Emphasis*, and also a few essays. And then other poems went into a collection called "In Another Light"; and a research project with the UP-SSHRC called *A Formal Approach to Lyric Poems* gave rise, in the course of writing, to other essays now gathered together in this volume.

Thus, it happened that, when I found a hospitable publisher, the manuscript consisted of poems and essays. They bear separate introductions: for the poems, my excuse is a presumption (perhaps immodest) that some readers may be curious about what the poet (not the critic) may have to say for himself; for the essays, my excuse is a concern (perhaps unwarranted) lest another critic demand some other mode of criticism or approach to lyric poems which, though valid and legitimate as it may be, is simply not my subject.

The poet's task, I suppose, is always to try and see things in another light; and the critic's task is merely a variation—to see the poem by its own light. The poet and the critic do not address themselves to the same task, and yet, the tasks are not incompatible. This, of course, is not the thesis of *In Another Light*: the poems are one realm, the essays, another. After all, the poet does not begin to write his poems by first being a critic: he will not be able to write a single line of verse, he will always remain agitated when it is important to have peace. Nor does the critic begin to write criticism by first being a poet: he will not be able to write a single line of criticism, he will always remain unfulfilled when it is important to submit. But the fact that poems and essays are equally negotiable by one and the same reader is, if I may say so, a disclosure of the unity of the present collection.

GÉMINO H. ABAD

Room 1060
U.P. Faculty Center
6 January 1976

[x]

Acknowledgments

I am grateful to Prof. Elder Olson and Prof. R. S. Crane of the English Department at the University of Chicago; to the U.P. Social Sciences and Humanities Research Committee; to my own colleagues in the U.P. Department of English, especially Prof. Francisco Arcellana, Prof. Ma. Lourdes Arvisu, Prof. Concepcion D. Dadufalza, and Prof. Winifreda Evangelista; to my own students in various criticism classes; to Prof. Pacifico Aprieto, Director of the U.P. Press; to Mrs. Erlinda G. Mariano, typist par excellence.

Contents

[xiii]

POEMS

To, speak, of, the, interior, of, light,
Requires, speaker, broken, by, light.
VILLA

The soul may be the part of you
that sees the dream.
BALAYAM

To the Reader of Poems

Whenever one is a critic, one seeks to rationalize whatever of the thing called a poem can be rationalized. Wallace Stevens might also have had in mind the critic's task as reasoning, argument, analysis of the analyzable, when he said: "The truth seems to be that we live in concepts of the imagination before the reason has established them. If this is true, then reason is simply the methodizer of the imagination."[1] It is important, I think, to distinguish between the discipline of criticism and the discipline of composition, between the art of explication and the art of poetry (making the object or thing called a poem). The difference, to put it simply, is that one is addressed to the reason, the other, to the imagination; not, of course, that the imagination is not reason, but that it is only the finest form of reason, the finest form of the human native intelligence.

Let me illustrate the distinction with that anonymous poem called "O Western Wind":

> O western wind, when wilt thou blow
> That the small rain down can rain?
> Christ, if my love were in my arms
> And I in my bed again!

We see a parallelism of structure between the first two verses and the last two: the first two express the speaker's ardent wish for rain, the last two express his passionate wish for his beloved. What is the connection, the poetic or imaginative link, not strictly rational or logical, between the first two and the

---

[1] Wallace Stevens, *The Necessary Angel*: Essays on Reality and the Imagination (Vintage Books, 1965), p. 154.

last two verses? We see that the *address* to the wind is not real, but imaginary, a figure merely or a device by which the poet depicts *someone's* wish for spring; we see that this wish is not quite the point yet, but that it only projects the speaker's condition, his yearning for his beloved who is obviously not with him. And we see that somehow spring would reunite the lovers, just as winter has somehow separated them, though we know nothing more specifically concrete as to just how either season has separated or would reunite them. And perhaps, when the lover in the poem speaks of "the *small* rain," we think of the other lover in e.e. cummings' "somewhere i have never traveled" who also imagines the rain as having "such *small* hands"; and then, we see that there is a difference. In the *dramatic* context of cummings' poem (the context of someone's action or experience as the poem simulates it), "small" indicates, like other words in the poem (which are the speaker's thoughts), the lover's delicate, sweet, almost feminine temperament; but in "O Western Wind," the same word indicates only a tenderness of mood not inconsistent with the passionate male force of the lover's yearning for his beloved.

So, then, we see all these things and are moved by them to respond to *the speaker's experience as the poem depicts it.* The poet does *not* need to see these things; he already understands them beforehand in his poet's heart, though he may not be able to articulate them as the critic does. They are merely the *means* for his poem, the poem he desires to write— the poem of the private event, one possible poem of the lover yearning for his beloved. He has other means, and he freely chooses among them because he already understands what the poem he seeks requires. But the critic, on the other hand, *needs* to see all these means and other possibilities as well in order to understand and appreciate the poem, to understand something about the specific, concrete, mysterious process of its composition, to see how the poet might himself have seen, as in a vision, the poem that he sought. The distinct and acute disadvantage of the critic is that the poet is always very much ahead of him in vision and revision. Of course, when he is critical, it is fair to grant that he is not always "twitching his skin like a horse that feels a flea"—as Marianne Moore puts it, but Marianne as poet, not as critic. Criticism, like any field of rational knowledge, has its limitations. But the mark of the educated man, says Aristotle, is that he does not require more than what his subject permits.

I want, then, to speak familiarly from somewhat the same standpoint as Marianne's, midway between the poet and the critic. I am not writing another poem "On Poetry," but only saying something that I think I know about my own poems. I don't think, of course, that I can *define* what a poem is, what any poem is, even if I can tell what its subject is, here or there,—I cannot define *the poem* because, in the light of any possible subject, there is always one more possible poem-of-it. But if I cannot define what a poem is, essentially, I can at least say something about how my poems came to be. This does not require that I know exactly what any poem is, essentially.

We speak, often enough, of the *freedom* of the artist, but quickly forget, in our enthusiasm or commitment to a particular disclosure of poetry, that there are other disclosures. It is good always to bear in mind that our commitment to any idea of the poet as rebel from all causes or as social reformer or as philosopher or as any number of other things involves an expression of *our* freedom that we cannot deny to other commitments to other ideas of the poet. Indeed, no artist is free or can grow in depth or stature without that appreciation and respect for other orientations of mind, other realms of sensibility, other politics, other mysticisms. This is why the poet must begin with the poem *as an artistic object,* he must first establish its *artistic value,* before he, as an artist, can even be said to be free. *Free*: with respect to his art and its values, and with respect to other things and other values.

I assert, then, that I am free. But what sort of poems, then, do I write? The best way by which I can answer that question, from a similar standpoint to Marianne Moore's, is to say something, not about how they were written, since that would take too long, but about how they came to be made.

Whatever I read, I want the poem of it. This is what happened when I read Barbara Ward's *Spaceship Earth* (a poetically intriguing title)—in fact, I did not, I could not, finish reading the book, for poetic reasons. As I was reading it, it suddenly became for me a poem, and I wanted to see it clearly as a poem, on the virgin page, as it were; and so, the desire translating into act, it took the form it had from the beginning, and became the poem I have called "A Study of River Politics." I was convinced that it was a poem, and so, I wanted another poet, Alex Hufana, to see it at once, the fire of its creation still hot upon it,—and Alex, because he is not only a poet, he is friendly. But what became the poem, by that title I gave it, was not only what Barbara said on some of her own pages, not only *Spaceship Earth* itself, though I had not finished reading it; what became the poem was also the desire to see it as a poem, and also, the act itself of translating the desire, the act itself of making the poem and the special energy of that act. What happened was something like this. After I had read a few pages of Barbara, the desire to see her subject as a poem, the desire to understand and appreciate it from the standpoint of the possible poet of it, became so strong that I stopped reading Barbara, so strong and violent that I felt I did not need to read her any further, that I felt I already knew what she was going to say next and next since I already saw the point of it, the whole poem-of-it. I could no longer read; I kept seeing the poem-of-it. I had to stop reading, or else, I would begin to *unsee* the poem-of-it, I would begin *not* to see what even Barbara saw. I had to protect myself from blindness; I had to see the poem-of-it, as clearly as now, or never again. I must catch the poem-of-it as it is even now, flying away. And if I cannot be writing it now, I must be making it now in the mind. And so, I wrote the poem-of-it as I saw it then and, since it now lives on the page, as I shall always gratefully see it. And so, also, many of Barbara's own words are in the poem, many of her own ideas or thoughts are in the poem (perhaps, even her own feelings) but they are really no longer hers, they are mine, or rather they are the poem's; in fact, since they are now the words and the thoughts and the feelings of the poem, not Barbara's in *Spaceship Earth*, nor mine, as I was thinking and desiring the poem-of-it, they are barbarously the words and the thoughts

[4]

and the feelings of other men as poets thinking poetically of *this* aspect of man's political reality, and desiring the possible poem-of-it.

That other poem called "Ariel Must Be Green" is in a similar case. Preparing to teach Shakespeare's *The Tempest,* I began to see the poem of some part of it, the poem of the essential Prospero and the essential Caliban, the poem also of Ariel and Trinculo and Stephano; I began thinking and thinking poetically of that human tempest called politics, and desiring one more poem-of-it, one other poem-of-it that I had not seen, that I had not written, until I had the very poem-of-it on the mind's virgin page, the poem in another light of another politics and the poem of the thinking and the desiring for the possible poem-of-it. The rage of that thinking and the rage of that desiring are equal to the rage of the object of that thinking, the subject called politics, and the rage of the object of that desiring, the thing called the poem, the thing that confidently proclaims that *Ariel must be green.*

Whatever I read, then, whatever I see, whatever I think or feel, whatever I do or whatever is done or happens to me—I want the poem-of-it. It is my temperament, a habit of mind, even the morality of my imagination. And so, all my poems are in the same case. *Everyone watches a fire*—the rage of that thought, as I saw a fire, suddenly became a poetic rage, a rage of thinking and desiring for the poem-of-it. And so the poem is called by what it announces, "Everyone Watches a Fire."

What is that thinking and that desiring for the *poem-of-it?*—say, the poem of the *fact* that one must be glad that someone among us is a poet; or the poem of the *thought* that the millipede may have a problem, or that the goat is more than his scientific name; or the poem of the *event,* that mysterious and momentous event, which takes place in secret when someone, in going over to Harvard, say, crosses over to one realm of thought or sensibility, and, in going back home, crosses over and back to the native realm of her own thought or sensibility. What is that thinking and that desiring for the poem-of-it? One possible poem—possible because it already exists—of *the mere fact* is the *poem* that decrees, "Be Glad He Was a Poet"; one possible poem of the mere thought is the poem that meditates on "The Millipede's Problem," or the poem that belies "Capra Hircus"; one possible poem of the event, a past event no longer past, is the poem that bares the "Islander in the Yard."

In this sense, all my poems are derivative. In fact, all poems are: a place for the genuine, says Marianne, having somehow been located in the very raw material of their poetry; an imaginary garden having somehow been established among real toads who, in that garden, may croak and protest as lustily as they may. There is the poem of the trivial (or what seems to be), and there is the poem of the profound. Both have the same value as poems-of-it. The *it* is the original poem; the thinking and the desiring, the original energy of the possible poem-of-it. The poem on the page is one disclosure of a poem's nature, and one disclosure of the thinking and the desiring for the possible poem-of-it.

The easiest way to talk about the poet is to say that he is the instrument of his inspiration. A *passive* instrument, since the inspiration, whatever it is, triggers the rage of the thinking and the desiring for the poem-of-it. The poet must submit to his rage. But also, he is *active*, because of the thinking and the desiring for the poetic disclosure, the disclosure of the thing (a fact, an event, a thought, a feeling), and the disclosure of the whole poem-of-it; because of the act itself of raveling and unraveling the mysterious disclosure, until the possible poem is made possible, being written down and done. The poem now, as it lives on the page, includes within its own nature and among its special disclosures, not only the object of the poet's thinking, the thing disclosed, the subject of the poem, which may of course consist of many things together; not only the object of the poet's desiring, the thing called the *poem-of-it*, the thing that proclaims the poem's subject and, in so doing, also discloses its own nature as a thing called a poem. The poem now, as it lives on the mind's page—the poet's and the reader's mind—also includes within its own nature and among its special disclosures, the inspiration of the poet, which consists of many things together: not only that which first inspired the poet, which triggered

the rage of his thinking and desiring, which may be one so-
litary thought or event or even a single word or the sound
of it; not only that which vitally constitutes the poem's sub-
ject or, since it is perpetually subject to change in the poet's
rage, that which has at least become a vital aspect of the
poem's subject. Not only *that* is the body and soul of the poet's
inspiration, but also that which adds to the poet's rage, or
strengthens it, those things which are gathered into that rage,
like innumerable sparks from contact with that rage, such
things as the words and their sounds and the rhythm of verses,
and facts, events, thoughts, feelings, and their intricate rela-
tions, essences of the poet's experience and essences of secret,
imagined lives, all those things that thrust themselves upon
the poet and claim a nativity in the poem that the poet de-
sires. This is why, when the poet is at work, almost anything,
almost the universe of his humanity, may be gathered by and
into his rage, and made a vital part of the poem a-borning.
The inspiration of the poet, then, does not mean only that
which goes into the poem after it has kindled the thinking and
the desiring for the poem-of-it, and so, becomes a vital dis-
closure of the poem's subject; nor does it refer only to all
those other things which are gathered by and into the poet's
rage of thinking and desiring, and so, have also become vital
disclosures of the poem's nature. The poet's inspiration also
means the poet's rage itself, the energy of the poet's think-
ing and desiring for the possible poem-of-it, which thus be-
comes part of the poem's subject, and part of its disclosure of
its own nature.

But how, then, can one tell the poem? How does the poet
know that he already has one possible poem-of-it? From words
and words and words to their poem is a very subtle, complex,
inexplicable process of *transfiguration.* We cross over the fig-
ures, the poet's words, the moat of his thought, to the poem.
This thing, this object we call *a poem*—when did it become
one? It became a poem just as soon as it shed all its words,
moulted all its figures. The words of the poem *are* the expe-
rience; the experience *is* the poem, the experience, that is,
of the speaker in the poem. The words no longer stand be-
tween us and the truth; they have already served their pur-

pose and do humbly now retire. The drawbridge has been raised and drawn aside; we are in the castle.

> Time and place, the well-lit palace of his mind,
> Without drawbridge to outer geography.

I admit, of course, that my poems are sometimes difficult; that the reader is sometimes at a loss what to make of them or how to respond to or be moved by them; that he is sometimes escheated of a cherished thought, or even envenomed by a thought that the poem had favored awhile; that he is sometimes brought to a different state of emotion or a different level of sensibility or a different depth at which the mind probes, different from what he had at first expected. All these I admit. But the reader, to begin with, if he desires to read poems, must desire above all to see the poetry of the poem's subject, the whole poem-of-it. Otherwise, he may be looking for something that the poem cannot satisfy. So then, he must read this poem or that, and read it again (and perhaps, again), because how he reads the poem is also how he perceives it, that is, how he perceives the poetry of the poem's subject. When the poem was made, what had at first belonged to the poet who was thinking of the poem and desiring it, had somehow passed into the poem; and this transformation of the poet in his poem has a way of communicating itself to the reader. He who has read any poem at all and submitted to its influence time and again "knows how the poem," says Wallace Stevens, "comes to possess the reader and how it *naturalizes him in its own imagination* and *liberates him there.*"[2]

Dylan Thomas' poems (merely to illustrate our point) are difficult; and his most difficult poem is perhaps "Altarwise By Owl-light." Elder Olson (my favorite critic) says that it is "a meditation on the fate of man."

> The hero of the poem is a man who, aware of his sinfulness and mortality, faces the prospect of death. . . .
> [Thomas'] symbols . . . set powerfully and quickly before us the state of mind of the man contemplating. Sonnet I, surely, sets us at once in a gloomy and terrible atmosphere

---

[2] Wallace Stevens, *Necessary Angel*, p. 50; underscoring mine.

where strange things are happening; we grasp this much before we realize that the gloom and terror come from the contemplation of the sin-ridden mortal flesh, utterly without defense against death. . . . The images tell, step by step, a painful story, in which the Heaven he had once hoped for spells out nothing but his doom, until the message is complete, and he realizes that sin, the venom of the Serpent, is to a merciful God nothing but the necessary condition of mercy.[3]

Now, our point is, Olson could not have perceived the subject of the poem, the speaker's experience that the poem depicts, unless he had first grasped the poetry of the poem's subject; unless, that is to say, the poem had first "naturalized him in its own imagination and liberated him there."

One other point should perhaps be made explicit: that the poet has an aversion of the explicit, the declarative. But to digress awhile. Such an aversion does not apply equally to every poet—Burns, for example, who is often direct and literal, and yet, is a very good poet. Here lies, very much alive, an important distinction that criticism would do well to observe: the distinction between any poetic rule (a concept of the imagination that the reason has established or methodized) and what is merely a matter of temperament or taste ("de gustibus non disputandum est"). Our essay, now, for example, seeks a disclosure of the poem's nature; but it is not, strictly, criticism since it has to do chiefly with my own temperament. And for all its little rage, it is not yet the possible poem-of-it. It is like the frog that seeks his imaginary garden, protesting all the while his pure desire for it.

But, as I was saying, I have an aversion of the explicit, the declarative, in poetry. The declarative has a way of obscuring the sense of what it declares, of even changing the subject of the declaration into something gross or something which

---

[3] See the fuller and magnificent analysis in Elder Olson, *The Poetry of Dylan Thomas* (University of Chicago Press, Phoenix Books, 1961), pp. 63-89. Compare with William York Tindall's analysis in his *A Reader's Guide to Dylan Thomas* (Noonday Press, 1962), pp. 126-43; the same analysis is found in *Master Poems*, ed. Oscar Williams (Washington Square Press, 1967), pp. 1063-72. Tindall, unfortunately, misreads Olson, saying (for instance) that Olson thinks the poem is "about Hercules in the zodiac"!

one had not quite meant to say. One reason for this is that it is often flat, uninteresting, saltless; it is often too concerned for its own selfish sense that it does not permit other, even more important, disclosures that would give its sense what we desire, above all, from it—rondure, élan, opulence; it even loses its hold upon its own sense because it does not invite or compel one to exert one's mind on it, and the mind that does not so exert itself can see nothing, or only a very little, in another light.

ISLANDER IN THE YARD
(For C. D. D.)

I

Her memory of the Yard was unlike other
    memories
Since it had singular root without tears.
It was the Yard only in itself
That stood out in the space
Which the mind carved out of years.
No one who had touched a nerve
In the delicate web of her feeling
Disturbed the purity of that space
Which invincibly niched the Yard
Amid time's tumult and wrack.

II

                Even now,
As she stands on the golden floor of air,
The sun lurches toward her return,
Toward the far-flung archipelago
Teeming with castles upon the fertile
    cloud;
But she looks toward the Yard,
The sightless hours like shafts aslant
    its tunnel of trees,
And perceives again how her life,
Where it aches and most requires,
Is so much like a death remote from
    rite.

III

She was a stranger there, the metaphors
Of whose mind drove a herd of antelopes
Across the Tropic of Capricorn,
And for whom the lotus wrapped
All the poetry of the East;
She alone who had crossed without tears
Over the cities of her mind's burials,
Descried the promised garden in the wheel
    of light
Where stars dipped their tranquil spears
To dance around the sleepy Bear.

[11]

IV

So, now

As her gaze shapes the Yard
To all her migrations,
She finds the squirrel kneels to winter's
Sumptuous feast, for whom trees are
Alcoves to her song and its tropical aim.
The wind raises a chorus of leaves,
Their colors autumn's last exiguous sheen,
But dies suspecting a hoard of stamens
In the uplifted tassel of her exotic name.

V

Ivor, strong of arm, man without guile,
Who mocked the fragility of her quest,
Did bare the subterfuge in the wordy cage.
Let the denizen out, Madam, to less subtle
Climate than the mind's, and own the peril
Of stumbling after an egregious sun
To fall upon the waterless rock of your
    stance.
But what was she to do who chose to see
Through the imperious need for her reality
A bird-bath as stoup for the reverent wing?

VI

How strange

To uncover again his writ
In a dry heap of leaves,
The smoke of his revelation in chancery
For that one bold gesture
Against the solitary gift of fire.
Ivor's head lies severed from the stalks
That once bore it up near the sun,
O, where his eyes had sent the humble roots
    down
To the raging core of that enduring light.

VII

Time forsook the Yard, its sole inhabitant
    her song
Through which the ghost of Ivor passed
    without tears;
And if there she lingered, yet was it only

A ruse to comfort since, in the tropic
    of resemblance,
The mind climbs on stilts like a tall
    flower
The dizzy hills of its cunning prolixity.
How, indeed, was she to know beforehand
That the trees would corridor the ruins
    of flight,
That on the narrowest of passage should
    open
The countries of infallible desire?

VIII

She is builded
Of her images, and borrows her rhetoric
From the far-flung kingdom of her requital.
Is it a procession of toadstools in the shade
That celebrates the monsoon of her grace,
Or is there exfoliation of the mind's sheaves
Toward the summits of her summer's restraint?
Gazing toward the Yard, she can no longer doubt
What the titlark must hold against the light
That falls sightless where its praises take
    wing.

IX

If she was a stranger there, she took
The nearest death and passed into the garden
Where the hours throbbed green in the trellis.
She had surmised the fathom of his ire
When Ivor spoke of the white antelope
That bore a star on its brow.
To what steppes in the East, Madam,
Does it carry away the mystic burden of your
    lore?
But when the moon rose over the garden
The planets swung their great censers
    in trine.

X

Poor Ivor,
Shall the ivy cover the dividing wall
That your own space deems essential?
What fantastic compost shall breed gardens
Beneath the scimitar of your severe gaze?

[13]

The sky has set with all its quiet stars
Since last you looked toward the East
And shook all its spears—
The way almost that the lotus shakes its
    petals
Over the cool tombs of reflected light.

WHITE BUTTERFLIES

It was enough
Since it healed her day on a
    sudden
To have seen a tree besieged
By white butterflies.
Her neighbors seemed asleep,
She could almost believe it was
    a plot
To diminish her against their
    silence
Since she would be left with a
    revelation
Even she had not consciously
    desired.
So again it was to be forever
    unshared
Like so many things that wake
    in the mind
And find no one else there
But a sleepy ghost whose smile
    drifts
Across their wordless ruin.

She had seen how the white ant
Wilts upon itself when one
      removes
Its small, delicate wings.
Is it the same when one sleeps
Against the sun, the mind
Slowly decomposing in a green
    shade?
O, she had never yet resented
What was freely given
In those impossible realms
    of vagary
Which the mind had blessed.
The butterflies shall lift
Their gentle siege to loose
Secret flowers in their invisible
    wake.

THE YEARS

Now of the same
Dust, worse traffic, more unwelcome
      summer,
Remembering how other couples more
      quietly separate
When the alien sun in the room makes
Unbearable any more intimacy,
Go with her to meet the small day's fate
And then return alone the same way,
The radio on louder for self-control
Since you imagine her at her desk
Bewildered by the strange cruelty
Of having to earn the means to live,
Because the means alone confer the
      right,
While through all that time of years
The very space of living is slowly
      devoured
By typewriters ceaseless like the
      clock—
O the years have turned to locusts
That batten upon the living grain!

            How does one stop the mind
When it does not itself know until
      late
That it has taken a deep measure
      of the past
And hurt itself incurably,
Only seeking more privately to rue
More private deaths than consciously
      borne—
Friend, show me if you know the route
To another summer not dishonored
By those ruins the mind stumbles on
When, weary of refuge or comfort,
It only dreams of a tranquil relation
To the past.

What dust, what unwholesome summer?
While these are indeed the invincible
Joints in time's own body,
You might imagine her differently,
Since there is nothing false, either,

From the other side.
In fact, you must not see her too
   clearly,
It presumes more than the truth
Which her absence quietly promulgates.
She must move invisibly through your
   space,
Which is how she repairs discontent
And weaves patiently through works
   and days
A skein of that wonder you had once
From the archaic light of her stance.
Go with her to share the small day's
   fate.
The locusts have more power in the
   mind
Than over the land they rudely wound.

Get me, said the prisoner,
Virgin paper.
The rats, sir, trouble my sleep
In which the wordless moon,
Thinking I have died,
Lies afloat, her long yellow hair
Wound about her old tired body.
I will sit here, then,
And invent novel speech
To compose the voyages of her mind's
Frail yearnings.
The past has no hold on me
Since it has been endured and at last
Forgiven,
And the time yet left to me
Is wide of wing
And legendary,
Like a bird at sea
Untroubled by the distance to shore.

She must not think of death
When she is companionless.
I will sit here
And invent what mind will not tell,
Wary of affliction
That lies in the word's ambush.
How often I have watched her rise
To my cell's window,
And wondered if she looked as desolate
From a bench in the garden below.
But I cannot bear thinking,
How does the garden look in the day,
Does it gather her into its trees?
When I am set free,
I will go there and wait for her
To renew her tale,
But I fear it may not be as I think
Since there may be nothing to see
Where one loves to be in the sun.

IMPRESSIONS OF A GUITARIST

If her hair were not golden
but dark,
dark, so that the light could not invite
to any thought of dawn,
        if her long robe were crimson
or red,
dark red, so that in the light
music could shape secretly
the perilous energy of her truth,
        how,
in that momentary dark,
could her audience survive
the quick and solitary pantomimes of her
        sound?
Or is that music they are rapt by
merely fictive,
a wreath laid upon the cold stone
of desire,
or is a deep stirring
toward her own truth
at last comforted, made gentle
upon the tide of her shoreless sound?

It is what you might call a skill
in the documentation of feeling,
every nuance and turn,
it is also what the old fool, the poet,
does with words you daily speak.
Her fingers tense for each note
like spiders dancing across their void
(where her audience dare not move)
to weave the invisible web
of her cunning
or erect from uninhabitable air
the impregnable ephemera
of her heart's tale or predilection.

What strange spiders
the sudden lives of those fingers
dancing upon the passive string,
running across the body of her sound
down and up and again,
restless for human prey,
and insatiable,

having traveled far
even to realms have not been broken
by the applause of comprehending hands!
So wide and deep is their estate
beyond the scope or hope
of a conquering thought,
their web may not be unwound again
or the ephemera be rebuilt.

THE EYRIE OF DESIRE

To imagine how desire may sleep
In its cage, he chooses the dark,
Not that darkness is the perfect
      choice,
But of late there has been too much
      light,
Speech lost the novelty of thought,
Too simple, too bare, the structure
      of the act.

What to imagine is not in question,
It is the manner of sleep shall
      soothe
The imperfect peril of his choice;
The cage is that shape which rebuts
      objection
To shut out his dream for excuse
And end the frail tenure of desire.

Since thought is exiled to dark,
It lies in state, as a leaf closing,
When the light is too westward for
      light;
But such sleep is a particular tone,
Like the voice in human sound,
In its particular cage.

It is a pure way of being:
The leaf closing when it will
By a green, infallible recoil
      of nerve.
Too westward for light is light:
The deed engenders its wreath, green
Wings of sleep folded in the eyrie
      of desire.

Why devise matter for sneering
As we grow old against those we
        love?
Was ever their youth, sacrificed
        to us,
Less hospitable for the fiction
        of their vows?
Though your hands might have worn
All its doors, you can't simply walk
Into someone's life.
Nothing there is definitely settled,
No one can help much.
To love long, and patiently,
Though without certainty,
And be made clean,
Like a tree stripped of its vines
—For this our world had no plan,
Neither can we design one
For future need.
            Sherwood, how smart we are,
How aptly we put things!
The wind over those woods
Bears no dry leaves for us.
We are too far out upon our hill.
            Just so.
But what is it we do not already
        know?
Let the sun take root in the eye
Or take hold
Of the last flowering thought
And requite it for so much bloom.

LOOKING FOR A PARTICULAR FLOWER

It was impossible from the start,
not only because the shops had, of course,
to mind other people with other needs—
a nude, a seascape, an abstraction
of something violently unannounced,
—and not only because the children
were at the zoo, looking for a giraffe
or a wild antelope carrying a bit of the forest
on its head, looking and dreading lest we come
too soon with our flowers;
      No, the reason had to do most
with the flowers we had needed to see,
captured once and for all in a particular way,
and yet dreaded to see,
the light falling in just that way,
as to wear the flowers for raiment,
so that it would not be easy to say
whether the light had first descended to their
      bloom
or the flowers had first ascended to it,
or they had only met halfway, as it were,
between their first conception and the last
      finishing touch.
      No, not this still life,
there is much of the desert yet
in the solitary grandeur of this sunflower
that endures the day's end;
nor this,
since the vase suggests a cold hospitality
to the weed's ghostly bloom;
and though that might do,
if the window were only half-opened,
yet something in the stir of the breeze
brings news of other flowers
that seem a deprivation of light;
and that, too, asserting itself on the beach,
the starfish imitating its lonely scope,
is it not possible it had once had
a depth of light at the sea's slimy bottom
which it had lost for having come ashore?
      No, the shops did not have
our particular flower,
since either the light had descended too soon
      upon its bloom
or the flower had ascended too slowly to it;

And since it was toward noon
and the children might already have tired
of the shy, magical giraffe,
or found the antelope a little sad
for the forest it always remembered,
we were leaving, tired of unsatisfactory
        flowers,
finding none that bore just that bloom,
and that the light gently claimed, —
we were just leaving, thinking of the giraffe,
her small head perhaps gently swaying
among thoughts of forest leaves,
and the wild antelope, his plural antlers
a study of those solitudes that gave him strength,
we were just leaving, Let us go,
the children must be impatient by now,
without dread of our flowers,
when we saw the peacock among nudes
and seascapes and abstractions,
and knew at once, as though convicted,
that he carried all the flowers of the world
and of the future,
that in him, when our children grew,
they might learn of our particular flower
and, thinking perhaps of giraffes and antelopes,
discover a dread of shops,
lest one identify in a picture
their particular flower.

BABY, CRADLE AND ALL
(For Tosi)

There was no help or quick or
potent enough. It was, clearly,
the end.
      And so he might be
forgiven a little bitterness:
the stars promised eternity
to his child's soul in a cold,
remote twinkle of obscure speech,
but it was not for succor he looked
to them, no, it was not for super-
natural space to contain this
loss.
      Full of that knowledge
that once had stood in the middle
of sleep and mocked the song,
he had no time to look idly
down a street and spend his mind's
recognition on a stranger.
      It was, clearly, the end,
it was that he had to meet again,
turning from the gate,
climbing the stairs,
inventing the words of comfort
where it had no shape,
except that his wife, who had not
seen the stars nor heard the fall
of their light, might also invent
the speechless word of their assent.
      Who could tell
if in that sleep his son,
too young for thought, learned
a motion toward their secret wish
that he look from his cloudy bough
where the wind rocked all his years
to rest,
      and cheer
the scape of their mind's sheer
plot toward a flowery wreck
of its presumptuous dream,
      cheer
with constant weather of his
innocence to help the mind
cradle the swing, the still
burden of that windy truth?

And so in later time,
the stars drifting in the wind,
a scatter of their cold light
all in stipple upon the tide
of a thought that once had seemed
to break upon a desolate shore,
it might be found that it was all
in song, but the sense of the words
different:
            the gust did nip
the stalk of his sound so the next
stroke and blow might gain a play-
ful touch,
so the next shoot of his ambitious
thought might learn to bend
and the bloom to come be made more
competent to endure its weight.

CHILDREN'S PARTY

Where they would have to dance if bidden,
The children claim their balloons and candy
 bars,
Then retreat from the music that threatens;
And soon lose interest in the enforced
 celebration,
Missing their paper boats in the ditch,
The familiar backyard, the deserted alley,
Where, though there are no balloons,
Except sometimes a yellow moon caught
 by the narra tree,
Time passes in the whirring of crickets
And seems to end too soon,
Their novel games not quite played out
Even in their sleep.

No, they did not look forward to this,
Even to wear a new pair of shoes;
They could not imagine the empty space
Which, till now, has not hurt them;
A hurt stranger than any fall
From a tree or in a dream,
Since they fall on nothing solid,
With sudden knowledge of their bodies'
 weight,
But only keep falling and falling
Through something that smiles at them,
Then looks away, still smiling,
Yet not with half the moon's light.

Their papas and mamas sit and talk
 of endless shocks,
Revelations of things they did not know
They had forgotten,
Yet only make merry for the occasion;
Their thoughts apart travel far inland
 of mind
Toward a merrymaking on a moonlit night,
And the antique moon they kept
Till their hearts ached in its light;
O, but they will not acquiesce to its
 rising
Nor acknowledge the late access of its
 tale,
Since one must not think too precisely
On what has already passed.

[27]

CAGAY REVISITED

And what about the town you only
remember?
Papa is dead
who used to gather fruit of the banana
with a long bamboo pole with a hook,
the great War hid from us
since we played in his shadow.
What have we to do now
with refuge?
A dog barks
and distance seems a loss of mountains.

And the moon has long set
so that the sky cannot hold
any thought across its dark,
except, of course, that Papa somewhere
with his long bamboo pole
may move toward morning
when children of yet another War
look to the mountain for their interrupted games.
To dream of another harvest,
tadpoles that live longer in water cans,
what bivouac in our time?

The town is lost
where the mountain drove our voices
into leaves and the bark of trees;
and perhaps the mind cannot reach it now,
it will first have to dissolve into rain,
move like mist through the trees . . .
except of course that Papa somewhere
may be moving toward morning.
He shall wake his old children
to their dream, to catch the fruit
his pole has chosen.

HER LONG PREVAILING

Who was it dreamed that truth
Was a dream all a-ripple
Beneath the dark keening tide
Restless for its shore?
For those eyes, with their hoard
Of kingdoms shut against our ken,
Shall a skiff of shallow draught
Venture upon the vaulting deep
To disembark its phantom crew
On the solid bar of their barren
    watch?

How many more lives must the soul
Pass through, enduring the coil
And waver of her own touchless
    gleam;
How much more steep and deep
The perishing climb of her flame
Through and through the smoky brows
Of the roil and foil of her counter-
    vailing;
Under the passing stars,
Lost brede and portent of her sky,
What deed shall perish her endless
    unravelling?

Of the world, in the world,
The mysterious angels of her
    wandering,
By which her feet shall quench
The wash and toil of the tide;
The minstrelsy of her mournful flame,
By which her eyes, before she was,
Shall weave wreaths for the phantom
    watch,
And so at last bring the lingering
    horde
Of passing stars, cresseted with her
    pasts,
Out of the durance of her long pre-
    vailing.

This is my body, he said,
And this is my blood.
Eat, drink, and be merry
Forever, he said.
But a thousand or more years
Was too long for the momentous,
The literal.
No word could hold it unwounded.
And we have ourselves invented time
And history, its patient and endless
Rewording of our survival,
Each one, for fear of the timeless
And space,
Content in the exquisite tomb
Of his saying.

This is my body, he said,
His speech made us delicate;
And this is my blood, he said,
Profound rhetoric of our need.
But not content with the event,
We interpret and reinterpret the sign,
And rise to take our own bait
And are duly fed.
A thousand or more years
Is too long
For the intimacy of his communion,
The scripture of memory
Too weak for a link
To hold us fast even to truth
Or to desire.

WHAT HE MEANT

He said what he meant,
Building his synagogue in the foxes' lair
And the field of blood,
But what he meant beckoned away
Beyond itself.
        And now,
Without our mortal dross,
And invulnerable like the air,
Will he not speak at our bidding,
Is he so estranged from us
Who had not had the courage
To understand?

His words hurt so,
Like the light on the blind man
Who had asked to see again.
We remember,
But would not die again.
His speech had power
To move us strangely into deeds
We would not do without further reason.
We feared the cripple
Who stood up in our midst
And wept when he understood
The weariness of human distance.

He meant what he said
But we would not enter
Into the kingdom of his word
Since we had sheep to tend
For our livelihood
Or women who offered forgiveness
Without much loss.
        To speak of him now
Is to think apart,
To lift a cry at the edge of the crowd
That mobbed his healing power,
Then left him a prey to his fearful
    meditation.

Oh, if in the valley of the shadow
Of his saying,
We were swiftly unsaid
That the lie may lie sheer

And wither,
Grass of our mind's summer;
Oh, if bravely enough,
By little and little,
We should take our part
Among these passing, irreversible Acts;
Oh, that the season of his grace
Wound the ground of our fearful need.

THE MIND IS CLOSED BY HYPOTHESES

The mind is closed by hypotheses,
We must let time pass
For other hypotheses to succeed
Who, in turn, bar the door
And down pull the blinds
Against the others who,
As once they did, press hard
And shiver and quaver without,
Unwelcome ghosts
To the smouldering hearth.

It was not any particular angle
    of vision
That mattered. What he needed
Was to have done choosing one,
      And then,
To remain seated where he was,
Faithful to what he saw from there,
And keeping pure,
Not confusing the things he saw
With what he was, or remembered,
Or desired to be,
Not even requiring a subject
Or an atmosphere
Which might authorize his stance
And cancel the element of choice.
What he needed, above all,
Was a mastery of that angle of vision
That he had chosen without intention
To promote a legend,
A mastery which meant that the things
He saw were seen —
Not for the sake of a subject
(Since the things then would become
Too definite and die as of shame) —
But only as the things themselves
Might see him if, seated
Where he was and only looking on,
They too had renounced memory,
Desire, the itch to promote
Their own deep legends.
      So, finally,
No difference would exist.
In the work which perfects his own
    seeing
And in the things themselves,
There would remain, root and crown,
His choice of an angle of vision
That in the end mattered above all.

THE MILLIPEDE'S PROBLEM

The millipede's problem,
That he has a thousand feet,
Is insoluble.
            Yet, if one foot
Cannot help itself, and two
Were enough for speed,
Why, indeed, may it not seem
A thousand would sweep
Swifter than thought?
            And then what
If one body were proportioned
To its thousand articulations?
What article in nature
Confounds the speculation?

Beg your pardon, sir,
But the millipede, perhaps,
Had better be asked for his
        opinion.
What, say, if he must needs
        crawl,
If a thousand feet, not more
        nor less,
Were apter than any number,
Bred merely of speculation,
For strange perhaps daintier
        uses
Than we could imagine
If we should be inclined to
        creep
Along the ground of his meek
        regency?

Consider that small body,
Its bright armor of soft metal
Beyond our skill in forgery,
And how it moves in the dust
Like a lesson in patience.
May it not be, rather,
That for his slow existence
Such equipment is requisite
As repels our profoundest
        observation

When we have only ourselves
For reference?

            To understand him, sir,
We must first learn to move
Toward that reality which even
    he suggests.

CAPRA HIRCUS

Children will chase a goat
Far afield
To force a crooked ride
Upon his back
Through pliant hours
Of their unfettered whim.
If he butts with his horn
Or tugs at the rope
Of their imagined war,
Will it bring him any closer
To the sere grass
Of his distraint?
      No, he will not
Take it unkindly,
This raucous breach of his
    leisure,
If some way be found
To make him view their concerns
At some angle of our sun
Where he will not miss his
    grass.

Was it so long ago
That, adorned with our chaplets
And cheered lustily on,
For the loneliness of his
    enterprise,
He was led to the desert's
    edge,
And his tracks,
As our seers observed,
Skirted oases
In favor of the burden
Upon his back?
      Other reports have it
That he threaded the eye
Of the simoom,
Then hung it on a withered
    bough
To dry blind.

What, then,
Are those fierce concerns
That drive children far afield
To establish a noisy pageant
Amid his preoccupation?
A piece of string, a broken
    eggshell,
A dead cat—
Do these hint
At business of some heat
If a vacancy of effect
Should rue the unpremeditated
    act,
And then ignite this project
On the still top of noon:
        A sudden procession
To the desert's edge
To test the truth
Of old reports,
That he will bide the storm
    yet to come,
And when his labor is done,
Disappear
Where his tracks end,
The storm buried in the sand.

An upheaval of grass
Shall cover the ancient spot,
Their green wave
Rolling through shoreless time,
Where once our children stood
Bareheaded in the sun,
And he, grazing at his leisure,
Had expected them to come.

THE OWL IS A BIRD OF PREY
(For Jonah)

No minstrelsy of fear has wrought that grace
By which a swift succor is won
For the creature brushed by his unexpected wing.

He quells quickly the sound might warn
Of the dark peril of his infallible eye,
Of the fell swoop of his sudden reign.

Rare and rank the ransom of his catch
If his thought be rapt to a further bough
For reconciliation of talon and wing.

What wisdom has plumage of his deadly toil,
Reek and rapine of his crooked beak,
Or hazard of his wing or mastery of his demesne?

He hoots at odd hours of his watch
To toll the ghosts back to their lairs
Yet tells no tale of the ambush of his aim.

He does not pause for poise in his climb
To pass through a cloudy round of desire
And perish upon a hush betrays his design.

The gorges of his eye endure no light
By which to unravel his ways and wiles
And make the venturous sum of his lore.

The owl is a bird of prey.
What wisdom has plumage of his deadly toil,
Or hazard of his wing or mastery of his demesne?

THE HUMAN JUG
(For Doming)

I

Oh yes, I have read the poem
Over and again. It's called
     The Human Jug.

II

But what is that we call
Human? What poem
Shall touch it asunder,
Then lure its parts back
To mind's wordy involucre?
A hard beginning for our
    analysis.
Let us say we understand
What is human.
       At once we see
It must qualify the content,
Not the container, this jug,
Which is merely accidental,
Like webs for what might have
    been feet,
Or fins for wings;
       Though the container
Is of some importance yet,
Whether it be of earth
Or glass,
    Or whether the liquid be cool
And clear
Beneath the small aperture,
Or whether the handle be easy
    to user
Who if he will may tilt this
Jug to the curious observer;
       But if the observer
Be an unknown factor,
Why should the jug's owner
Do him favor? Does his jug
    suffer
From lack of observation?

III

The poet must ask questions
Though his leman scoff
At things and jugs, and point
To the infinity on hand:
The thing has an indwelling
Beneath the exactitude of its
 clime,
And there persisting,
Delicately shaped,
He must name it with the word
 most apt
At the depth at which he sees
This jug—
Not demijohn nor grail—
Since it happens it is part
Of a poem's rare career
To imitate the nightingale's
 note
Presiding over the precise
 plight
Of lovers beneath the golden
 bough.

IV

  This jug
Is the exact shape of human
 solitude
Beneath the rampant augury
 of the word.
  Whether it be
Of earth or glass,
The native grain of it matters.
It will make a difference
How it breaks,
How the intimate pieces lie;
  Or whether
Its ghost-stippled draught
Lie to a poise and steep
Beneath the lovely-imminent
For the gush, for the flush
At the brim;
  Or whether
The handle be not fragile
To the skillful hand,
The will to tilt the jug

To the curious stranger.
      For be
His drink or sour or sweet,
The grace of it persists.

V

     And certainly,
If the drink be offered
Without stint, will it be far
From the tippler's mind,
That nightingale
Who, in the dark, complains
Of her fate?
     However,
To one merely inquisitive,
And not strict of palate,
There may not be a sense
Of the murk,
Since what is apparent
Is an absence of the sun,
And in that spell,
Why indeed must he imagine
A nightingale in the heart's
    boskage
To investigate a complaint?

VI

You too must read this poem
Over and again. It's called
    The Human Jug.

OUR MAN IN THE PARK

He was sitting in the park
Reading an old newspaper.
We could not get through to him,
But who he was we knew,
A man of our imagination.
This was why, above all, we could not
Establish contact
Except, but rarely, at a level
His own mood had dictated
To which then we paid heed
When undistracted by the antiquity
Of what news he might be reading.
We wanted to see him reading our private
        wars,
And gave him that paper too willingly,
Only making sure that it was old;
And we wanted him to sit in the shade
Of ancient firetrees that no longer
        needed rain,
In a park that did not exist
Except as we had willed it
In the space that had become too inhuman
For intercourse.
But we could not get through to him
Though we had thought it would be the best
Of our difficulties,
Since, of course, we had only invented him
As a hypothesis to set against
The endurance of lives that yearned
For farthest speech.
There was something—perhaps, a pretext
For cheer in his presence—
Something in the way we made him up,
That, once he came into his own,
Our metaphysical homunculus,
Made him resist at once our effort
At conciliation.
Why, we had read his news before him,
But had wanted belief in catastrophe,
So that we waited if he would
So much as let fall a tear
To make our own terror more solid
Than his bench or shade of his tree.
We did not expect that he would refuse

To have character
And cover his face with our newspaper
To sleep and dream in the park that,
If we had not wanted him there,
Would not at all have existed.

A STUDY OF RIVER POLITICS

Believers have to mark time
And not lose count in sullen assent
Whether or not they have elaborated
Upon the Experiment, the demise
     of power,
The great anachronism.
        Meanwhile,
The essential task is to hold
Communities or Colonies intact,
To keep the hope of Unity alive.
        If one Community
Be destined to grow into the State
Yet none would have it be
— This is the critical point,
The axis on which the future spins.

        A national income,
Composed of customs receipts,
If centralized,
May be enough as the underpinning
Of the ideal Federation;
        Or levies
Against internal wealth
Conferring power on the grave
     Commissioners;
        But such measures
Compel the uneasy Communities
To withdraw their support,
Then await the next move
     of displeasure.
For the Communities still prefer
The weary run of the war-ridden
     reign.

        Ruing of past
Humiliations is not the aching
     root.
The mystic sense of the State
     inspires fear.
What need to sign ententes
Toward a final reconciliation
When no Community may be able
     to cope
With awkward surpluses of peace?

One nice political justification
    must be left
To throw besotted rascals out
Who strut on stage
And misinterpret catcalls
    for acclaim.

      Here, then, is less
Obtrusive role cannot be played
    out,
To strengthen the will to Unity
Along lines that respect the separate
    vocation
And anchor freedom in those dangers
That give it breadth without claim
    to be proof.
      The role, of course,
Of the crocodile cooperating
With a timorous school of mudfish
Is never easy, since affection,
Like anger, can produce disaster.
To be large and loved,
With whiplike tail and innocent
    jaws,
This is complex feat, often
    misunderstood,
It may never cease to lament
The world's failure to give
    due thanks.

      Yet, here again,
Is that critical point.
The future rolls into a coil
On its axis,
The apex still and magical
At the center
Like a new, unexpected frond.
      What minute egg
From that precarious coil
May suddenly break and drop
The squiggling creature upon
    the river's bank—
The crocodile's benevolent heir
Or mudfish swimming upon Silurian
    fins,
Indifferent to the Colony's flag?

ARIEL MUST BE GREEN

Neither Stephano nor Trinculo can see
    the island
Or hear flute music upon the balmy air.
Stephano has an idea of the commonwealth
In which the magic of Prospero
Would soothe his subjects with superior
    sack,
So that a primitive like Caliban
Would gladly bury thoughts of his dam
Where he digs mussels for the endless
    feast.
        But first he must dehorn the beast
That butts against the trunk of his idea
With talk of the moon and airy witches
By using tricks of surprise learned
During sleepless voyages in the hold
Where he and Trinculo wagered
On the veiled bride at the voyage's end.
What if Prospero's wand be filched,
Might he revert to his former state,
All his books wet in a leaking boat,
Be ready to have his daughter tupped
By a heavy spirit of the woods
So the heir to the island's beast
Might ride the enraptured beast
    to his lair?
        Trinculo, on his part, dreams
East and south of his sea of sack,
Riding dolphins down and up the windy
    troughs,
Oblivious to all else but a simple
    trick
By which he could make the sun stand
Still at his mind's inventive center
And drink up the fogs to clear his dream
Of a shipwreck blessed his time of life
With rarest casks beyond the dissolving
    reach
Of Prospero's magical, despotic stick.
O, let Stephano rule and be Caliban
    his slave
And time unwed lest it grow old again
And lose a further skill for his vintage.

And yet, if none could see the island
From its dragon's mouth to the tip
        of its tail
And compute the longitude of that
Green round of sleep which shelters
The deep woods of a promised meed;
If neither the butler who would be king
Nor his mate with his flagon of sack
Could hear flute music floating
        upon the tide
To make gentle the reefs of that fate
Cast ashore a kingdom in quest of an heir,
And, falling fathoms deep for an old man's
        eyes,
Restore a lustreless pearl to its original
        clam
Where the furies lie dreaming on a sterile
        curse;
How shall Stephano find that secret lore
To make straight the staff of his regal
        conjecture,
Or Trinculo, that vintage of a famulus'
        thought
To steer clear of the grosser taste
Spoils the ripening sleep of his precious
        casks?

Beyond the circle of Stephano's plot,
Further beneath the foggy ride of his
        mate,
The island lies open to balmier influence
Of a rule requires no magical sceptre
If the trunk of thought mure not
A musical spirit has yearned for more
        space
Than the reaches of its ambitious aim.
O, the invisible Ariel must be green,
Green the raiment of his mind,
Greener than the morning of Prospero's
        timeless pasture,
The object of his present schemes
More green than Prospero's youth
And its proud chaplets of conquest.
So the music of his invincible flute
That wafts upon the wreck of the unreal
        storm
Weaves deepest magical fabric

For that reality where innocence finds
Its most perfect rite.
                    Well, then,
Might Stephano yield his claim
At last to his fawning beast
For the rude and mechanical aim
Of a plot too obvious for his faith,
And Trinculo, admit the staleness
          of his drink
For secret toasting of that bride
Who swooned at his last voyage's end
Upon a sandbar in his foggy dream.

THREE POEMS FOR MY FATHER

THE WHEEL OF HIS SPOOR

I

After the uneventful action
And repetition,
Without horror because without knowledge,
Living according to circumstance,
Misled by the evidence,
An obsolete machine only running down,
You will arrive a stranger
In the familiar district,
In the middle of a forgotten calamity,
The clew found in the obvious place,
And learn a salutary loneliness
Of the judicial eye,
Rejecting the role of spectator,
The secondary suffering, the secondary
    fear,
Since evasion brings only a temporary
    release
In the private puzzle, the private
    abstraction.

II

There was indeed time
For the fruiting body in slime mold,
There was time for country practice
Of whatever was real,
Time of illness in the holidays,
Incubation of the incurable future,
When you fed upon the carcass
Of unfulfilled intention,
Authority without passion
Arranging auspicious flowers
Without belief,
Time beyond diagnosis
Or exorcism,
Fog of static voices,
Its long distances undiminished
By hope of returning.

III

It does not come from thinking
Or observation,
It is something you did not know
You knew,
Life persisting
But shrouded by lying voices
Not noticing the change.
Explaining will lead
To worse misapprehension,
Setting you farther away
From reconciliation.
You bring only your own landscape
Returning to the point of departure
Where knowledge is deeper, steeper,
Than all the senses gathered together
At the still point of thought.

IV

For the time you have to live
And the future that awaits its end,
There remains a knot to be untied,
An unspoken word to disinter,
The eye adjusted to the luminous gloom.
To grasp the unreal aberration,
Or whatever was too real to alter,
No revision of perspective is essential.
The wheel is come full circle,
There is no provision for escape
In a void of the mind:
After the play is played out,
There is no need to moralize
On what has passed and is to come,
The chorus unattended on stage
After the hero has been shot.

V

There remains outside the wheel,
Yet part of the still revolution,
Ever approaching,
Like a lost hunter to the circle of light,
Like a wounded quarry to the sheltering
    bush,
Drawing nearer to the final reconciliation

Beneath the obtuse design,
Against the sinister direction,
Someone the shards of whose sound,
The splendor of whose spoor,
Lie all about, gross and particle,
Separating the eye from the routinary
    seeing,
Compelling the rondure of the dream
    folded in reality,
The synergy of the reality invented
    in dream.

THE FIGURE OF HIS SPHINX

I

He did his work well
Because his heart was not in it.
It was essential to be indifferent
When the need for authenticity ran counter
To every other need.
What he had to do he did quickly,
Even boldly,
Before the desire overtook its long shadow,
So that afterwards the deed looked monstrous,
Like a bird with wings too small for flight
Since the desire had come too late
To give it or shape or aim.

II

As he had catalogued each grief or desire,
There was nothing he did not already know
By its own proper name.
No bellows would stir up fire
From his prodigal ash.
The ebb and flow of indefeasible order
About the bold reef of his hypothesis
Only provoked a feat of survival
That lacked the fortune of a shore.

III

And so at last,
He grew strange toward human sentiment
And felt ridiculous in his pew
Where he read the names of donors
That breathed the odor of a forgotten
    catechism.

Shall typhoons renew him?

He had only seen
The lights of distant boats
Drowning in the lusty squall.
No dream could raise
Against his survival
A raucous flock of long-winged
Sea gulls.

From prayer books
He had only sipped maigre gruel
That would not drag the rickshaw
To his door.

No sibyl with sickle
Eyes in the soul's wilderness
Could unriddle the wastes
Of his dissolution.

IV

He had laid to rest long ago
The noisy symbols of his youth
Since the appetite for reason was a disease
Of the antique mind, too poor in secular
     history.
And yet, by what virtue or destiny
Did the rebel once bear his love for custom
To the holy roots of his eternal disquiet?
Were his speeches left only for mice,
His last ally, in archives to criticize?
Why should now the strobils of his mind
Rain continually on the arid land?

V

So a rood of his mind slowly grew
Where a star raised the siege
To make amends for the clangor of his
     quest.
The wages of dead years fell like scales
From dry places of the soul embowered
     in weed.
It took no finding, it lay all about,
The compass of disillusion,
Like corrupt readings of other words
Than the imperious text of his obsession.
He sailed near the wind in discourses
That battened purposeless on time,
And found the pageant absurd
In which he alone was real,
The sound of his storming eye
Lifted for transport above his dusty
     saints.

THE LEXICON OF HIS SPACE

I

Light began to fail early
And everywhere the leaves were falling.
The river-borne mist crept in
Across the grey ruins of light
Till it caught in the trees
Where the fireflies hung their tiny, fitful
      lamps.
Uncertain figures wandered under the arches,
The familiar bells tolled of last year's
      memories.

Under the first stars
One spoke less than the truth
As foil to the spent illusion.
Where was the legendary hero,
The old, comic jinn,
Leagues from reality, a fawning monster,
Holding his golden bell,
The crooked tree flowering at his feet?

II

He read in humdrum tapestries
The note of fantasy,
Exquisite, unrepentant,
Like the cloistral hush which fell
Upon the butt-ends of each day's disaster.
Larger matters seemed at stake,
Intimations of doom cloud-bound
Where offal floated green.

There was a low door in the wall
To the enchanted garden.
Astride memory,
Among the delusive flowers,
He listened with half the mind only
And died of an untranslatable word
      at the heart,
Delicious, archaic,
After long captivity.

But he forgot his cues, garbled his lines,
Was ever in two minds as to grosser passages
That cried for ballast
Against the squalls of conjecture.
What was there more to understand
If the present had no fixed word
And were irreversible
Because it had no direction?

The particulars of his case
Had small, clear voices beneath the wind
And yet had no fixed language.
Might a kingfisher suddenly flare
Across the straits of sleep
But leave a fragment of explanation
Where all the past was present,
Invulnerable to tears?

IV

O, he was ringed with solitudes
That quelled the mind's quick exfoliations.
His voice no longer seemed equal
To their immensity,
His hand lay weak upon those things
That once steadied his heart's composure.
Only toward his life's end
Did he understand the childhood of the word.

The word thrust slow, plural root
Into the compost heap of silence
And achieved a foreseeing of all journeys
So that, in the end, its history
Became its own singular will,
Deep and fragrant
As each change that shaped
The labyrinth of mortal solitude.

V

And thus he recognized the separate reality
Of what he understood and needed to know
Beyond his choice of fiction,
That hoard of light,
Rising and setting upon the entranced mind,
Repeating itself
Or evolving routes of evanescence,
Like a history of the touchless seasons.

[56]

The lexicon of that space which mourned
      his years
Was travelogue of wordy lives
Stilled in the beneficent dusk of an old
      man's love,
Rich and sudden in foreseeing,
Since each name spoke from a native depth
At which its progenitor first descried
The fugitive transparence
Of his re-echoing, contradictory world.

THE FIGURE OF THE HERO

To heave against the havoc of his seas
Or the wrecked fathoms of his eye
Where his long-tressed sirens swathe
His wounded mind in song
Still requires the fell and dark which drives
The battering ram of his faith.
But what at last shall he present to light
As meed of his striving and pride
Amid the blather and bluster
And steep ascent of his despitous age?

None but he has the seamanship
For the squalls and stormy buffets
Of his thralldom
Where the eye descends farther than light
To cancel the gust and scripture
Of his rage
Or where his sirens raise a subtle chorus
To drown his sense of rarest earth
And lure him back to the watery provenance
Of his name.

Of his thralldom
May the seers sing lusty proverbs
For the spindling youth of another time,
And of his rage
May the burrows of the mind brim
Till the lightning and toil of the blood
Burn the prologues to kingdom come,
But of his name
Which paraph shall demolish
The forgeries of the phantom sun?

EVERYONE WATCHES A FIRE
(For Franz)

Everyone watches a fire,
Its funnel afar off
Proclaiming a frenzy of change
Sparked by a chance
Has found its murky aim:

The air rife with conjecture,
Increase of daring,
Brooding on the mysteries,
While smoke enisles a hapless sun
In script and swirl of its billowing
     mane.

What wind shall promote a contrary
     vane
To spare the tall flowers
Of a crowding thought
Pays no heed to the worsted grief,
Would worship the ineffable wrack?

Who might settle his wager
With fire with a greater blaze
Than this prolusory to gall and gash?
Is there one whose endragoned thought
Shall put chance's bilious eye out?

What mysteries shall he brood on,
By weirder, more sudden fabulist,
If, enlaced with his rampant flame,
Their dreadnought roots have reached
Into his heart's core of a thirstier
     fire?

Everyone watches a fire. Let none
Conjecture on the smoke of its vane.
The sun droops like a flower
Past its bloom, its wreck seeks
A farther grace than grief's aim.

No daring of hand or eye,
Snell or sly, may yet suffice.
The blaze guttles half the mind
Wrestling for mastery of the change
That mobs the sky of his assent.

He must make his mind's bow taut
For his fabulist's shaft
To strike the tocsins of his tale
And shape the wailing chaos of his
    eye
In the fierce blast of his heart's
    thirsty craft.

IN CELEBRATION OF MIND
(For Ric)

The mind has no object
Other than herself.
She speaks in images
That the words barely reach
At second hand.
No threat stalls a paramour
Whose predicate is a looking glass.

By her regal solicitation
The humblest, nameless thing
Entrusts its lode to her coronal
As she stands guard over her sorrows
And makes free
With secret places of the spirit
Swaddled in words.

What is the shape of a sensibility?
What is the form of the wind
Beneath the most tranquil wave?
What careful speech,
The sky dark with tumult of fowl?
Who will ask questions
And hide the sun from his rising?

The mind has no object
Other than the possible.
She shapes her speech
According to the brunt of the questing
    wave
Or the white gull sweeping down
As the sun postpones his light
To trick the curious fish.

What figure for the mind in torrid
    weather?
Or under the green cumulus
Of her leisure,
What trope to signify
The satrapy of her eye
Despite the passionate clamor
Of rival claims to her patient rule?

She dances for her favored mate
As in a vaudeville show,
The coronal of her speech
Lifted like a flowery wand
So that no shadow dare approach
The burning circle
At her heart's meridian.

THE ARCHIPELAGO OF OUR WORDS

I

Between the Equator and the Tropic of Cancer,
Engorged with sun and the truculent plumage
    of the real,
Repetition is inevitable
Since at cockcrow all the evidence truckles
To a small, windy archipelago of our words.

What delicate task with mind's bold rood
    to probe,
To track our truant x-eyed mole to his lair,
Then, at the hour of triumph, not relent
    to his tropes,
Nor contemn the music of their subtle band,
Nor provoke contention with their happy
    rabble.

II

Sir, mark well the sign our elders veiled
    in strangest script;
The lodestone of our knowledge is a simple
    anodyne
To cheat our nerve for a false report.
Through what sleight of demise shall we
    transfer
Then our estate to time's dandies or apes?

Or shall we ourselves grow beards,
Then pose for the immortal blurb?
Sitting at our ease in our professorial
    garb,
Shall idiot antics inveigle our everlasting
    smile
And fuzz the burden of our jest?

III

O tempora, O mores, cried the poet;
The simple truth, however, is much simpler,
Merely skin-deep and staler,
Spelt large in children's letters,
Exhibits A to Z in the mind's public stalls

[63]

—But spilled upon the ground, sir,
Of proof and reproof;
But stalled, sir, with ancient curiosities
Or comfortable resident ghosts
In league with our brash next of ken.

IV

Read rarest poems of the late T'ang
Or consult the humpback seer, the tricycle
    man,
For the delicate vocabulary of the fates
    brooding
Over a country gutted with eating places
And beauty contests for matrons and wenches.

Meanwhile, fishes have drowned for lack
    of air;
They wait ashore to go out with the tide.
The fisherman's wife repairs his net
    in the shade
While he dreams of grace given at the last
To curb the lust of his fiercest shark.

V

The sun is up; the wind rises;
The stricken fishes are withdrawn to the
    deep.
The shark patrols the provinces of his
    lust.
What benison shall confine this ravener
To a remote atoll of his horrible myth?

The fisherman may be his next of kin,
Though his legends reach only each day's
    end,
The islands of his mind all staked out
For simple terminology of his most final
    need.
His silences are only such as repair his
    dream.

VI

But lest the eye's torrid zone
Foil the flight of the precious sphinx,
The bird woman who collects tribute of our
    learning,

[64]

Let our sun invent data upon the tricky
  dew
To compass her airy range or correct her
  loot.

The iteration of the real is her new
  mythology:
At cockcrow when the world's dew is spent,
Our doctors of gossamer shall rehearse her
  monstrous sums,
Her molten wings duly clipped,
And test the delving senses of her every
  word.

VII

What ceremony shall be found without horns
To mate our gaudy sphinx with our exuberant
  mole?
What blessed hole, at the hour of reconciliation,
Shall propagate the reckless metaphors
By which to music all contention be stilled?

All scripts shall bear only bars
To chant the care for custom,
And magic shall lodge in the nerve's précis
So that the inheritance of mind's estate
Shall quickly escheat to the superior geste.

VIII

Then borrow time's moustache for the final
  conceit,
And sit upon the windy stool of reputation
To shape a lush glossary for jargon
Or fiddle upon the wordy themes of academe
And catch the exact chime of their survival.

Who shall advertise the alphabet to his
  forbears
Or tame to syllables their eternal gibber?
One may smile and smile yet remain no
  wiser
Nor larger than the letters he stalls with
Nor proof even to buffets of his ghosts.

IX

Who is the poet shall lay the fatal kiss
Upon the private intercourse with truth
And singe the cheeks of the public seer?
The wordsmith by whom our curiosities are
    healed
And proof made invulnerable to reproof?

In our guts shall all his poems live
Where he threads the eye of the sphinx
Or spins the voluble fantasies of the mole
That, as subtle founder of our dynasties
    and cuisines,
He may yet survive interpretation of his
    word.

X

Should the tricycle man continue to ride
The wordy engine of his public wisdom;
Our mole, beneath the limen of sense,
To prophesy the plumage of mind's summer;
Our sphinx, to unriddle the jargon of our
    minute survivals;

Then shall hold, since the scenery persists
Of eating places and beauty contests,
The imperious law of the hinter mind,
To see or perish, to muster its nightmares,
And note, with a cold eye, matter for
    burning.

THE NEED FOR THE POEM
(For Alex)

The word only names a certain need,
Is quite unlike its object,
Meeting the mind halfway
To make possible the poem
For a singular nerve.

The need may be for tenderness,
Or for private space,
Though its blank gaze or inclement gesture
May hood the vein of its intent
Or the rigors of its hermitage.

It does not recognize a norm
But forth may spring from wells
That long had not had rain,
Or from the heart's stintless motion,
Incautious of the perils of its clasp.

It is not possible to determine
By the heart's solitary vane
The weather of its infinity
For its seasons are quicker than change
And still more deadly.

The object is quite unlike
The sound or script of its name,
The difference creating immortal space
By which the mind is chastened
Beyond its sylvan speech.

It may be the listening sky
Or the wars of earth's childhood
Whose emblems move the mind
To endure the invisible
Without relief of certitude or belief.

And be the mind's speech as green
As any its fertile invention,
Still shall the speechless world
Mock the mind's enterprise or bold
    machinery
With the simple blaze of its cunning
    reity.

Yet there shall the poem build its demesne
To meet the tragic-gestured need
And name the world to itself,
Heedless of that blazonry by which it
  interprets
The wordy pulse of its sweet demise.

BE GLAD HE WAS A POET

Be glad he was a poet only,
Mind of sundry,
Measurer of the exact titre,
Who, middling or great, in this
    world
Could not do very much harm:
A few ears not a little vexed
By his odd diapasons,
A mind or two even envenomed
    by his words;
O bless, rather, the flummery
Of his brief, so brief rule:

For finches in his mind
Whose quick, trenchant notes
He caught on the wing
But did not care to transpose
Lest he abate the burden,
The sweet skill of their sound
By which the mind,
Rathe and nimble in the grove,
Adverts to sudden alms
Of the unmitigable desire;

For the mind's fell abuttals
That, obedient to logic,
He aimed at,
Then opposed with firm
    conjecture,
So that, laced with stress
Of his unpredicable theme,
He luffed toward the giddy sun
Of his world's summer malison,
Toward the gold coinage
Of his mind's azurous lists;

O bless, rather, the stocks
    of his yield:
It was enough his finches had
    their sound,
He did not look to accipiters

Wild of wing
For the hurl and the stroke
    of his stress;
Enough for the mint of his
    voyages
That, lashed to abrupt fiction
Of his clashing shores,
The mind yet struck the tale
And telling of his sun.

A LONELY TOWER

What need to speak in riddles
If it were plain we measure outward
With meek calipers of the mind
Circling the might and pain of a change
That the fixed eye has blessed
For its dark and late descending?

Let us be candid: we will not house
And haggle beneath wordless eaves of the
        dream
To conjure the skill for countervailing.
What fruit beneath its quick seizures
Does the thought cloister close,
Fraught with rondure of the ripening
        doom?

The last settlement, dreaming of diamond
        mines,
Left undecipherable tablets on the moon,
The flotage of their bold enterprise
Not enough to tip the dusty tail
Of a diminishing star
And blazon forth the hurt and hurtle
        of their blast.

What remains, beyond meter readings and
        tautologies,
Is an expansion, a resonance of the mind,
After our words have become unimportant,
The mind, like a lonely tower,
Scaling a steep horror of height
Upon the febrile stalk of its perilled
        appointment.

The petals of its oracular images
Are turned back in the storm and wrack,
But straddling the time of discontent,
Of purposes embalmed in the deed's nitre,
It reaves the doom that the moon heaves
Upon the dreaming shells of its beetling
        aim.

So time again to plant the new years
That the late rains shall fresh and bend
To make grow without hands,
And hearing speech of their green, sudden
    tongues,
Not to let the blind, gilded worms
Smother and wreck in the deep wreaking
    of their slime.

ESSAYS

*There's no theory in that profession;
only practice.*

HONORÉ DE BALZAC

*If it is worth thought, thought ought
to be worthy of it.*

ELDER OLSON

Introduction: The Basic Modes of Criticism *

I

The crucial problem in literary criticism is one of method since no statement about literature or a specific work has a determinate meaning apart from its logical status and function in the critical discourse. The logical context of any critical statement is, first of all, the precise question, usually implicit, which it seeks to answer; consequently, a just comparison between pronouncements on a specific work is possible only when propositions are addressed to the same underlying question. Moreover, any question in literary criticism is a function of its conceptual framework, i.e., any question about a literary work is dependent upon basic assumptions concerning literature in general or the specific literary work on hand—assumptions, for example, as to what sort of thing the work is, or under what aspect it is viewed, and how knowledge for its appreciation is reached. Since they have different frameworks, Aristotle, for instance, cannot be said to have refuted Plato on poetry; and what seems at first to be conflicting or contradictory among various critical positions on literature (when doctrines are isolated as self-contained assertions) are often only differences of concern among critics due to different aspects of literature which interest each one.

If critical theory of a sort is inescapable, what is necessary is its refinement. But since critical statements are relative, we ought to regard the various theories of literature,

* This introduction is a revised and expanded version of an essay I was asked to write for *The Philippine Collegian* (March 2, 1972) where it appears as "The Criticism of Literature." In turn, that essay derives from R.S. Crane's "Questions and Answers in the Teaching of Literary Texts" in *The Idea of the Humanities*, II (University of Chicago Press, 1967), 176-93.

[73]

from which they ultimately derive, only heuristically, i.e., as useful techniques, each appropriate for different ends. We would then avoid the dogmatic stand that this or that theory of literature is the *only* valid one or the most adequate for *any* question that might be asked about a literary work.

Critical questions may be grouped, as R.S. Crane suggests, according to particular *aspects* of a literary work to which they are addressed: (1) the verbal elements and devices of a given literary work, regardless of kind, by which thought, action, and emotion are revealed; (2) the structure or form which distinguishes one kind of work from another, whether, for example, it is a lyric poem or a novel of one sort or another; (3) certain qualities of the author's sensibility or thought which his work embodies; (4) the historical circumstances of the literary composition; and (5) certain moral, religious, social, or political values that the work sets forth or assumes. These *lines of inquiry* constitute the *distinctive subject matters* in the corresponding modes of criticism.

The "criticism of elements and devices" regards the literary work as essentially a *verbal composite*. Meaning (or content) and diction (or style) are its principles of analysis: they determine its distinctive framework and, therefore, the kind of questions that may be raised. *Meaning* "embraces everything from the individual significations of the words and metaphors, through the implications which these set up, to the structure and import of arguments or actions, and the signs, in the discourse, of character, emotion, and action."[1] *Diction* refers to "that aspect of discourse which appears when we ask about the kinds of words, among the alternatives available for a given purpose to the writer, which he has selected to convey his meanings, the particular phonetic, rhythmical, and syntactical patterns in which he has chosen to arrange his words, and the devices of imagery, metaphor, antithesis, paradox, and so on, which give to his writing such dynamic quality as it has."[2] The critical procedure commonly called *explication de textes* is useful whatever the nature of the writer's me-

---

[1] R.S. Crane, "Questions," p. 182.
[2] *Ibid.*

dium (prose or verse) or the nature of the work itself (an essay, a lyric poem, a history, a play). The interpretation of meaning and the sensitive appreciation of stylistic devices and qualities which the explication makes possible can then serve as a basis and means of control for the other modes of criticism.[3]

The criticism of form or structure (formal criticism or "poetics") views a literary work as an *artifact of a certain determinate kind*. A short story, for example, has a peculiar nature which distinguishes it from a play; and a lyric poem on the order of Hopkins' "Spring and Fall" is different from another lyric poem on the order of Browning's "My Last Duchess." Moreover, from the formal standpoint, meaning and diction do not exist simply for the sake of immediate or local effects but also for the sake of a determinate kind of artistic whole which they ultimately achieve in a given work. The principles of analysis in formal criticism are the *parts* which constitute a literary structure and the *organizing principle* (or *formal principle*, both general and specific) by which such parts are ordered into a whole of a certain kind (that is, a lyric poem or a play of one sort or another). Content and style remain the basic structural elements, but they are oriented to both a general and a specific artistic end or function that determine the nature of the literary whole. The general artistic end may be *didactic*, i.e., "the inculcation of an argument of some sort," in which case content and style, as structural elements, would be resolved into "the component premises and devices of proof or persuasion."[4] When, further, we consider the

---

[3] The analysis of individual literary works by the so-called "New Critics" regards the literary object as essentially a verbal composite. See, for example, I. A. Richards' distinction between "statement" and "pseudo-statement" in "Science and Poetry" in *Criticism: The Foundation of Modern Literary Judgment*, ed. Mark Schorer, *et al.* (Harcourt, Brace, 1958), pp. 505-23; or Cleanth Brooks' concept of "Irony as a Principle of Structure" in *Literary Opinion in America*, ed. Morton Dauwen Zabel (Harper Torchbooks, 1962), II, 729-41; or John Crowe Ransom's definition of the poem as "a logical structure having a local texture" in "Criticism as Pure Speculation" in Zabel, II, 639-54; or Ransom's distinction between Physical, Platonic, and Metaphysical poetries in "Poetry: A Note in Ontology" in *The Great Critics*, ed. James Harry Smith and Edd Winfield Parks (W.W. Norton, 1951), pp. 769-87; or William Empson's *Seven Types of Ambiguity* (Meridian Books, 1955).

[4] R.S. Crane, "Questions," p. 184.

specific means, manner, object, and effect of various works sharing the same didactic end or function, we may discover various *distinctive kinds* (as having different specific organizing principles in view of different specific artistic ends) : for example, *Everyman* (dramatic allegory), *The Divine Comedy* (epic allegory), *The Faerie Queene* (allegorical verse romance), *Pilgrim's Progress* (allegorical prose narrative) ; *The Rape of the Lock* (satirical mock-epic), *Mac Flecknoe* (mock-heroic poem as invective), *Gulliver's Travels* (satirical prose narrative), *Animal Farm* (satirical fable) ; etc.[5] Or, again, the general artistic end may be *mimetic,* i.e., "the representation of a human experience of some sort' for its own sake as meaningful experience, artistically rendered, with a distinctive emotional power; in which case, content and style, as basic structural components, would be resolved into the constitutive elements of "plot" or of a human experience of one sort or another (such elements as action, thought, character, emotion) and "the various technical expedients by which thought, character, emotion, situation, action are brought before us."[6] When, further, we consider the specific means, manner, object, and effect of the representation in various mimetic works, we may discover *distinctive kinds* as, for example, different tragic or comic forms in drama. *Oedipus the King,* for instance, is a different sort of tragedy from *Macbeth,* and both tragedies are different from *Death of a Salesman*; *Lysistrata* is a different sort of comedy from *The Alchemist* or *The Importance of Being Earnest.* Evidently, what is essential is a more discriminating apparatus of concepts and distinctions (than we now have) by which specific organizing principles may be formulated for analyzing the variety of conception and handling of parts in various *specific kinds* of poetry, drama, and prose fiction that belong to either general class of didactic and mimetic works.

But the criticism of form cannot by itself tell us why *King Lear* or *The Brothers Karamazov* is a *great* work for,

---

[5] Our intention here is merely to suggest (not to define) the variety of distinctive forms or structures within the general class of didactic works.

[6] R.S. Crane, "Questions," p. 184.

in strictly formal terms, *Treasure Island* is at least equal to either one. Their greatness lies beyond their purely technical aspect for we are moved through these works by a particular way of viewing the human condition. So, then, a different approach is requisite: the "criticism of qualities" by which we examine certain qualities of sensibility or moral vision that inhere in the content and style of profoundly moving works. Its principles of analysis are those general categories that Longinus speaks of: *thought* (the writer's unique conception of reality), *emotion* (the peculiar qualities of his sensibility), and *expression* (a certain distinctive style by which such thought and emotion are realized). Since the procedure is necessarily comparative, such criticism, when it is not merely impressionistic or too general and vague, rests on a rich knowledge of literary works, a keen intelligence, and a highly refined sensibility.

The "criticism of circumstances" involves questions that are relevant to literary history. More useful than schemes and formulae concerning various literary periods and movements are "a grasp of essential chronology," "a sense of period styles," and adequate information on the occasions, sources or models, philosophic "commonplaces," and artistic conventions and traditions by which certain other kinds of differences among various works (all great, say, and having essentially the same form) may be fruitfully discussed.[7]

Finally, the "criticism of values" (moral, religious, social, political) asks questions regarding the uses or functions of literature in relation, say, to education or to society (as in Plato's *Republic* or Aristotle's *Politics*). We cannot remain unperturbed or uninfluenced, at least to some extent, in our conception of reality or moral behavior by Camus or Saint-Exupéry; therefore, we ought to raise questions concerning basic propositions about life and conduct that certain works set forth or assume. We should, of course, avoid narrow-mindedness, dogmatism, and boorishness by availing ourselves of other critical modes as preparatory basis and means of

[7] *Ibid.*, p. 187.

control for our statements, and by examining the assumptions
that underlie our own judgment of certain values.

These, then, are five distinct modes of criticism, each de-
termined by its own basic assumptions about literature or
about some aspect of the literary work, by the kind of ques-
tions that are deemed appropriate within the framework of
those assumptions, and by the data deemed relevant in view of
those questions. It is, of course, true that criticism is an
organic whole since its object—the literary work—is itself an
organic whole. The various aspects of literature that we have
distinguished as the proper subject matter in each critical
mode are fused together in the literary work. And yet, it is
also true that those aspects have each an independent status.
It is best to regard the various critical modes heuristically as
techniques, each with its own powers and limitations, for a
fruitful and intelligent way of discussing various aspects of
the literary work.

II

R. S. Crane's classification of the basic modes of criticism
is itself a heuristic schema. Indeed, each mode comprehends
a variety of *specific* critical approaches, and a given critical
work could also employ a variety of modes. The chief point,
however, is that, in a given criticism of a particular work or
author, one mode alone, one specific critical approach, would
ordinarily govern the analysis since it would otherwise lose
its focus. The analysis might employ other modes, other critical
approaches, but it would nevertheless have to return to that
particular aspect of the literary work under consideration
which, in fact, constitutes the subject matter of the analysis.

To illustrate our point: compare Kenneth Burke's "Sym-
bolic Action in a Poem by Keats" with Cleanth Brooks "Keats'
Sylvan Historian: History Without Footnotes."[8]

Burke's essay exemplifies one *specific* approach in the
"criticism of elements and devices." Its basic assumption is
that, since language as employed in poetry (i.e., literature)

---

[8] See Burke's *A Grammar of Motives* and *A Rhetoric of Motives* (Me-
ridian Books, 1962), pp. 447-63; and Brooks' *The Well Wrought Urn*
(Harvest Books, 1947), pp. 3-21, 151-66.

s "a mode of action," a poem (any literary work) is "an
act, the symbolic act of the poet who made it—an act of such
a nature that, in surviving as a structure or object, it enables
us as readers to re-enact it." Such an assumption implies
that a "criticism of circumstances" would at least be helpful,
if not necessary, for a fuller analysis of the poem. Keats' "Ode
on a Grecian Urn," as symbolic action of the poet, can of
course be considered "only in itself, as a series of internal
transformations to be studied in their development from a
certain point, and without reference to any motives outside
the Ode"; that is, transformations of meaning in the ode
itself without reference to Keats' own life and times. How-
ever, "to understand its full nature as a symbolic act, we should
use whatever knowledge is available." Thus, in considering
the poem "as an enactment in a particular cultural scene,"
Burke arrives at the *motivation* of the ode (motives found
outside the ode but transferred or referred back to it) : Keats
needed to proclaim the unity of truth and beauty "precisely
because here was the basic split responsible for the romantic
agitation (in both poetic and philosophic idealism). That is,
it was gratifying to have the oracle proclaim the unity of
poetry and science because the values of technology and busi-
ness were causing them to be at odds." The transformations of
meaning in the Ode "were necessary for the romantic philoso-
phy of a romantic poet to transcend itself (raising its roman-
ticism to a new order, or new dimension)"; they constitute
the poem into a verbal object or structure which, as it sur-
vives, enacts the poet's symbolic act or "strategy" and enables
the reader, in his turn, to re-enact it.

Burke is not averse to employing the methods or the
results of other modes of criticism—or, for that matter, of
other branches of knowledge—in the analysis of a poem. "Lin-
guistic analysis," he points out, "has opened up new possibil-
ities in the correlating of producer and product—and these
concerns have such important bearing upon matters of culture
and conduct in general that no sheer conventions or ideals
of criticism should be allowed to interfere with their develop-
ment." The chief point, however, is that Burke never loses
sight of that aspect of the work which has determined the

specific subject matter of his criticism and defined his ap-
proach: the poem *as symbolic action of the poet*.[9]

Brooks' own essay exemplifies one other specific approach
in the "criticism of elements and devices."[10] Its basic assump-
tion is that "paradox is the language appropriate and inevitabl
to poetry." The poet is "forced into paradoxes by the natur
of his instrument," i.e., the language appropriate to poetry. H
has, "within limits, . . . to make up his language as he goes
. . . [but] He must work by contradiction and qualification.

> the poet has to work by analogies. All of the subtler state
> of emotion, as I. A. Richards has pointed out, necessaril
> demand metaphor for their expression. The poet mus
> work by analogies, but the metaphors do not lie in th
> same plane or fit neatly edge to edge. There is a continua
> tilting of the planes; necessary overlappings, discrepancie
> contradictions.

The poet, though he "makes up" the language of his poen
has yet no choice about the nature or characteristic of tha
language: the words in the poem "are continually modifyin
each other, and thus violating their dictionary meanings"; the
"cannot be kept out of the poem; [they] can only be directe
and controlled." But what directs and controls the words i
the poem? Brooks answers: "The paradoxical situation out c
which the poem arises." But this "paradoxical situation" i
not, from Brooks' standpoint, the human situation which th
poem seeks to represent for its own sake (or, as in Burk

---

[9] To my mind, the analysis of a given poem which employs Burke
approach would, however clever, remain gratuitous or conjectural at tl
center. Is it to be assumed *a priori* that any literary work is a symbol
act of its author? Does its language necessarily undergo a series of tran
formations of meaning which dramatize the author's symbolic enac
ment? Is Browning's "My Last Duchess," for example, a symbolic act
the poet? Almost anything in Browning's life or age might be used
explain whatever transformations of symbolic meaning are perceived (t
virtue of the hypothesis) in the poem, but there would be no way t
either confirming or refuting the alleged evidence. And what about poen
whose authors are unknown? Shall we ever "understand their *full* natu
as symbolic acts" of the poets who made them?

[10] Brooks himself recognizes the difference of his own approac
from Burke's: "I am happy that two critics with methods and purpos
so different should agree so thoroughly as we do on the poem [Keat
"Grecian Urn"]. . . . the emphasis of my essay is sufficiently differe
from Burke's . . ."

the poet's own situation which the poem symbolically enacts), but rather, the *paradoxical meaning of the poetic discourse.*[11] The poem does not represent or symbolize an experience; rather, it exemplifies a paradoxical relation of meaning which underlies it. The poem is, then, essentially an argument of sort: its form or structure is essentially that of an argument, "poetic" in the sense that it develops and resolves, in terms of its meaning, a paradoxical point; its "dramatic context" is the context of the terms of the argument, not the context of the human experience (the experience of the speaker in the poem) which the poem, since it happens to be an imitation, has rendered. Thus, Keats' ode is, in Brooks' analysis, "obviously intended to be a parable on the nature of poetry, and of art in general"; thus, *character* in the ode has to do, not with the speaker in the poem, but rather, with "the Urn's character as a historian."[12]

III

R. S. Crane's classification of the basic modes of criticism rests only on a distinction between the subject matters in the various modes. But, elsewhere, he maintains that any critical discourse is constituted by its "method," i.e., "a particularly formulated *subject matter* and a particularly determined *mode of reasoning* about it."[13] Therefore, "all critical utterances, whether statements of doctrine or observations on works, [are necessarily relative] to the critic's choice of *basic terms* and

[11] Herein is Brooks' essential difference from Burke. "Our specific question is not what did Keats the man *perhaps* want to assert here about the relation of beauty and truth; it is rather: was Keats the poet able to exemplify that relation in this particular poem?" (Underscoring mine.)

[12] To my mind, Brooks' approach is pre-emptive, like Burke's, and severely restricted to the analysis of metaphor. (See also Brooks' "Irony as a Principle of Structure" where he regards the poem as essentially "structure of meaning," i.e., meaning on the verbal plane.) His interpretation of Keats' ode, for example, assumes *a priori* that the poem is governed by a central paradox on the verbal plane—the paradox of a speaking urn; therefore, his analysis (what Olson would call purely "grammatical") is confined to a study of the poem's meaning which its words convey, that meaning, precisely, which the verbal connotations set up and develop, and which finally clarifies and resolves the alleged paradox.

[13] R.S. Crane, "Introduction" to *Critics and Criticism* (University of Chicago Press, 1952), p. 8; underscoring mine.

operational devices—i.e., to the methodological principles which
as hidden premises, determine the sense and validity of hi
arguments." [14] A critical statement is meaningful and valid onl
within its own special critical framework, and differences be
tween critical judgments are owing to differences in concept
and methods. The *adequacy* of a critical method is, moreove
"a function at once of the analytical precision and the rang
of the compendent concepts it affords within the confines c
its special view."[15]

Elder Olson also holds the same "pluralistic and instr
mentalist view":[16] possible critical positions are determine
by "two principal considerations: (1) the number of aspec
of a subject which can be brought into discussion, as constitu
ing its *subject matter;* (2) the kinds of basic dialectic whic
may be exerted upon that subject matter."[17] The *subject* is "wha
is talked about," e.g., poetry, whatever in itself it may be; b
the subject matter is that subject as particularly formulate
or "in so far as it is represented or implied in the discussion."
Thus, the subject matter of a given discussion may be certa
aspects of a literary work considered as a *product* of its art-
such aspects, for example, as its verbal medium or the pow
it has to elicit a certain kind of response. Since there a
various possible formulations of a given subject and vario
possible modes of reasoning about it, any "given discussi
is a function of its subject matter and of the dialectic, i.
system of inference, exerted upon that subject matter."[19]

Whatever aspect of poetry constitutes the subject matt
of a critical method, its nature is usually explained in ter
of certain causes or reasons. If, for instance, the *product*
the poetic art, i.e., the literary work in itself, were the subje
matter, the *nature* of the work *as product* may be sought
one, several, or all of these *causes:* its matter or medium (t

---

[14] *Ibid.;* underscoring mine.
[15] R. S. Crane, *The Languages of Criticism and the Structure
Poetry* (University of Toronto Press, 1953), p. 36.
[16] R.S. Crane, "Introduction," p. 9.
[17] Elder Olson, "An Outline of Poetic Theory" in *Critics and Cri
ism,* p. 547.
[18] "Any discussion of a 'subject' is relative to its formulation." (Ols
"Outline," p. 547.)
[19] *Ibid.,* p. 548.

oet's language); the subject represented or depicted (the idea
r experience which a particular use of the language renders);
he depictive method of the poet (the manner by which he
epresents an experience or conveys an idea); and the end or
ffect of the product (its power to move its reader or auditor).
hese causes point to aspects of the literary work *when it is
iewed as a product of art,* and constitute the basic principles
f its analysis.

Considering only "a single characteristic of dialectics—
heir concern with likeness or difference, or both," the mode
f reasoning that may be employed in the analysis is either
f two general classes: "the integral or likeness-dialectic
which] reaches solutions by combination of like with like"
nd "the differential or difference-dialectic" which reaches so-
ations "by the separation of dissimilars."[20] Thus, *integral* cri-
icism "resolves its questions by referring poetry, for example,
ɔ some analogue of poetry, finding characteristics of poetry
ɣhich are shared by the analogue"; and *differential* criticism,
by separating poetry from its analogues, finding character-
stics which are peculiar to poetry."[21] When, for example, a
ritic regards the literary work as a product and seeks to
xplain its nature in terms only of its matter or medium, his
ɪode of reasoning may be *integral,* as when he seeks "general
riteria for all literature, whether poetic, historical, philosophic,
r personal, on the ground that all literature employs words";
r *differential,* as when he seeks "to discriminate poetry from
rose by differentiation of the kind of diction employed in
ach, in order to discriminate appropriate criteria for each."[22]

[20] *Ibid.,* p. 549.
[21] *Ibid.*
[22] *Ibid.,* 550. "Given the same formulation of the basic *subject matter*
f criticism, it is still a matter of choice for the critic whether his *reason-
ɪg* concerning it takes one or another of several radically divergent forms.
. makes all the difference in the world for our interpretation and judg-
ɪent of a critic's statements whether—to mention only the more signif-
ant diversities of procedure—he moves from assumed general principles
ɔ their applications by dialectical division and resolution or from observed
fects to their necessary and sufficient antecedents by hypothetical causal
ɪference; whether he argues concerning the relation of parts to wholes in
ɪrms of the literally discriminable functions of the parts or in terms of
ɪeir reflection of, or participation in, the characteristics he ascribes to
ɪe whole; whether he holds his terms constant and varies his treatment of
ɪings accordingly or holds things constant and allows the meanings of
is terms to vary from context to context; or whether he resolves his prob-
ɪms integrally ... or differentially." (R.S. Crane, "Introduction," pp. 7-8.)

IV

The essays that follow are essays in *formal* criticism the criticism of form or structure. The "Aristotelian" method formal criticism, developed by the "Chicago school" of critic has for me a strictly pragmatic value. I owe my understandir of it to R.S. Crane and especially to Elder Olson; howeve they are not accountable for my own errors.

It is not my intention to construct a theory of the lyr poem or, what could be even more ambitious, a theory literature. My aim is chiefly to show the value and usefulnes in practical criticism *and for certain critical purposes onl* of that critical method for the analysis of individual lyr poems which derives ultimately from Aristotle's *Poetics*.[23] B I also wish to contribute a little to the development of criticis as an aspect of our knowledge of literature. I hope to add or, at the very least, to clarify some of "the multiple but co pendent differentiations of the specific method,"[24] i.e., that m thod which seeks the *internal causes* of poems which accou for the peculiar construction and effect of various *distincti kinds* of poems considered as concrete artistic wholes. I hor in short, to be able to contribute to "a broad base of asce tained literal knowledge about poetry"[25] which, more than a abstract theory of literature, promotes a *specific* and *concre* appreciation of the literary works themselves.

The primary concern, in our essays, is to appreciate, concrete and specific terms, "what a poet does *distinctively a poet,"* which is, "by means of his art, to build materials language and experience into *wholes of various kinds* to whic as we experience them, we tend to attribute *final* rather th merely instrumental value."[26] On this view, criticism is "p marily an inquiry into the specific characters and powers, a the necessary constituent elements, of possible kinds of poet wholes, leading to an appreciation, in individual works, of hc well their writers have accomplished the particular sorts

---

[23] See Elder Olson, "The Poetic Method of Aristotle: Its Powe and Limitations," in *Aristotle's Poetics and English Literature*, ed. wi introduction by Elder Olson (University of Chicago Press, 1965), pp. 175-

[24] R.S. Crane, "Introduction," p. 24.

[25] *Ibid.*

[26] *Ibid.*, p. 13; only the first underscoring is Crane's.

poetic tasks *which the natures of the wholes they have attempted to construct imposed on them.*"[27] But the prevailing modes of criticism today—the criticism of the *poetic means,* for instance, which chiefly engages the "New Critics" (Brooks, Warren, Empson, etc.)—do not provide the necessary analytic tools and concepts for the kind of problems raised by the concern for the distinctive natures of various poetic wholes. For purposes of formal criticism (or the criticism of form or structure), we need concepts and devices that will enable us "to discriminate the *various species of wholes* that poets have made; to determine the number, character, and ordering of their functional parts; and to define *the often quite different conditions of success or failure implied by the nature of each.*"[28]

Our first essay, "The Poem Itself," discusses a concept of form or structure that is valuable for the understanding of poems as concrete artistic wholes. It is based, of course, upon the Aristotelian idea of *imitation* or *mimesis* which, though now hardly understood among some critics (who, indeed, reject its corrupt sense as though it were Aristotle's), yet remains a valid and fruitful concept.[29] Some critics and teachers of literature discuss only the poet's "thought" ("theme" or "message"), considered as the content or subject of the poem, sometimes even using the poem as a springboard to discuss society, politics, psychology, and any number of other topics; others discuss only the poet's verbal and rhetorical devices (metaphor, irony, etc.), considered as the "poetic" technique; still others discuss both aspects of the poem, employing some vague or general notion of the union of "form" and "content." Inevitably, however valid the methods or concepts used within the critical framework of the discussion (often a rather elusive framework), and however necessary even these are for purposes of *formal* criticism, the discussion usually remains *inadequate* in its presentation and elucidation of *the poem as a determinate kind of artistic object.*

27 *Ibid.;* underscoring mine.
28 *Ibid.;* underscoring mine.
29 For a fuller discussion of the concept, see Richard McKeon, "Literary Criticism and the Concept of Imitation in Antiquity" in *Critics and Criticism,* pp. 147-75; and his "Imitation and Poetry" in his *Thought Action and Passion* (University of Chicago Press, 1954), pp. 102-221.

The next two essays attempt to clarify the hermeneutics of a lyric poem. It seems to me that some of our difficulties with criticism stem from our failure to distinguish between interpretation and criticism, and from too facile interpretations of "meaning" that we hardly ever question. When Prof Ma. Lourdes Arvisu lent me her copy of Elder Olson's "Hamlet and the Hermeneutics of Drama," I began to ask myself what the hermeneutics of a lyric poem might be. I used Robert Frost's "Stopping By Woods on a Snowy Evening" as my poetic specimen. "Edward," in the next essay, illustrates a common problem in interpretation of "meaning" which, to my mind, is best resolved by examining carefully one's own response to the poem. Brooks and Warren, on whose critical method most of us may have been brought up, happen, among other critics, to illustrate some of the unhappy excesses of the critic of "elements and devices."

The essay on "O Western Wind" is a criticism of criticism a short exercise, you might say, in critical vigilance. It indicates the *inadequacy* of the "criticism of elements and devices" whenever it seeks to discuss poetic form or structure; i.e., whenever it inquires into the peculiar construction and effect of various *kinds* of poetic wholes. The criticism of the poetic *means* simply does not have the necessary concepts and distinctions for such an inquiry. Its results are, at best, a partial account and at the worst, a serious distortion, of the *distinctive nature* of a given poetic whole.

The essay on Pound's "In a Station of the Metro" distinguishes between the poet's declared intention and (to adapt a term from Burke) the poem's own motivation. Between the poet and his own poem, the final authority, in *formal* criticism is the poem itself. As in our analysis of "Edward," a careful examination of one's own response to the poem is the means by which one is able to perceive the *specific nature* of the poetic whole in terms of its own "working power" (*dynamis*) or effect

"A Few Poems on the Order of *Spring Day*" is an exercise in the delineation of *one* kind of action or experience (a particular behavior of the "speaker" in the poem) which the lyric poem, when it happens to be an imitation, simulates. The speaker's *action* is viewed as *a specific organizing principle* (among others) which constitutes a given poem into a poetic whole of a certain kind. Most readers of poetry, it seems to me, see only the *thought* or *abstraction* that the words in the poem convey (as though all poems are didactic pieces). The *haiku*—or rather, their translations—are meant only to illustrate the possibilities of form or structure (with respect to the depicted action *alone* as an organizing principle) among the terser forms of lyric poetry.

"The Serious and the Comic in Lyric Poetry" seeks to clarify a useful distinction (but also a thorny problem) in criticism; i.e., the distinction between the serious and the comic *as the distinctive power or effect* in various literary works of the mimetic and didactic kind. The distinction is best seen by comparing "comic" with "serious" lyric poems: T. S. Eliot's "Aunt Helen," for example, with Emily Dickinson's "The Last Night That She Lived"; or Robinson's "Miniver Cheevy" with Pound's "Ballad of the Goodly Fere"; or Herrick's "Upon Julia's Clothes" with Baudelaire's "A Girl Too Gay" (*À celle qui est trop gaie*). The first two pairs happen also to be *lyric accounts* (or lyric poems in the narrative mode); the last two, *lyric enactments* (or lyric poems in the dramatic mode). I was especially struck by the first pair (Eliot and Dickinson)—for my purposes, a happy serendipity.

"The Poet's Use of Language: W. H. Auden's 'Musée Des Beaux Arts' " attempts to show that (1) poetry, considered as an "art" of language, is chiefly concerned with it as a *medium of imitation*, i.e., as permitting the simulation of a human action or experience; (2) the "poem" (be it a lyric poem, a short story, etc.) is not merely a verbal composite since, precisely, it renders someone's behavior or experience; (3) one's "poetry" is a matter neither of certain devices nor of certain qualities of diction but, rather, a particular use of language for purposes of a given imitation; and (4) "poetic diction" is *any* kind of diction at all required by a given imitation. Of course, we are dealing only with the literary work (a lyric poem, a short story, etc.) that *happens to be an imitation of a given kind* (e.g., a reflective lyric on the order of Auden's "Musée").

[87]

The last two essays on Angeles and Eberhart are detailed *formal* analyses. They bring to bear on individual poems the entire critical apparatus of concepts and distinctions (so far discovered) for the appreciation of lyric poems as concrete artistic wholes of various distinctive *kinds*. While I do not claim that the critical procedure employed is adequate for *all* critical purposes, I do assert that, if we wish to define the distinctive *nature* or *form* of a lyric poem *considered as a product of its art* (or as a concrete artistic whole), such a procedure is the most adequate and the most fruitful. I also submit that such a concern for the lyric poem as a determinate kind of artistic object would not only help us avoid hasty generalizations about poetic "structure" or "form" or "organizing principle," misinterpretations of "meaning" or "theme," and similar faults and excesses which have undermined the critical task in its various modes, but also, on the positive side, enable us to contribute to "a broad base of ascertained literal knowledge about poetry" upon which a theory or "poetics" of lyric poetry might be more solidly established.

The Poem Itself: A Concept of Form [1]

In other modes of criticism than formal or technical, the discrimination of specific forms or structures of various literary works is not particularly important. If, for instance, the critic is concerned with "vision of life" or "social relevance," he need not distinguish *La Via* as one kind of poem from *The Bamboo Dancers* as one kind of novel. But, on the other hand, for certain critical problems, the distinction between literary species is crucial. In general, it is prudent, in criticism as in other matters, not to treat things as similar, or the same, when they are in fact different. A given literary piece may be different from another even when they look alike: *The Frog Prince* is a different sort of work from *The Little Prince,* and the odes of Horace are not quite the same as Keats'. Again, a writer may be good in one literary kind but not in another: NVM Gonzalez now writes fiction but not poetry or drama, and he writes such novels as *A Season of Grace* but not such as *Tom Jones* or *The Marble Faun.* Or, again, the criteria for excellence in one literary kind may not be appropriate for another: a good judge of poetry may not be as good a judge of fiction or drama.

Indeed, we always distinguish at one level or another, for merely to mention "art" or "lyric poem" is already to differentiate it from something, or everything, else. The chief

---

[1] This essay, except for the brief discussion of Frost's "Stopping By Woods," is based on a mere portion of Prof. Elder Olson's "Introduction" (MS.) which he had kindly shared with me in 1968. A long and brilliant introduction to his theory of lyric poetry (which, since that time, I have been anxious to see in print under the title, as he promised elsewhere, of *General Criticism and the Shorter Forms of Poetry*), it has helped me numberless times in the delicate task of criticism.

point is how general or how specific we ought to be in terms of our critical purposes. At a certain level of generality, distinctions even between the larger classes of literary kind (prose fiction, drama, poetry) tend to disappear: when one, for example, distinguishes in terms of certain characteristics or qualities of language or the verbal medium (as when one dichotomizes between "prose" and "verse," or between "scientific" and "poetic" discourse). Conversely, at a certain level of specificity, distinctions between literary works of a given kind (say, lyric poems on the order of Keats' Odes) tend to be *sui generis*. The critic ought, therefore, to seek a reasonable mean between these extremes such that, for example, the criteria for excellence in a given kind of lyric poem (say, lyrics on the order of "Sailing to Byzantium") are neither so general as to apply to other kinds (say, poems on the order of "La Belle Dame Sans Merci") nor so specific as to apply only to Yeats' poem.[2] Certainly, the formal critic has to be specific—as far as necessary; but the discrimination of literary forms is, most certainly, not meant to obviate either their development or the growth of new forms. Indeed, such criticism does in fact point to the infinite possibilities of development and growth, since it respects the dynamism of art.

But what, then, is *form*? What do we mean by "specific literary kind" or "poetic species" or "a lyric poem of a certain order"?

It is generally agreed that a poem is a meaningful organization of words. The problem, if we hold this view, is to differentiate the poem as one kind of meaningful verbal composite from such other things as scientific treatises, histories, sermons, even telephone directories and ordinary conversation. Some critics hold that it is primarily a certain *content* or *subject matter,* in the sense of "meaning" or "theme," that makes the poem a different sort of verbal composite.[3] Maud Bodkin, for example, finds that poems embody "archetypal patterns"

---

[2] If it is improbable that no other poem, on the order of "Sailing to Byzantium," exists, it is just as improbable that there are no other forms of the lyric poem, or that other forms will not emerge.

[3] By "poem" or "poetry," in this essay, we refer to such things as short stories, novels, plays, and lyric poems. It is a pity that English does not have a generic term like the German *Gedicht.*

of human experience, while Kenneth Burke finds that poetry names typical, recurrent situations in real life and, in so doing, symbolically employs strategies for dealing with them. Other critics assume that certain characteristics of the *language* employed make the poem a poem or "poetic." William Empson, for instance, holds that what makes a poem is the rich ambiguity of its diction, while Cleanth Brooks holds that in "poetic" discourse, statements are always qualified by their context, since the words continually modify each other and enter into new and sudden combinations that balance and support each other. Neither critical position is without basis since, as Olson puts it, a meaningful verbal composite always "implies both some principle of organization in the meaning and some principle of organization in the language." Thus, critics holding either position can discuss what they call "poetic form" or "poetic structure" since "the *subject matter* can always be discovered to reveal patterns of experience, structures of symbols, or organizations of themes, and the *language,* similarly, to reveal structures of metaphors, ambiguities, or paradoxes." One with the requisite critical stamina can probably devise a comprehensive index or calculus of those organizing principles —certainly, for example, more than seven types of ambiguity.

Obviously, then, a single poem may contain a number of different structures, and critics examining one and the same poem may discover different structures or forms and analyze these differently. As Olson points out, Marvell's "To His Coy Mistress," considered as a meaningful organization of words, has a *grammatical* form or structure; as syllogistic reasoning, a *logical* form; as an effort at persuasion, a *rhetorical* structure; as a metrical composition, a *prosodic* structure; and other forms or structures, as well, may be discovered in the same poem—structures of ideas, of symbols, of images, etc. And each kind of structure is, of course, a whole with certain functional parts; but each whole is different from another, and consists of different parts that function differently.

But *the* form of a *given poem* is that which makes it a certain *kind* of poem. It is what Olson calls "subsumptive form," i.e., "that towards which all other forms or structures in the poem tend, and in which they are included." By the same token, the *function* (power or *dynamis*) of the poem as poem is its "subsumptive function," i.e., "that toward which all other functions tend, and in which they are included as a whole."

Suppose we consider a few terse compositions. The first three were made up by Olson, the last one is a translation of Issa's *haiku.*

(1) *On the Death of Caesar*
   Julius Caesar
   Was assassinated in
   Forty-four B.C.

(2) *On Bones*
   A bone consists of
   Organic and inorgan-
   Ic materials.

(3) *Notice*
   Smoking and spitting
   Are strictly prohibited
   On these premises.

(4) *Spring Day*
   Departing, the spring day
   Lingers
   Where there is water.

It is what something is *as a whole* that determines its nature or form. The form, or structure, then, of (1) and (2) is that of a *proposition,* the only difference between them being that one is a historical, and the other, a scientific, proposition. The purpose or function of a proposition is to convey a fact; the primary consideration, therefore, is whether it is true or false. You don't consider the circumstances under which either statement is made; e.g., the character of the speaker, his mood, etc. Both propositions have, of course, the same *grammatical* form, i.e., that of a declarative sentence; and the same *prosodic* structure, i.e., if we only count the syllables per line; but such forms or structures are subsumed under the *logical* form: (1) and (2) as propositions.

"Notice" has the same grammatical and prosodic form as (1) and (2), but it is not a logical proposition: you don't consider whether it is true or false. And it is not merely a statement: the statement is made only as it is entailed in an act prohibiting something. The final or subsumptive form is, therefore, that of an *action,* i.e., an order or command. The meaning of the statement is subsumed under its structure as an act. It calls for a specific kind of response or behavior; and the proper response is action that complies with the prohibition or command.

Here, then, is an instance which demonstrates a certain character or power of language, i.e., that it can reach beyond meaning or constitute an act. Olson cites another example: a speech that incites its audience to treasonous behavior is not judged only grammatically (in terms of the intelligibility and correctness of its statements), or logically (in terms of the truth or falsity of its propositions), or rhetorically (in terms of the persuasiveness of its argument). Grammatical, logical, and rhetorical structures or forms are all subsumed under the nature or form of the speech as action; and, therefore, the consideration of the speaker's character, his motive, and all other circumstances of his action would be appropriate and relevant, just as in the consideration of any other action in life.

But if speech may constitute action, it may also *simulate* (or, as Aristotle would have it, *imitate*) action. The human face, for example, is bounded by lines or planes; by reproducing these, you can draw or sculpt a human face. Similarly, since an angry or grief-stricken man will tend to do certain things by means of speech (denounce or lament), to use a certain tone of voice, certain rhythms of speech, etc., by reproducing these, you can simulate the speech of an angry or grieving man.[4]

---

[4] Simulation, says Olson, is either a mere *copy* or a *representation.* The cast of a hand of a *particular person* is a copy: the sculpture of a human hand *in general* is a representation. You can copy or reproduce a certain particular thing; but you can also represent only the *kind* of thing that that particular is.

Simulated action is, of course, quite different from *real* action. In real-life action, for example, this angry man, in particular, is speaking and acting in this way because he is this sort of character suffering this particular sort of emotion. But in simulated action, the reverse is true; i.e., the simulated speech and action are of a given order because any angry man of a certain character *would* do or say such and such things. In one, you have a particular fact; in the other, the particular is substituted

Consider, now, that translation of Issa's *haiku*, "Spring
Day."[5] It is more than a mere statement, grammatically cor-
rect and intelligible; and more than a proposition, though
it is true as a statement about an optical phenomenon. All
these, as forms or structures, are subsumed under its structure
as *simulated action*.[6] The poem is a depiction, i.e., it offers a
likeness or "imitation" of someone's mental activity. What
is important for the poem (since it determines our response
to it) is our sense of a human person observing the close of
a spring day and comparing the continuing brightness of
watery places to a lingering-on of day. It is not a mere "ex-
perience" as such that is communicated; it is a mental activity
of noticing and comparing on someone's part (i.e., the speaker
in the poem). The poet, Issa, has selected a crucial detail—
the fading light of a spring day reflected by watery places.
It activates our imagination (if we are responding to the
poem): we visualize an encroaching darkness, the last bright-
ness in the spring sky, the still-bright watery places and, by
implication, the darkened places where there is no water. And
the comparison of spring-day to someone departing, and yet
lingering, is significant: it can occur only to someone in a
tender, melancholy mood, someone regretful over the day's
closing; someone, therefore, who endows the day with his
own feeling since he imagines it as lingering, reluctant to
depart. The effect or power of the poem is to make us share
the speaker's mood. There is no need to interpret the "mean-
ing" of his experience on some symbolic plane.[7]

by a general probability. The difference is very well exemplified by an
audience's reaction to tragedy: they enjoy the tragedy because, first of
all, the tragic action is simulated; if it were real, actually transpiring
on stage, they would be horrified or repelled.

[5] We are not, strictly speaking, considering Issa's *haiku*, but only one
possible translation as a definite *kind of lyric poem*.

[6] It is different from "Notice" in that the latter is on the order of
real action since you are supposed to respond to the command by com-
plying. In "Spring Day," the final end or function is in the poem itself.
The depiction exists for the sake only of what it depicts as having a
certain power or effect. Whether or not you respond properly (emotionally)
to the piece has no further consequence than that you have or have not
responded properly; but, in the other case ("Notice"), your response has,
evidently, a further consequence.

[7] It is not as though, without discovering a further "meaning" in
the poetic experience, we would not be able to respond to the experience

From such a consideration of "Spring Day," we arrive, says Olson, at a few useful inductions:

1. A lyric poem may be *mimetic,* i.e., a simulation, likeness, or imitation of some human activity.[8] Its form or structure is that of *someone's experience* as poetically rendered, and its function, as poem, lies in the power or capacity of the depiction to move us emotionally in some determinate way.

2. A lyric poem on the order of "Spring Day" represents or imitates a single, indivisible action on someone's part.

3. We are affected by the simulated activity as it is represented to us, not as it exists in nature or real life.

4. The probability of the action is not natural, but general or "poetic," probability, since the imitated action is universalized, i.e., restricted to what a certain *kind* of person (sensitive, pensive, etc.) *might necessarily or probably* feel, think, or do.

After discovering one *specific form* of the lyric poem— i.e., in terms of the depicted action, the imitation of someone's mental or emotional activity, single and indivisible,—one may then proceed to explore at least some of its possibilities by considering other poems that have the same specific form: such poems, for example, as the anonymous "O Western Wind," Landor's "Dirce" and "On Lucretia Borgia's Hair," Dickin-

---

on its own terms. Clearly, the experience *sans* symbolic interpretation is not by itself meaningless. Also, such interpretation, over and above the experience, is in actual fact a process of discovery *ad infinitum,* depending not so much on the poem itself (the depicted experience) as on the critic's ingenuity. Certainly, the reader, if he so wishes, may experience the poem at his own level of experience or even at several (if he is not so easily confused); but, on the other hand, he must needs experience the poetic depiction *first, at its own level,* before he makes free with the poem. In general, too, when we respond to "meaning," we are really responding to an abstraction of one sort or another (to which the poetic experience has been reduced) rather than to the concrete individual human experience which the poem depicts. Besides, we really do respond immediately to the experience itself which the poem simulates without any irritable reaching after some other, further meaning which it may seem to suggest.

   [8] Other lyric poems (Emerson's "Fable" and "Brahma," Shakespeare's "The expense of spirit in a waste of shame," Housman's "Infant Innocence," etc.) are *didactic,* i.e., they inculcate a particular moral or idea. See Oscar Williams, *Immortal Poems.*

son's "Presentiment," Pound's "In a Station of the Metro," etc.[9]

But suppose, now, we consider a lyric poem of a different order, say, Frost's "Stopping By Woods on a Snowy Evening."

> Whose woods these are I think I know.
> His house is in the village though;
> He will not see me stopping here
> To watch his woods fill up with snow.
>
> My little horse must think it queer
> To stop without a farmhouse near
> Between the woods and frozen lake
> The darkest evening of the year.
>
> He gives his harness bells a shake
> To ask if there is some mistake.
> The only other sound's the sweep
> Of easy wind and downy flake.
>
> The woods are lovely, dark and deep.
> But I have promises to keep,
> And miles to go before I sleep,
> And miles to go before I sleep.

The traveler in the poem is aware at the outset that "stopping here" is not quite right in his situation. That he should think of the woods' owner indicates immediately his uneasiness: "He will not see me stopping here." This, I think, is even why Frost's poem begins the way it does. For if the woods' owner is not by to comment on the traveler's action, yet does his own mind misgive: he considers that even his horse "must think it queer" on practical grounds alone to be "stopping here." Being troubled at heart, he also imagines, when his horse "gives his harness bells a shake," that it must be "to ask if there is some mistake."

But the traveler does stop by these woods and tarry at least long enough to take in the woods and find them a restful and inviting sight: "lovely, dark and deep." The admission suggests not only that, when he finally decides to continue on his journey, it is not without some regret, but that,

[9] See "A Few Poems On the Order of Issa's 'Spring Day'," pp. 140-52.

also, his fanciful speculation about his horse may be a kind of subterfuge for doing awhile exactly what he feels uneasy about. This is why, as it seems to me, the horse, or rather, what the speaker imputes to his horse, takes up half of the poem. As subterfuge of a sort, it does not quite strike at the root of his uneasiness, though clearly it projects his state of mind, even as his final decision reveals its real cause or source. And perhaps, there is an element of wry humor in the speaker's situation—a kind of sudden embarrassment. His "little horse," for example, has the better end of the "argument" as the traveler becomes self-conscious—for it is as though he catches himself doing something on the sly and finds that his own horse has noticed it, too.

But, evidently, "stopping here" is not his intention or conscious will since he finally decides to go and not linger a moment longer. It is not on purpose but on impulse that the traveler tarries awhile by these woods. Precisely, given his moral sensitivity of a sort, he examines that impulse—first, by way of what his horse "must think" of the "mistake," and then (with some effort—since he seems to pull himself together, to take his eyes off, as it were, from the lovely sight), by reminding himself that he has "promises to keep ... before I sleep."

Is not an inner conflict of sort involved in the action as depicted? Certainly, since at the end of the poem, it becomes clear that the traveler has chosen between alternative courses of action: enjoying a possible respite or postponing it in order to keep promises. He resists an impulse, he overcomes a temptation, if you will. To say, however, that he is divided against himself, that he is resolving an inner moral conflict, or that there is a moral dilemma or crisis, would be to over-read the experience as poetically rendered; it would over-interpret the thrust of the poetic imitation, put too much stress on an aspect of the experience which the imitation does not seem particularly to warrant. Similarly, the analysis of "irony," "tension," or "paradox" in the depicted experience is likely to misread or overstate some aspect of it.

Is Frost's lyric a *symbolic* poem? I think not, if by a symbolic poem we mean a poem on the order of Blake's "The

Sick Rose" or Housman's "Infant Innocence." But in deny-
ing its symbolic nature, we are not saying that it is not open
to a further range of significance than that which the ex-
perience itself, as poetically rendered, presents. We are mere-
ly stressing the fact that we can respond to the poem on its
own terms as a representation of an individual experience,
and do not need to interpret it further on some symbolic
plane. This is a fact that needs to be stressed in view of a
current tendency in criticism toward symbolic interpretation
ad infinitum.[10]

To sum up: In "Spring Day," the depicted action is *mo-
mentary,* i.e., a single act of comparison made by someone in
a melancholy and tender mood. But in Frost's poem, the de-
picted action is *sequential,* i.e., someone's single but continuous
line of deliberation over a certain period of time. And it is
complex in that it involves a *reversal* or *turning-point*; i.e.,
the depicted action is like a bent line: it moves first in one
direction—the traveler stops by some villager's woods to watch
them fill up with snow; and then, it changes course, and
there is a reversal—for the traveler, made uneasy by his
tarrying there, examines the impulse to enjoy the lovely sight
and finally decides against it. We can also distinguish the
form or structure of "Spring Day" from that of Frost's poem
in terms of the *power* or *effect* of the simulated action. In-
deed, it is the power of a given literary work which finally
determines its specific nature or kind since, when the work
is considered *in itself,* the power is the end or function for
which it exists. In "Spring Day," what we are offered is
merely a mental and emotional activity of reaction to a scene:
we can infer the speaker's mood but not his moral condi-
tion. Our response, then, to the poetic depiction is based sim-
ply upon human sympathy. But in Frost's poem, the speaker's
action exhibits his moral character; i.e., we infer that he is a
man who has a fine moral sense since he decides finally to

10 Robert Penn Warren, for instance, is much more concerned with
"theme" or "meaning" than with the experience which the poem renders;
otherwise, he might not only have found the experience more meaningful
in itself, but also, he might have arrived at a somewhat different for-
mulation of the poetic "theme." See his "The Themes of Robert Frost"
in his *Selected Essays* (Vintage Books, 1966), pp. 118-24.

keep faith. Indeed, the principal part of the poetic imitation is his choice or moral action, and to this, primarily, we respond—with moral approbation or a kind of moral relief based on an ethical consideration. Needless to say, this is a *formal* comparison, not one of literary merit; for, as poems, both are artistically excellent in that each achieves its own specific end or power.

Lyric poems that happen to imitate a human action or experience belong to the large *mimetic* class of various literary kinds. The *specific form* or *structure* of a given lyric poem within that class may be defined in terms of the depicted action which, primarily, endows the poetic imitation with its peculiar power to move us emotionally. Hence, also, form may be defined in terms of the power or effect of a given imitation since, ultimately, it is that power which governs everything else about the poem. But only a specific formal analysis of lyric poems can discriminate among their various kinds for purposes of evaluating their excellence in terms of their own particular requirements.

Interpretation is prior to criticism. It makes a great difference, for the analysis of poetic form, whether we take the "meaning" of Frost's poem to be *symbolical* (perhaps, even allegorical) or *literal,* i.e., simply that meaning which emerges when we regard only that concrete and particular human experience which the poem has in fact rendered. For, on the first view, Frost's poem assumes the form or structure of a species of *argument* in which the experience as depicted is merely illustrative of a particular "thesis"; but, on the second view, the poem assumes the form of a certain class of poems that renders an individual and concrete experience, *not to enforce an abstraction, but to evoke the experience as rendered for the sake of its emotional power.* Interpretation, as concerned with a choice among variant constructions of its meaning that a poem tends to support, is not the same thing as criticism, which elucidates the nature of a given poem as an artistic whole of a determinate kind and judges of its excellence according to criteria appropriate for each kind.

[99]

Stopping by Woods: The Hermeneutics
of a Lyric Poem [1]

I

Some readers of poetry think of interpretation as the
art of discovering the almost infinite variety of meanings
which a poem, if it is a good poem, may be made to yield;
others, when confronted with variant readings that conflict
or contradict each other, assume that interpretation is, after
all, a matter of taste or opinion. On either view, interpreta-
tion becomes a free and endless improvisation on themes or
ideas that are discoverable in a given poem. No criteria exist
by which one appraises it as valid in relation to the poem.
But unless we are to accept an interpretation on the basis of
its novelty, ingenuity, or some other virtue of inspired read-
ing, rather than on cogency of proof, we ought to be able to
judge between variant interpretations from a knowledge of
the laws of evidence.

We are, to begin with, interpreting a lyric poem, i.e., the
poetic text alone; we are not interpreting human experience
itself viewed through the poem. For there is a difference be-
tween action, thought, emotion, and character as these appear

[1] First published in *The Diliman Review*, XX, No. 1 (January, 1972),
25-40; here revised. The essay is an application to lyric poems of a given
kind—the kind that happens to be a representation of a human ex-
perience—of principles and problems of interpretation as I understand
these from Elder Olson's "Hamlet and the Hermeneutics of Drama" in
Modern Philology (Feb. 1964), pp. 225-37. All quotations in my essay
refer to this article, unless otherwise indicated.
Our specimen of the one kind of lyric poetry that we have in mind
is Robert Frost's "Stopping by Woods on a Snowy Evening"—a familiar
poem to most readers and, therefore, convenient for our purposes. But
comparisons with other lyric poems are of course inevitable.

in real life, and as these constitute a certain kind of lyric poem; and consequently, there is a corresponding difference between their interpretations. Action exists, or is represented, in a lyric poem in view of some artistic end, i.e., the power to move us that its representation would have; it is, like thought, emotion, and character, a functional part of the poetic whole. Action occurs in real life in view of some good to be achieved; and that good is definable only in relation to that life as lived. Hence, the laws of evidence that are specifically relevant to problems in imaginative literature are quite distinct from those that are relevant to problems in real life.

Interpretation, moreover, is not the same thing as textual and linguistic analysis, though it rests thereon, since the text must first have been established and the meanings that arise from the words and their syntactical relations must first have been explicated. And formal criticism, in turn, rests on interpretation; differences in analyses of structure and evaluations of poetic merit may therefore arise from differences in interpretation. But interpretation, as concerned with a choice among variant constructions of its meaning that a poem tends to support is not the same thing as criticism, which elucidates the nature of a given poem as an artistic whole of a determinate kind.

It makes a great difference, for the analysis of poetic form, whether we take the meaning of Frost's poem to be *allegorical* (e.g., "Life is a journey by which the soul is tried; the woods' owner is either God, putting Man to the test, or the Devil as tempter;" etc.) or *literal*, i.e., simply that meaning which emerges when we regard only that concrete and particular human experience which the poem has rendered. For, on the first view, Frost's poem assumes the form or structure of an allegory of sort, and on the second, the form of a certain class of poems that renders an individual and concrete experience, not to enforce an abstraction, but to evoke the experience as rendered for the sake of its emotional power. Such differences in poetic form necessarily involve differences in the conception and handling of the poetic parts. Therefore, the principles of critical analysis and evaluation will also differ.

When a critic takes the meaning of Frost's poem to be allegorical, he would regard as the basic structural parts of the poem the component premises of its argument or the component ideas of its unifying theme which, precisely, constitute it into a lyric poem of the *didactic* kind. He would assume that the poem is organized according to the principles of allegorical construction, i.e., the elements of experience, such as character, action, etc., are so employed as to convey meanings independent of the experience that their peculiar organization renders. He would also try to specify its nature or kind within the didactic class (whether, for example, it is an allegory, a parable, a fable, etc.) by comparing it with other lyric poems that are similarly constructed. And he would distinguish it from the symbolic poem on the lyric order (like certain poems by Blake or Yeats) by noting, for example, that in the symbolic poem, such elements as action or situation, are not so organized as to parallel certain meanings that these serve, in an allegory, to body forth.

When, on the other hand, the critic interprets Frost's poem literally, he would regard as its basic structural parts the various elements of a human experience in its particularity—such things as the situation of the speaker in the poem, his particular actions, the sort of character he manifests, his own thoughts and feelings, etc., which, through their interrelation with each other and the whole (i.e., the complete and concrete experience as represented), constitute the artistic whole into a lyric poem of the *mimetic* kind. For, on this view, one is not responding to a universal human experience (such as that which is abstracted in allegory), but rather, to a specific and individual experience. The critic would also assume that the parts of the poem are so organized as to render that experience and endow it with power to move its readers in a way appropriate to it. And he would try to specify its kind as a lyric poem by discriminating among lyric poems of the same mimetic class in terms of the means, the manner, the object, and the end or effect of the representation.

If, then, the question of choice among alternative hypotheses as to the meaning of a given poem is prior to formal criticism, it is *a fortiori* also prior to any other critical discussion which proceeds from the analysis of poetic form: whether, for instance, Frost's poem is a *great* poem in terms, say, of the quality or character of the poet's vision or sensibility, when we compare it with such other lyric poems as Lovelace's "To Lucasta, On Going to the Wars," Tennyson's "Ulysses," and Yeats' "Sailing to Byzantium"; or whether, in relation to such things as education or society, and judged according to appropriate standards in view of such a relation, it has social, political, moral, or religious values over and above the purely artistic.

II

An interpretation of meaning in a given poem is essentially a hypothesis. Only proofs of probability, not an absolute demonstration (as in the physical sciences), can establish such a hypothesis as certain, i.e., beyond reasonable doubt.

But since a lyric poem like Frost's is made up of such parts as action, character, thought, emotion, etc., our hypothesis would necessarily be complex, i.e., it would entail subhypotheses as to those parts and their interrelations with each other and with the whole that they constitute. Therefore, its probability would depend on that of its concomitant subhypotheses. In fact, the propositions that make up a complex hypothesis in interpretation are of various kinds: *basic, inferential,* and *evaluative.*

"*Basic* propositions are about facts or occurrences," and the evidence for them is that they "exist or occur in the work itself." In a lyric on the order of Frost's poem, basic propositions involve only the speaker's thoughts and at least· the "apparent form" of his verbal action, e.g., that he is reflecting or deliberating. Whatever else make up the whole experience represented in the poem can only be inferred, e.g., the speaker's character, his emotion, the "real nature" of his action or experience, etc.

"*Inferential* propositions are about facts or occurrences implied by basic propositions"; therefore, the evidence rests on basic propositions from which they are inferred. You infer, for instance, that Frost's traveler does not think it quite right to be stopping by woods because his reflections imply

[103]

that attitude. For it seems to him that his "little horse must think it queer"; when his horse "gives his harness bells a shake," he alone interprets it as asking "if there is some mistake"; finally, he bethinks himself of "promises to keep ... before I sleep."

But consider also the following instances:

1. That the speaker is a traveler and is now stopping by woods are inferred only from what he says.

2. The "real nature" of his verbal action, that he is choosing between alternative courses of action, or that he is trying to resolve a moral question that confronts him in his situation, is only implied by the train of his reflection.

3. That he feels somewhat weary (physically or spiritually) is also inferential, since he is "stopping here" though he still has "miles to go before I sleep" (the repetition of that thought, in the speaker's situation, reinforcing our impression of his physical or spiritual weariness).

4. Likewise, it is inferrable that the woods' owner is less than friendly to the speaker since the latter shows a concern lest the owner "see me stopping here to watch his woods."[2]

All these instances show that, "while formally all inference is necessary in the sense that the premises necessitate the conclusion ... a conclusion can never be stronger than the premises upon which it depends." Thus, inferences may be assertoric as in (1), necessary (2), probable (3), or merely possible (4); for "probabilities can never establish necessary propositions, and possibilities can never establish probabilities."

Evaluative propositions are also inferential, but "they have predicates qualifying an action or an agent ... and the qualification always involves reference to a standard of some kind." Therefore, the evidence "consists in part of basic and inferential propositions, in part of some standard, established as appropriate, to which these are referred." That Frost's traveler has good moral sense and a fine sensibility or imagination is an evaluative proposition which rests on the follow-

---

[2] But such an inference is dubious since the whole experience, as the poem renders it, does not seem to warrant it. That the woods' owner is less than friendly is irrelevant to the lyric speaker's experience.

ing basic and inferential propositions: he finds the woods "lovely, dark and deep"; he considers the implications of "stopping here"; he recalls "promises to keep" which are opposed to watching a lovely scene and the need for sleep. All these propositions, when referred to an appropriate standard of human conduct, yield a judgment of the speaker's action and character.

The evidence for evaluative propositions is not as simple as it may seem. Consider, for example, the proposition that Frost's traveler is "tarrying," not merely "stopping." First, we must interpret the traveler's thoughts not merely as a train of ideas but as signs of certain things he does (stopping, watching; imagining, deciding), certain conditions of mind (uneasiness, admiration, regret), his particular situation, etc. Next, we must consider the specific act of "stopping here" in view of all circumstances that may be known from taking his thoughts as signs of other things: for example, why does it seem important to him that the woods' owner "will not see me stopping here"? or, how significant to him are his horse's imaginary objections? And finally, we must refer the act of "stopping here" to an appropriate standard by which we may, having weighed all its given circumstances, judge of it.

An interpretive analysis of Frost's poem would thus consist of a complex network of inferences of various kinds, basic propositions on which these rest, and certain standards by which one may evaluate certain aspects of the poetic experience. For the poem represents directly only an individual's train of reflection, but we must needs infer and evaluate, if we are to respond properly to the poem, the whole experience which his reflection implies.

III

A lyric poem, like any other literary work, is generally either mimetic or didactic. The didactic lyric presents an argument, the mimetic represents an experience. Compare, for example, Longfellow's "A Psalm of Life" with Marvell's "To His Coy Mistress": what is merely argument of a sort in one is someone's action in the other. When we respond to a lyric poem, it is always on the basis of opinion concerning the elements of an idea or theme as they correlate and constitute the whole argument, or concerning the elements of an experience, such as action and character, as they interrelate and constitute the whole experience. If, then, a lyric poem is to have a determinate effect, it must furnish data to support certain opinions and deny certain others; and we must ask, in interpretation, what the poet has done, in a given poem, "to afford data or to warrant implication or evaluation."

Frost's poem is mimetic, and has the form of verbal action or speech as action, i.e., its significance lies not only in what is said but also in someone's saying it. We have not merely a series of declarative statements (speech), but also, someone's deliberative activity (speech as action), and implied thereby, a particular sort of response to his own situation by a more or less individualized character (the "real nature" of the represented experience).

There is a difference between language as such and the "language" of action: language is analytic, but action, synthetic. Language, to convey an experience, to express its synthesis, distinguishes between the man and his activity, gives each a name, and then integrates, to say, "the man is deliberating"; but experience presents the synthesis as the-man-deliberating; and such a synthesis is similarly represented in turn by verbal action, such as that which Frost's poem renders.

Frost's poem, considering the *manner* of representation, is "dramatic." For someone speaks in his own person, and therefore, language, as employed in the poem, performs directly his action (deliberating) and renders, by implication, its "real nature"; you witness the-man-deliberating. And you are responding to his experience, now, as he undergoes a crisis of sort and comes to a final resolution of it. Compare, again, with "Psalm of Life" or Pope's *Essay on Man*. Both are didactic, and have no intrinsic "dramatic" interest, i.e., our response does not depend on a particular human experience which either renders. One is merely speech on the order of a Sunday exhortation—the didactic poem as sermon; the other is a moral treatise in verse—the didactic poem as tract.

Not all poems, however, of the mimetic class are "dramatic" on the order of Frost's poem. Keats' "The Eve of St. Agnes" is a mimetic poem, but it is not a lyric since it involves plot such as that which you have in a short story like Joyce's "Araby"; and it is *narrative* in manner. Keats' "La Belle Dame Sans Merci" is also a narrative poem or "story poem," rather than a lyric, in that its organizing principle is plot. It is essentially narrative, for the manner is only *pseudo-dramatic*, i.e., one character asks another for an explanation of the latter's condition, and the latter recounts his experience to explain it. We respond primarily, not to their encounter, as in "Lord Randal" or "Edward," but to the knight's experience *as narrated*. Compare this with a "dramatic" lyric involving more than one character like Browning's "The Bishop Orders His Tomb," where we respond to a confrontation between the Bishop and his illegitimate children.

The problem then of the poet, if he is to reconstruct a human experience in a "dramatic" lyric, is to make an object whose medium is not simply language as such but language *as action*. The title of Frost's poem employs only language as such; but the poem itself is language as action. The poet conveys the experience "primarily by verbal action, and conveys that alone directly, conveying everything else indirectly, that is, by implication." When, for example, a physical action is involved ("stopping here"), the poet can only imply it, since all we have, directly, is someone's deliberative activity. Similarly, any internal condition of the speaker can only be inferred, e.g., that he is inwardly troubled. His "speech" is a "thinking aloud" which the poem renders directly, but its "real nature" as action can only be inferred also; e.g., that he is really coping with a moral crisis of sort, but decides finally to keep faith.

Interpretation seeks to determine the "real nature" of the represented action or experience; but the basic proposition concerning it can state only its "apparent form" as verbal action. When we note that the statements in Frost's poem are declarative sentences which mean such and such, we are considering only their grammar (language as such): Frost himself is merely saying that he thinks he knows whose woods these are, that the owner's house is in the village though these are his woods, etc. When we say, "Someone is deliberating," we are stating the action of a character who exists only in the poem, but not adequately, since "deliberating," in the speaker's circumstances, implies more than someone's having such and such thoughts.

The basic proposition as regards the lyric action is, nevertheless, essential in interpretation. For, first, the verbal action constitutes an essential structure of the "dramatic" lyric. The basic proposition which it warrants is not subject to conjecture and evaluation, for otherwise our response to the lyric action does not rest on any foundation. Secondly, though the "apparent form" is "not necessarily the same as the real nature of the action ... it remains a thing done, regardless of what constructions may be placed upon the doing of it." And thirdly, both the "apparent form" and the "real nature" of the verbal action are determinative of the inner structure or form of the lyric poem.

The truth value of basic propositions depends on "whether their predicates are definitions convertible with the statement of the verbal action." In "someone is deliberating," the predicate is a definition immediately convertible with a statement of the verbal action which the poem renders. "The predicate, furthermore, must never contain a metaphor, for all metaphors involve ambiguity," and therefore, inference; "and it must also never involve any term of evaluation, that is, anything that involves a judgment of the action," for that would be an evaluative inference. We cannot say, "The speaker in Frost's poem desires death," because "desires" evaluates the drift of his thoughts, and "death" is a metaphorical meaning for "sleep."

We must, nevertheless, make inferences and evaluations to determine the "real nature" of the verbal action by considering the conditions or circumstances under which it is done. We infer, for example, that the speaker is on a journey "to keep promises," tarries, enjoys the woods, is inwardly troubled, resists a temptation of sort, etc. A very complex process, but necessary, for otherwise we would never be able to state the "real nature" of his experience.

The circumstances of an act are, "generally, the agent, the act, the person or thing on which the act is done, the purpose, the result, the instrument, the manner, the time, and the place." In any literary work, all or only some are rendered or implied, and all or only some are further specified in various ways, according to the sort of effect that a particular action or experience, as so represented, is to have on us. But in a lyric poem, all circumstances of the verbal act can only be inferred, since no basic proposition can be made except one that concerns only its "apparent form," and all other basic propositions involve only the speaker's thoughts. Moreover, the circumstances of an act are either "substantive," i.e., they "constitute the act as an act of a particular nature," or merely "incidental." That Frost's speaker has a sense of duty is a "substantive" circumstance which has to do with the character of the agent; it determines, significantly, the nature of his deliberative activity. But that it is a snowy evening is merely "incidental," since it does not affect the character of the deliberation. If it were not evening, or snowing, would that change or in any way affect the speaker's basic attitude? The poem does not indicate or hint that it would. Again, it is the *purpose* for which the journey has been undertaken that makes it a "substantive" circumstance; and therefore, the journey in itself is not "substantive."

IV

In formal criticism, a literary work may be distinguished in terms of the means, the manner, the object, and the end or effect of the representation. Considering only the *object* of representation as a principle of differentiation, lyric poems of the same mimetic class may then be discriminated as to their specific kind in terms of the verbal act represented. In Hopkin's "Spring and Fall," for example, someone is also reflecting or deliberating; but the action is different from that in Frost's poem because the circumstances that constitute its nature as an act are different. A mature person is addressing in his mind a weeping child; he understands Margaret's grief from the vantage point of an older person who knows from experience that "sorrow's springs are the same"; he would comfort Margaret but she is too young, too innocent, to understand that "It is Margaret you mourn for." Where, therefore, Frost's speaker is deliberating, i.e., making up his mind, arriving at a moral decision of sort, Hopkins' is contemplating a human condition, "the blight man was born for." Again, in the anonymous "O Western Wind," the "apparent form" of the verbal act is that of an outcry; we only infer that a lover is longing for an absent beloved. (Strictly speaking, the speaker is either man or woman.) In Marvell's "To His Coy Mistress," also, someone's argument is directly represented as a specific sort of verbal act; but we infer its "real nature" as that of a clever act of seduction. An aggressive and passionate lover, who is also shrewd and witty, is persuading and urging his "coy mistress" to yield herself to him, now.

In all these instances, both the "apparent form" and the "real nature" of the verbal act are determinative of the form or structure of the lyric poem. Obviously, too, when the object of representation is different, the poetic power or effect would also be different; and here, we have another principle of differentiation among *kinds* of lyric poems. In Hopkins' poem, we feel *similarly* as the speaker; i.e., the poem puts us in a pensive frame of mind much like that of the speaker. We contemplate the same object that the speaker contemplates, i.e., "the blight man was born for," so that we perceive, as the speaker does, that Margaret "'weeping over Goldengrove unleaving" is really, even now, already mourning her own inevitable death. Therefore, we feel similarly as the speaker because what causes his emotion is also what causes our own response: i.e., the same perception of the human condition. But in Frost's poem, we feel *differently* from the speaker because what causes his emotion is different from what causes our own response. The speaker feels a quiet sense of moral triumph over a difficulty resolved; he is uneasy and tense until he finally chooses to continue on his journey and keep his promises; it is not without regret that he foregoes the lovely sight of woods filling up with snow; he feels a deep weariness (perhaps only physical, but perhaps, also spiritual) as he drives away and thinks of

the "miles to go before I sleep"; but, at the same time, despite
the regret and the weariness, he feels a kind of moral relief.
This is the dominant feeling or emotion of the speaker at the
poem's close since it alone dispels the tension and misgiving
which initiated his deliberation and gave it a moral cast. Clear-
ly, the reader does not feel similarly as Frost's traveler, be-
cause he responds to the poetic depiction only through sympa-
thy (for the traveler in his situation), and on the ground of a
moral judgment that the depiction promotes. In Hopkins' poem,
we share the speaker's thoughts and are led by them to agree
with his conclusion; since these alone are the ground of his
mood and that of ours, we feel consequently as the speaker
does. But with Frost's traveler, it is not a matter of sharing
his thoughts and agreeing on some universal truth which con-
duces to a certain attitude or mood. The traveler is responding
to his own situation at the moment, a situation which requires
a moral decision of sort on his part; the reader, on the other
hand, is sympathetically responding to the traveler's action or
behavior and judging it on some ethical ground. The reader is
not himself engaged with the same problem of choice that the
traveler deliberates on; therefore, even if he shares through
sympathy the traveler's uneasiness and relief, he does not him-
self feel what the traveler feels. He admires, for instance, the
traveler's fine moral sense, but the traveler cannot be said to
be admiring himself. Again, when the traveler feels a kind of
moral relief at the poem's close, the reader does not himself
feel that kind of relief (since he does not have the traveler's
problem of choice); or, if the reader does feel that kind of
relief, it is yet different in character since it has a different
source—that is, for the traveler, the cause is his final resolu-
tion of an ethical problem, but for the reader, the cause is
his sympathy for the traveler and his own judgment that such
a choice as the traveler made, in any such situation, is right.
The relief the reader feels is also a kind of release from the
uneasiness and tension that he sympathetically feels from wit-
nessing the traveler in his situation; here, again, the reader's
uneasiness and tension is different in its essential character
from that of the traveler since they have different causes—that

is, where the traveler's uneasiness is, because of his situation, moral in nature (a misgiving), the reader's uneasiness is merely sympathetic (an emotional tension).[3]

Verbal action in a lyric poem represents, generally, either (1) someone who is moved by some emotion, as in "O Western Wind"; or (2) someone whose private activity of thought is exteriorized in speech, as in Frost's poem, where it is essentially deliberative, or in Hopkins', where someone is not so much comforting a child as contemplating a human condition (hence, the child's grief is merely its occasion); or (3) someone who is acting upon another character existing only as the object of his action, as in Marvell's poem, where the lover is persuading his mistress. In all cases, we interpret not only what someone's thoughts mean, but also, what their meanings imply in terms of the speaker's action, character, and emotion. And therefore, verbal action is the sign, not only of the "real nature" of someone's activity, but also of character and emotion in a lyric poem.

By character, we mean the sort of person the speaker in a poem is given out to be: whether, for example, he is one who has a fine sense of moral duty, as in Frost's poem; or whether, as in Hopkins', he is a pensive thinker or philosopher of sort. Other traits are of course involved; for example, one is sensitive to beauty, and the other, a gentle and compassionate person; but what we are trying to specify is their distinctive character. Thus, character may be precisely defined as "the potentiality of the agent for action of a certain kind, . . . or to put it differently, it is what determines the necessity or probability of a given action in terms of its agent." Character is an internal condition, a potentiality, and hence, it can only be

---

[3] Another illustration: in "O Western Wind" and Marvell's "Coy Mistress," our response is quite different from what their speakers feel since the causes of the speakers' emotions and our own are different. In one, we do not find ourselves in the same condition of passionate longing for a loved one, and in the other, we do not share the lover's own desire to possess his mistress. For in both poems, the cause of the lover's longing or desire—namely, his own ardent love—is not the cause of our own response: in one, we respond to the lover's yearning, and so feel a certain pity for his condition; in the other, we respond to the intellectual adroitness or wit of the lover's argument, and so feel a delighted admiration for the lover's clever mind.

inferred from action which manifests it. And therefore, also, action is the principal part of the *object* of imitation in the lyric poem; i.e., verbal action, both its "apparent form" (e.g., an emotional outcry or private mental activity or persuasion) and its "real nature" (e.g., longing, or making a moral or ethical choice, or seducing).

Both character and emotion are inferred through signs and probabilities as these arise from the agent himself through his verbal act, primarily, and everything else that his action may imply. We infer by sign that Frost's traveler has a fine moral sense from a prior inference that he decides finally to keep faith; and by probability, also, because one who keeps faith is generally a morally sensitive person. Again, we infer that he is uneasy because he exhibits signs of uneasiness in his own thoughts (note his concern lest the woods' owner "see me stopping here," and what he assumes his own horse "must think"); and also, because anyone, given such a character as our speaker has, in a similar situation, would probably feel uneasy.

Most lyric poems represent only "a single character acting in a single closed situation"; by closed situation is meant that the speaker's activity is "uncomplicated by any other agency."[4] Thus, character is not usually as highly individualized as we find it in most drama and prose fiction. But the degree of particularization varies among poems according to the sort of emotional response that the poem is to evoke. Frost's traveler is about as individual as Hopkins' contemplative; but the lover in Marvell's poem is more individual than the lover in "O Western Wind," i.e., Marvell permits more inferences about his lover's character; but also, less individual than the lover in Browning's "My Last Duchess."

The degree of specificity that the poem permits in our moral judgment of action and character qualifies our emotional response. Compare, for example, our responses to the lovers in "O Western Wind," "To His Coy Mistress," and "My Last Duchess." In the first poem, we consider only the speaker's

4 Elder Olson, "An Outline of Poetic Theory," in *Critics and Criticism*, ed. R.S. Crane (Chicago, 1952), p. 560.

emotion, a lover's passionate longing for a beloved, and to that alone we respond; we can make no further consideration (as to whether, for example, the emotion is licit or illicit). In the other two poems, however, our judgment of the speaker's character is necessary for the proper response. In Marvell's poem, we respond primarily to the lover's resourceful wit, the intellectual adroitness of his arguments, by which he seeks to fulfill his passionate desire. But we cannot evaluate further his action and, hence, his character. The effect of the poem is, in fact, to make us side with him rather than with his "coy mistress." We are delighted by his argument and we admire his mind. But in Browning's poem, the opposite is true: we are repelled by the lover's cruelty and blind pride; we judge of the Duke as a villain. He has caused the death of his last duchess, whom we favor, and is now taking a new wife, for whom we fear, since the Duke's message to the Count is a veiled threat.

The magnitude of the lyric action (that of a single character acting in a single closed situation) necessarily restricts inferences concerning action, character, and emotion, i.e., they rest on a single instance in an individual experience. Therefore, only natural signs and natural probabilities are usually the warrant for inferences from signs and probabilities in the lyric speech; and only a universal standard of morality is usually called for in evaluative propositions.

A relevant question in interpretation is, therefore, one posed by the represented action or experience in a given lyric poem; and what determines the validity of any answer to it is the total experience as represented in the poem directly and by implication. Moreover, formal criticism can rest on no other foundation than a valid interpretation.

"Edward": A Problem in Hermeneutics [1]

EDWARD
(Anonymous)

"Why does your sword so drop with blood,
          Edward, Edward,
Why does your sword so drop with blood,
     And why so sad go ye O?"
"O I have killed my hawk so good,
          Mother, Mother,
O I have killed my hawk so good,
     And I had no more but he O."

"Your hawk's blood was never so red,
          Edward, Edward,
Your hawk's blood was never so red,
     My dear son I tell thee O."
"O I have killed my red-roan steed,
          Mother, Mother,
O I have killed my red-roan steed,
     That once was so fair and free O."

"Your steed was old and you have got more,
          Edward, Edward,
Your steed was old and you have got more,
     Some other grief you drie O." *
"O I have killed my father dear,
          Mother, Mother,
O I have killed my father dear,
     Alas, and woe is me O."

---

[1] We are here concerned with only one version of the ballad, the same
version that is analyzed in Cleanth Brooks, John Thibaut Purser, and
Robert Penn Warren, *An Approach to Literature*, alternate 4th ed. (Ap-
pleton-Century-Crofts, 1967), pp. 290-92.
* Vocabulary note: *drie*, endure

"And what penance will you drie for that,
          Edward, Edward,
And what penance will you drie for that?
    My dear son, now tell me O."
"I'll set my feet in yonder boat,
          Mother, Mother,
I'll set my feet in yonder boat,
    And I'll fare over the sea O."

"And what will you do with your towers and your hall,
          Edward, Edward,
And what will you do with your towers and your hall,
    That were so fair to see O?"
"I'll let them stand till they down fall,
          Mother, Mother,
I'll let them stand till they down fall,
    For here never more must I be O."

"And what will you leave to your children and your wife,
          Edward, Edward,
And what will you leave to your children and your wife,
    When you go over the sea O?"
"The world's room; let them beg through life,
          Mother, Mother,
The world's room; let them beg through life,
    For them never more will I see O."

"And what will you leave to your own mother dear,
          Edward, Edward,
And what will you leave to your own mother dear?
    My dear son, now tell me O."
"The curse of hell from me shall you bear,
          Mother, Mother,
The curse of hell from me shall you bear,
    Such counsels you gave to me O."

If we examine how exactly we are led by the poem to re-
spond to the depicted experience at each stage, as it were, of
the encounter between mother and son, we would not, I think,
be too easily misled by facile interpretations of the poem's
"meaning" or "experience."

The *first stanza* begins on an ominous note with the mo-
ther's query: "Why does your sword so drop with blood, Ed-
ward, ... and why so sad go ye O?" We are here moved by
a mother's fear and anxiety; and with the son's response,

we not only feel his sorrow but surmise that perhaps the killing of his hawk was an accident. We have no ground as yet to suspect that it might have been deliberate.

In the *second stanza,* after the mother has expressed her disbelief ("Your hawk's blood was never so red"), our foreboding increases with the mother's growing anxiety (we certainly do not suspect her at this stage); and with the son's response, we begin to doubt somewhat the sincerity of his grief since we suspect he may be lying and feel that perhaps he has done a more serious deed. He seems to deny that it was his hawk that he has killed; so perhaps, too, it was not his steed. He seems unwilling to confess just exactly what he might have done. (In "Lord Randal," we feel, toward the poem's end, that the son may not be telling all to his mother, but not that he may be lying.)

Our suspicion is somewhat confirmed when, in the *third stanza,* Edward's mother again shows her disbelief. "Your steed was old" (hence, it could not have made your sword drip with so much blood), and besides, "you have got more" (hence, there is no reason to be "so sad"). Edward, then, must be lying, or, he must have committed a more grievous deed: "Some other grief you drie O." Edward then comes out with the truth, and we are moved *chiefly* by the horror of his deed, though we are also touched with pity for the son's remorse. We feel he is *not* lying: the expression of grief rings true (we cannot feel it is merely put on); we have been emotionally prepared for it by his mother's suspicion of a more terrible deed; we may also feel that Edward is himself impressed by the horror of his deed such that he could not quite tell it directly; besides, in the next stanza, Edward's mother no longer doubts her son's deed.

In the *fourth stanza,* there is no need to feel that the mother's reaction is a little strange. Why isn't she aghast? Why does she seem so detached? I don't think it immediately occurs to us to question her reaction, to grow suspicious of it. Certainly, Edward's mother might have reacted differently, but there is really nothing particularly questionable about it. That she does not appear emotionally upset, at this point in the encounter, does not necessarily indicate that she must be cold-hearted—or that she already knew about Edward's crime and had only been leading her son to his confession. After all, she too is somehow prepared, after her questioning doubts, to accept her son's shocking revelation. The deed is done; what remains is her son's remorse and penance. She is not thinking, here, of herself; rather, she is addressing herself to a very serious moral problem: what terrible penance will you now endure for the parricide? (Even in the light of the *last stanza*, we cannot conclude that, necessarily, she is merely being hypocritical.) And her moral concern is, as a matter of fact, quickly taken up by her son's moral decision on self-exile as the necessary penance. Edward takes his mother's question seriously although he has already (we know this in the final stanza) lost his respect for her. (And, incidentally, Edward's decision removes any doubt regarding the parricide or his remorse.)

In the *fifth stanza*, the mother, realizing the implications of her son's self-imposed penance, begins to protest against it. It can be pointed out that Edward is now the heir to his father's estate and that his crime has not freed him from filial obligations. But this does not seem really to be the basis of his mother's appeal, for she calls attention rather to the pity of "your towers and your hall . . . *so fair to see*" falling into ruin for neglect. It would seem, then, to her mind that Edward's self-imposed penance is not quite right merely from a material consideration, just as though such a concern might outweigh the moral consideration with which she began. There is no question here regarding the sincerity of her moral concern in the preceding stanza; after all, a mother's natural, if selfish, desire to keep her son by her may now be motivating Edward's mother. In any case, her objection seems an instance of "such counsels" as she is used to giving her son.[2] The son's response certainly shows his deep regret for

---

[2] May it not be that the mother's objection, as phrased, is simply a manner of speaking? That is: she may really be appealing to her son's sense of filial obligation at the same time that she shows, quite unconsciously, her emotional attachment to those towers and hall "so fair to see." This interpretation is kinder, if not fairer, to Edward's mother. In any case, the emotional attachment does color, or tend to subvert a little, the ground of her objection.

A PROBLEM IN HERMENEUTICS

For Brooks et al., the interest of the poem lies chiefly in the "story" and its "meaning." The story, they say, is as follows:

> Edward, the hero of the ballad, is a knight. His mother and father have *presumably* had a deadly quarrel. In any case we *know* of the desire of the mother to dispose of the father. The mother has gradually played on the son's feelings until he worked himself up to the point of killing the father. The mother has therefore accomplished her purpose without making herself actually guilty of murder. She discovers her son with a bloody sword in his hand; and in a mixture of curiosity, gratification, and horror, now that the deed is actually accomplished, she questions Edward...[3] (underscoring mine.)

I do not know by what sort of sleuthing Brooks et al. have ferreted out their "facts," but the alleged "story" seems to be a consequence of their supposition that what you have is a narrative, "not 'told'... [but] rather, presented in direct form as a dialogue between the two principal persons of the story." What you really have is a *confrontation;* the dialogue is merely the principal device of representing it.

We know that Edward is a knight or nobleman "because of the reference to his towers and hall." But "how do we know of the relation of father and mother? The last line of the poem established the mother's desire to get rid of the father." But does it, really? It establishes, rather, the ground or reason for the son's curse against his own mother by establishing the son's awareness that his crime is a direct consequence of his upbringing on "such counsels" as she gave him. All we can infer is that her counsels were somehow morally deficient; we cannot be certain as to whether she had somehow goaded her son to a parricide that she herself had secretly desired.

"How do we know that Edward is suffering remorse before he confesses?" We know from Edward himself when he laments his deed: "O I have killed my father dear, / Alas, and woe is me O!" But, we are told, we know it on some other ground:

[3] Cleanth Brooks *et al., An Approach to Literature,* pp. 290-92. All quotations, unless otherwise indicated, refer to this critical write-up.

> [Edward] refers to his "hawk so good," his only one, and
> to his "red-roan steed," that before was "fair and free";
> but this regret for loss *is really a statement of regret for
> the loss of the father,* who may be taken to have been "so
> good" and "fair and free." There would have been no more
> reason for killing the father than for butchering the hawk
> or the horse which had served him well. (Underscoring
> mine.)

Now this is certainly a case of twisting your evidence. Why
should one statement of regret over one loss be considered
as a version merely of another statement of regret over an-
other loss? Besides, we really do not need some such other
ground for supposing what is already quite plain. We would
feel insulted.

It may also be pointed out that it is not because Edward
is "overcome with his growing remorse" that he finally "con-
fesses to the crime." For Edward's intention seems, rather,
to show his mother, with a kind of vengeance, the disastrous
effects of her counsels. He is *not* confessing. He is sorry
(we cannot doubt it, finally) for hawk and horse, and re-
morseful over his father's murder, and owns his guilt; but
more than that, he has come home before sailing away to
lay the chief blame on his mother. For why indeed does he
begin in his "confession" with hawk and steed, both dear to
him, before he tells with great anguish of his parricide? It
is apparently with the same sword that he has actually killed
his hawk, his steed, and at last his own father in a violent
emotional fit (there is no ground to suppose that the killing
of hawk and steed is merely a metaphor for the parricide!);
and he is apparently showing his mother just how irration-
ally destructive her counsels have made him. It is not Ed-
ward's mother who is leading her son on to a "confession"
(which occurs soon enough); it is rather Edward who is
leading his mother on to her "penance."

And "how do we know that the woman is a hard and
calculating woman? Naturally, we know it from the accusa-
tion at the end." But, as we have noted earlier, the accusa-
tion as such cannot establish her character as "hard and cal-
culating" since it does not allow us to infer that she had her-
self instigated her own husband's murder.

But there are three significant indications that do something to define her earlier in the poem and to give an effect of mounting suspense. First, when Edward says that he grieves over the horse, she says, "why, the horse was old," ignoring any sentiment a person might feel for a faithful animal. To her it is only a piece of property.

She is not exactly saying, "why, the horse was old!" with that implication which Brooks et al. conveniently (in view of their hypothesis) read into that statement; rather, as they themselves assert, she is saying that if he has killed his horse, "he would not be [as] sad" as he now looks "because he has other and better ones." The point, then, would seem to be her disbelief: "Some other grief you drie O." Indeed, the fact that she does not know what greater sorrow her son bears would seem to indicate that she has not earlier desired "to dispose of the father" (thus clearing her at least of an unjust charge). But may she not be merely pretending that she does not know? This, too, would be unjust since the poem offers no evidence for supposing it.[4] The mother's disbelief enforces a growing fear on her part that Edward has done a more grievous deed than he is willing to admit.

[But] Second, she asks, "what penance will *you* do?" She attempts by the way she frames the question to separate herself from all responsibility. The normal reaction would have been one of grief or at least momentary astonishment, but she is so cold and self-controlled that she first attempts to clear her own skirts.

The stress on *you* is of course Brooks' et al. I have already commented on this aspect of the depicted experience. The above interpretation is neither necessary nor probable even in the light of the son's accusation.

Third, when she addresses him in the last stanza she refers to herself as his "own mother dear," trying to ingra-

---

[4] We are not, most certainly, playing counsel to Edward's mother. We are merely trying to show what correct inferences we can draw about the situation which the encounter reveals. For we cannot respond properly to the confrontation unless we have judged in all fairness the *dramatis personæ* on the evidence only that the poem presents. What it presents is intended to determine and control our response.

tiate herself with him, when she is really his worst enemy and has ruined him.

Certainly, she is "trying to ingratiate herself with him," but how should that mean that she is therefore "hard and calculating"? It seems perfectly natural, in an emotional relationship, to try and cling to the object of one's attachment, especially when a separation threatens.

> What is the meaning of the poem? We know the story, but what kind of effect does the story give? It gives an effect of tragic irony. A crime has been committed; and presumably the person most guilty, the mother, will suffer. But the son, whose moral nature is much superior to that of his mother but who has been influenced by her to commit the crime, must suffer too. Even the absolutely innocent persons, the wife and children, must suffer, for they will be abandoned to beg through life. The same question lies behind this story that lies behind the great tragedies: what is the nature of justice? But the ironical effect is not single, for it has certain cross references as it were, within the situation. First, only when the father is dead does Edward realize the father's virtues and his own better nature that brings him to remorse and penance. Second, the mother, who should be the greatest guardian of the son, has ruined him. Third, the mother who expected some profit or satisfaction from the crime, is left with only a curse from the son whom, in her way, she loves. Fourth, the wife and children, who are innocent, must suffer too. The irony of "Sir Patrick Spens" is more simple.[5]

To Brooks et al. the "meaning" and "effect" are apparently the same; i.e., we are moved precisely by the "meaning" of the poetic experience. What the poem, or the depicted experience, "means" is precisely its power to move us emotionally in some determinate way. But "meaning," for Brooks et al., is over and above the experience to which we respond; more specifically, it is the *ironies* that might always be perceived in any human situation. "Meaning" is abstracted from the experience: "What is the nature of justice?" To have

[5] Again, gratuitous inferences: (1) only when the father is dead does Edward realize the father's virtues (because of hawk "so good" and steed "so fair and free"? because of his remorse?); (2) Edward's mother expected some profit or satisfaction from the crime.

responded directly to the poetic experience does not seem to be enough; we must look beyond the experience, as it were, for some further revelation of "meaning."

The "irony" is there, of course, but is it "tragic"? Or what can Brooks et al. mean by "tragic"? Certainly, the depicted situation is "ironic" as well as "tragic" if by that we mean, for example, that the mother should have been the last person to ruin her son ("ironic"), or that the misfortune is so great that even the innocent (Edward's own family) suffer ("tragic," assuming, gratuitously, that Edward is a noble character). But the *immediate* impact of the experience, as soon as we apprehend it, is not to make us see that it is "ironic" or "tragic": that seems primarily an *intellectual* effort, a careful consideration of the "data" which the poetic experience offers for the abstracting mind. We see that it is indeed "ironic" and "tragic" (more precisely, "pathetic") only after our *emotional* response to the experience has been evoked; only after we have apprehended the experience *as a concrete individual experience* and have been moved by it; only after we have carefully examined that experience, not simply now on its own terms but in relation to the universal human experience, such that, for example, we can ask questions like, "What is the nature of justice?" The "ironic" and the "tragic" elements (indeed, the "ironic-and-tragic" structure) of that experience, which the mind abstracts, do *enforce* the power or effect of the poem, but they *do not*, therefore, constitute the actual effect of the experience as poetically rendered. The effect is not, essentially, intellectual but *emotional;* but the emotion, of course, is founded upon an intelligent, though also instinctive, apprehension of the whole concrete, individual experience. The *actual and immediate effect* of the ballad, the *essential power* of the depicted experience, is to move us with a moral sort of horror: we are horrified by Edward's mother, we disapprove of her on moral grounds, since "such counsels" as she gave her son have led to senseless killing and parricide. We do not need to know just exactly what "such counsels" were; we see clearly enough their evil consequences. Indeed, if we know what those counsels are, our consideration of their exact nature may very well lessen the effect of horror: for, if they were patently evil, we may not be so easily convinced that the mother could be so evil (unless more grounds for the opinion are given); but if, on the other hand, they were not so morally deficient, we may begin to hold that the mother is not so much to blame after all. In short, the poet would have involved himself in an unnecessary difficulty when he had only wanted, *in the first instance,* not a perception of the "tragic irony," for example, of human experience *in general* (of which, then, Edward's "story" is merely a concrete illustration), but rather, a dramatic representation of a final confrontation between mother and son, an evocation of the moral horror (the emotional power) of a *particular human situation.*

Meaning has *two senses:* (1) an abstraction or theme implied by such a question as "What is the nature of justice?" which is *assumed* to be the poet's "thesis"; i.e., a "meaning" over and above the particular experience depicted; and (2) the meaning of the experience itself as poetically rendered since, as a concrete and particular human experience, it is already meaningful in and by itself; this meaning entails, for example, the peculiar nature of the confrontation between Edward and his mother, the character of the mother, etc. Our chief point, then, is that if we *begin* with "meaning" (sense 1), we tend to ignore or gloss over our own immediate reaction to the experience as poetically rendered, to treat rather cavalierly such an experience and, in view of a particular hypothesis as to its "meaning," even to distort the poetic experience for the sake of our own favorite hypothesis or theme. Interpretation of meaning (sense 2) must *precede* formal criticism, which is already concerned with the nature of the artistic object, called the poem, considered as an imitation of a particular human experience. But we cannot interpret meaning (sense 2), nor choose between alternative "meanings" (sense 1), unless we look closely at the experience as poetically rendered and consider our own reaction to it in every part of it and as a whole. Such a reaction, while essentially emotional, is grounded on inferences we make at every stage as the poetic experience unfolds, and is finally determined by our apprehension of the particular human experience *as a whole.*

Three Critical Comments on "O Western Wind":
A Criticism of Criticism

O WESTERN WIND[1]
(Anonymous)

O western wind, when wilt thou blow
That the small rain down can rain?
Christ, if my love were in my arms
And I in my bed again!

Three critical comments on "O Western Wind" illustrate
various approaches to the poem which are either inadequate
or invalid primarily because of the critics' failure to con-
ceive of the poem as *more than a verbal composite*.

> A. Two lines of description, two of emotion. And for
> description, the eliminating of everything but the wind
> and the rain. Then, for the sake of sharpness, the two ad-
> jectives—the "western" wind, the "small" rain . . . The
> words are exactly chosen, even to the sound of the *w's* in
> the first line and the droning *n's* in the second. But more
> than that, the poem has been made intense by a rigorous
> narrowing down to two simple elements.[2]

Western wind and *small rain* are certainly "description,"
and as such, elements of the poetic *means* (verbal medium);
and the economy of such description doubtless contributes to
a certain intensity of poetic effect. But they are not merely
description; they have a *dramatic* context: i.e., the speaker

---

[1] In Sir Arthur Quiller-Couch's *The New Oxford Book of English
Verse* (1939), this poem bears a title which describes its speaker's action:
"The Lover in Winter Plaineth for the Spring."
[2] Donald A. Stauffer, as quoted in *The Case For Poetry*, ed. Frederick
L. Gwynn *et al.* (Prentice-Hall, 1954), p. 13.

is not describing something that has yet to occur; he is, rather doing something more definite—wishing for rain to come.[3]

The poem is not rigorously narrowed down to two simple elements: description and emotion. Emotion, after all, is involved in the wish for rain. Description is an element of the poetic means, and emotion, an element of the poetic *object* (what the poem represents).

The poem happens to be an imitation. As imitation, its elements are, in the order of importance, its effect or power, the object, the manner, and the means of imitation. As one form of imitation, the poem is an instance of a poetic species which may be generally defined in terms of *all* its parts, thus:

> 1. The *object* of imitation is a serious action of the first order of magnitude, i.e., one involving a single character acting in a single closed situation. The speaker in the poem is performing an act which actualizes and instances his condition as a lover (passionately longing to return home to his beloved) ;[4]
> 2. The *manner* is dramatic since the character speaks and acts in his own person;
> 3. The *means* are the words embellished by rhythm, rhyme, alliteration, etc.

[3] Why is it that we assume the lover in the poem is a man? The assumption rests on a mere convention that the poem does not seek to controvert; i.e., the popular notion that in love the man plays the *aggressive* role. Owing to such a convention, we find it easier, for example, to refer the blasphemous oath, "Christ," to a man in a passion rather than to a woman (who must always behave like a lady).

Why does the lover say *"small* rain"? Where the lover in e.e. cummings' "somewhere I have never travelled" speaks of the rain as having "such small hands", thereby suggesting a sweet, feminine delicacy of temperament, likewise, our lover's imagined perception of "small rain" bespeaks a tenderness of mood not inconsistent with the passionate force of his yearning for the beloved.

[4] The address to the western wind, harbinger of rain and spring, is imaginary, not an actual address. It is a rhetorical device called apostrophe by which the poet depicts someone's ardent wish for rain. But the lover's wish for spring, while real, also projects his desire for the beloved since the rain or spring would somehow make their reunion possible. Such a possibility explains the nature of the "parallelism" (which Bateson sees differently) between the first two verses (the wish for rain) and the last two (the wish or yearning for the beloved). That spring would somehow reunite the lover's points, moreover, to winter as having somehow caused their separation; but, certainly, we cannot ever know *more specifically* (since our only evidence is the poem) just how winter separated, or just how spring would reunite, the two lovers.

4. The *effect* is a general sort of sympathy, the sort we feel for *any* lover in distress. No moral judgment of the speaker's action is involved.

The poem, considered as an imitation with a certain disnctive power, has in relation to that power (which is its *sential* form, "soul," or structure) the following parts in is order of importance: the activity itself of wishing or nging; emotion or passion, which the activity actualizes;[5] ought (i.e., the content of the lover's plaint), by which the motion is made manifest; and last, diction (i.e., the vehicle ' the lover's thought). The order of importance is estab-shed by the poetic power; it indicates the governance of part ' part in relation to the whole which they constitute in such ise as to endow it with a certain distinctive power.[6]

B. The lover, grieving for the absent beloved, cries out for relief. Several kinds of relief are involved in the appeal to the wind. First, there is the relief that would be had from the sympathetic manifestation of nature. The lover, in his perturbation of spirit, invokes the perturbations of nature. He invokes the beneficent perturbation

Western wind, when will thou blow,

as Lear invokes the destructive,

Blow, winds, and crack your checks!
rage! blow!

Second, there is the relief that would be had by the fulfillment of grief—the frost of grief, the drought of grief broken, the full anguish expressed, then the violence allayed in the peace of tears. Third, there is the relief that

---

[5] We omit *character* as a qualitative part of the imitation since all can really infer about the speaker is that he is a *lover* (which is not at we mean by character), and *passionate* (which is not character her, in this particular instance, but rather, an emotional condition of lover).

[6] It would be interesting to compare "O Western Wind" (generally reed to be a "lyric poem") with Francisco Arcellana's "Trilogy of the rtles" (generally agreed, I suppose, to be a "short story"). Is Arcellana's tory" a *short story* or a *lyric poem?* The question deserves more than footnote, since any adequate answer to it involves a distinction between *lyric* and a *non-lyric* poem (say, Keats' "Ode on a Grecian Urn" and eats' *The Eve of St. Agnes*), and a distinction between *lyric poem* and ort story; both distinction, moreover, would have to be made more con-ete and more specific through the analysis of various possible forms kinds of the so-called "lyric poem" and various possible forms or kinds the so-called "short story."

would be had in the excitement and fulfillment of love it
self. There seems to be a contrast between the first tw
types of relief and the third type; speaking loosely, ..
the first two types are romantic and general, the thir
type realistic and specific ...

In the last two lines, the lover cries out for the spe
cific solace of his case: reunion with his beloved. But ther
is a difference between the two lines. The first is genera
and romantic. The phrase, "in my arms," does not seer
to mean exactly what it says. True, it has a literal mean
ing, if we can look close at the words, but it is hard t
look close because of the romantic aura—the spiritualize
mist about them. But with the last line the perfectly litera
meaning suddenly comes into sharp focus. The mist i
rifted and we can look straight at the words, which, w
discover with a slight shock of surprise, do mean exact
ly what they say. The last line is realistic and specific. I
is not even content to say,

And I in bed again!

It is, rather, more scrupulously specific, and says,

And I in *my* bed again!

All of this does not go to say that the realistic ele
ments here are to be taken as canceling, or negating, th
romantic elements. There is no ironical leer. The poem i
not a celebration of carnality. It is a faithful lover wh
speaks. He is faithful to the absent beloved, and he i
also faithful to the full experience of love. That is, h
does not abstract one aspect of the experience and call i
the whole experience. He does not strain nature out o
nature; he does not over-spiritualize nature. This name
less poet would never have said, in the happier days o
his love, that he had been led to his Sweet's chamber win
dow by "a spirit in my feet"; and he certainly would no
have added the coy disavowal, "who knows how?" Bu
because the nameless poet refused to overspiritualize na
ture, we can accept the spirituality of the poem.[7]

Warren's comment is a case of *over-reading*: a commo
excess among critics who discuss poetic form or structure mer
ly, or primarily, in terms of the poetic medium. The words i
the poem cannot be their own principle of order; the contex
of meaning which the words establish is governed by some

[7] Robert Penn Warren, "Pure and Impure Poetry," in his *Selecte
Essays* (Vintage Books, 1966), pp. 8-10.

ing more than the total meaning asserted or implied on the
rbal plane.

It is true that "the lover, grieving for the absent beloved,
ies out for relief... for the specific solace of his case: re-
ion with the beloved." But to assert that "several kinds of
lief are involved in the appeal to the wind" seems neces-
ry merely in view of the critic's gratuitous assumption that
e poem consists of "romantic" and "realistic" (or "pure
d impure") elements. There is no evidence—so far as the
em goes—that the lover seeks relief from nature's "sym-
thy" (the rain falling like tears?) and relief in weeping.
ch kinds of relief are perhaps suggested by the words (or
ther, by an implicit assumption about "pure and impure
etry"); but verbal implications are strictly controlled, in
e poem, by the dramatic context: the lover, as Warren him-
f is aware, is crying out for reunion with his beloved. "The
mpathetic manifestation of nature" as source of relief is,
spite Lear (a rather superficial similarity), immaterial, or
erely incidental, to such a context. What is important for
e poem and our own response to it is the suggestion that
ring will somehow make it possible for the lover to return
his beloved; this must be the reason why he is impatiently
shing for rain.

The necessity in Warren's interpretation springs only
om the antithesis between "romantic" and "realistic" *qua-
es of the poetic diction* which has been assumed to be the
derlying structure of the poem considered *chiefly* as a ver-
composite. He wishes to see a difference between the third
d the fourth line of the poem; consequently, "the phrase,
my arms,' does not seem to mean exactly what it says";
sequently, he discovers "with a slight shock of surprise...
perfectly literal meaning" of the next line. Consequently,
poem exists for the sake of the critic's own hypothesis.
w does Warren know—to cite another instance—that the
aker in the poem is "a faithful lover?" He even seems to
w what the lover would have said or refrained from say-
"in the happier days of his love!"[8]

[8] A similar misinterpretation of the poem is to be found in *Under-
iding Poetry*, ed. Cleanth Brooks and Robert Penn Warren, 3rd edn.

C. Here 11. 1-2, addressed to the west wind, are
prayer for rain for the growing crops, and 11. 3-4, a
dressed to Christ..., are a prayer for the return of th
lover. And the parallelism of form overcomes the co
trast of content. The effect is to suggest that the lov
whose return is desired so passionately is also involved
the natural cycle of the seasons. In spite of appearanc
to the contrary spring will eventually come again, a
the speaker tries to attribute a similar certainty to t
return of the lover. By a blasphemous implication Chr
is in effect assigned the role of a fertility spirit. T
"sides" in this poem are therefore (a) the non-hum;
processes of growth, and (b) human self-fulfillment
sexual love. To define the content of the poem in mo
abstract terms would be to distort its meaning.[9]

Bateson's comment is a more serious case of *misreadi*
due to the assumption that the poem expresses the poet's
tion, i.e., the speaker in the poem is not the lover but is,
ther, a kind of surrogate or "mask" of the poet. Thus,
effect, the poet is doing two things: praying "for rain
the growing crops," and praying "for the return of the love
It is the poet, not the lover, who is praying; and he is pr
ing, first, to the west wind, and then, to Christ who pla
"the role of a fertility spirit." As it finally turns out, ho
ever, it is not so much "prayer" as an argument of sort.

It seems that the "blasphemous implication" is rather
instance of "the parallelism of form [overcoming] the contr
of content"; at least, the contrast becomes less acute if, l
the west wind bringing rain, Christ were also a fertilizi
agent. The other instance is, of course, the parallelism betw
the lover's return and the return of spring. The poet p
sionately desires the lover's return (note this dramatic
versal!), but since, "in spite of appearances to the contr;
spring will eventually come again," the poet then "tries
attribute a similar certainty to the return of the lover."

Bateson has completely succeeded in doing exactly w
he had wanted to avoid. Perhaps, he is aware of it, for he sa

(Holt, Rinehart and Winston, 1960), pp. 245-46. The same "roman
realistic" antithesis is used, plus another necessity in the critical re
toire, "the depth and complexity of experience" or "poetic sincerity."
9 F.W. Bateson as quoted in *The Case For Poetry*, p. 13.

"To define the content of the poem in more abstract terms would be to distort its meaning." Considering the poem as essentially an *argument* of sort, he finds that the basic terms are "(a) the non-human processes of growth, and (b) human self-fulfillment in sexual love." Can anything be "more abstract"? In any case, the poetic content has been reduced to an abstraction. The "dramatic" context is only what it is in Brooks: merely a certain collocation of terms that interact toward a balance or reconciliation of contraries (what Brooks calls "invulnerability to irony").

Conclusion

Since, without the words, we cannot apprehend anything of the poem at all, we must of course deal with the poem *as a verbal composite.* Nevertheless, when the poem *also happens to be an imitation,* the meanings of its words, syntactical relations, and linguistic and rhetorical devices must, first of all, be strictly relevant to a particular human experience (what we mean by their "dramatic context") which these words and devices serve to simulate; otherwise, nothing hinders the critic from referring their meanings to some hypothesis or other as to their *structural principle*—e.g., Warren's *assumed* antithesis or balance between "realistic" and "romantic" elements. Also, as we observed in our essay on "Edward," the theme or "meaning" over and above the experience as poetically rendered, such as that which Bateson sees, must be validated by, since it rests thereon, the meaning of the whole experience in and by itself; otherwise, the theme we perceive in or foist upon the poetic experience may distort or even contradict it.

"In a Station of the Metro": Ezra Pound on His Own Poem

Writes Ezra Pound:

> Three years ago in Paris I got out of a "metro" train at La Concorde, and saw suddenly a beautiful face, and then another and another, and then a beautiful child's face, and then another beautiful woman, and I tried all that day to find words for what this had meant to me, and I could not find any words that seemed to me worthy, or as lovely as that sudden emotion. . . . I wrote a thirty-line poem, and destroyed it because it was what we call work "of second intensity." Six months later I made a poem half that length; a year later I made the following . . . sentence:
>
> The apparition of these faces in the crowd:
> Petals, on a wet, black bough.
>
> I dare say it is meaningless unless one has drifted into a certain vein of thought. In a poem of this sort one is trying to record the precise instant when a thing outward and objective transforms itself, or darts into a thing inward and subjective.[1]

As an account of the poem's *genesis,* Pound's statement is incontestable. The subject of the poem, however, is not discovered by what the poet says he had wanted to do or accomplish, but rather, by what he has actually done or accomplished; and for this, there can be no evidence other than the poem itself. The poem, not the poet, is the final authority.

But let us consider what Pound says is the subject of the poem since, after all, the poem itself may confirm it. One day,

[1] As quoted in *The Case For Poetry,* p. 287. Also quoted in Brooks and Warren, *Understanding Poetry,* p. 90.

as the poet got out of a train, he saw "beautiful" faces in the crowd, and later "all that day," he "tried . . . to find words for *what this had meant to me,*" i.e., what the event meant to him at the time he saw those beautiful faces. He wrote a thirty-line poem but destroyed it since the words did not seem to him "worthy, or as *lovely* as that sudden *emotion.*" Apparently, then, the *meaning* Pound wishes to convey in the poem is a certain *emotion* he had felt.

But the poem, as we have it now, is "meaningless" unless one is able, by its means, to "drift," as it were, "into *a certain vein of thought,*" i.e., a certain frame of mind. For the poet, "in a poem of this sort . . . is trying to record the precise instant when a thing outward and objective transforms itself, or darts into a thing inward and subjective."

The subject of the poem is, then, a certain feeling or emotion as the meaning of a particular experience: something "outward and objective" (faces in the crowd) has transformed itself, or darted into "a thing inward and subjective." The process of transformation involves, apparently, the perception of faces in the crowd *as beautiful;* the perception of beauty is part, if not the whole, of "that sudden emotion" which Pound had wanted his words to convey a sense of. In short, the subject of the poem is beauty: not, however, as an abstraction, but as an experience, an "inward and subjective thing," a "sudden emotion."

Unfortunately, however, the poem by itself makes it difficult for the reader to "drift" into Pound's own "vein of thought." "Petals," by itself, is the only word in the poem that may suggest beauty; but its context (verbal) tends to qualify that suggestion. Something supernatural, perhaps even eerie, is suggested by "apparition of these faces in the crowd." One also receives, from the first line, an impression of disembodiment, of a sudden and unexpected appearance.[2] "Petals

---

[2] Thomas A. Hanzo (as quoted in *The Case For Poetry*, p. 287) notes that

> The faces are not those of a crowd, but "these faces in the crowd," a selection which emphasizes the special, even unique, quality of an apparition and, since only faces are mentioned, reinforces the idea of a bodiless substance.

Obviously, the reader (unless he is reading too closely) would in all probability immediately think of those faces as *of* the crowd at the staon a wet, black bough" seems also to reinforce the sense of disembodiment. Of course, those petals are not necessarily of any particular color that would contrast with "black" of wet or rain-stained bough. But if "apparition" suggests "white" petals, that color would be ghastly, death-pale. In any case, the contrast does not seem to be the main point of the line. More important is the suggestion that the petals are *stuck or clinging* to "a wet, black bough."[3] The suddenness of the comparison (faces/petals) and the isolation of "petals" (only petals) on the bough seem also to accentuate the startling unexpectedness and distinctness of the "apparition" to the mind's eye.

I do not think, then, that the immediate impression one tends to share with *the speaker* in the poem is *necessarily* of something strikingly beautiful about "these faces in the crowd." Brooks and Warren say of the poem

> that a new and surprising comparison is exactly what Pound gives us. The petals on a wet, black bough, the *white faces against the dimness*—the comparison does embody a leap of the imagination, a shock of surprise. And yet, in the midst of the novelty, we sense that it, too,

tion; and therefore, "the idea of a bodiless substance" would most probably not occur to him. And "faces" is an obvious instance of synecdoche. Nevertheless, an ambiguity of sort does exist; and if we assume that it is *not* accidental (we know that Pound worked hard and long on this poem, and in any case, it is fairer to assume *that* for any poet), then, certainly, the ambiguity must be poetically functional: i.e., it serves to emphasize a supernatural quality of the apparition.

To this, however, there is counter-argument of some weight: granted the ambiguity is there, it is not necessarily intentional (and therefore, poetically functional), since the poet might not have had any choice. What, after all, is an alternative, unambiguous statement that would convey the sense and rhythm of Pound's line? Besides, the poet could very well depend on the reader's good sense (grammatical): "faces in the crowd" has the immediate sense of "faces of the people in the crowd." The reader must take the immediately obvious or literal meaning of the line unless there is strong evidence to the contrary.

Is "apparition," then, a strong enough evidence? Does it not suggest a possibility that the faces in the crowd, *as* an *apparition*, may not be those of the actual individuals in the crowd? One cannot deny the poetic probability.

3 "Wet" seems to be the more important word (than "black") in that it accounts for the "black" of bough and the presence of "petals" upon it. For we infer from "wet" that it has rained; that the rain has stained or made the bough appear "black"; that the rain may have caused the petals to fall upon the bough and cling to it. Incidentally, there is a seeming ambiguity in the phrase "on a ...bough." Are those petals sprouting from it? But the word "petals" is rather unusual if the poet had wanted to suggest sprouting buds.

has a logical basis. The poet has simply focused upon the *significant quality* for the comparison, discarding other qualities, more obvious qualities. And the shock of surprise takes us to the poem's meaning.

A new and surprising interpretation is exactly what Pound's new and surprising comparison gives us. Even in this most unlikely place, we catch a glimpse of *something beautiful, fresh, and pure,* and in that momentary lift of the heart, sense an interpretation potentially applicable to a great deal of experience.[4]

A different sort of reaction to the poem is, however, just as reasonable (at least) in that the poem may very well evoke it, too. We have already indicated the basis for such a reaction. The first line of the poem tends to qualify our impression in that it suggests something supernatural (or preternatural), something ghostly, disembodied, about "these faces in the crowd." We have to do, after all, with an "apparition" (though Brooks and Warren suggest that the word *apparition* is only a metaphor).[5] And the next line seems to reinforce our impression of disembodiment, and suggests further a sense of immobility (petals stuck "on a wet, black bough") and something like a state of prostration or ruin (since the petals have fallen

---

[4] *Understanding Poetry,* pp. 89-90 (underscoring mine). "Exactly what Pound gives us" is not a comparison, but *someone's experience;* not an interpretation on some general plane, but that experience as already in itself meaningful. "The significant quality," according to Brooks and Warren, is the similitude between *"petals* on a . . . *black* bough" and *"white* faces against the *dimness"* in a station of the Metro. But the similitude does not necessarily convey an impression of "something beautiful, fresh, and pure" (unless one had read beforehand Pound's own statement on the poem). For "wet, black bough" does not quite help support such an impression, and "white faces" in an apparition more immediately suggest something quite ghastly. "A year later," says Pound, he wrote *this* poem: the lapse of time and the series of poetic revisions may well account, too, for the transformation, in the poet's mind, of the *original* perception (or emotion) that he had wanted to catch in a poem.

[5] The apparition *is* the event in the poem: not *necessarily* an actual apparition, the appearance of ghosts (though we cannot entirely discount the possibility) but, at least, a *mental event;* i.e., exactly how the lyric speaker perceives "these faces in the crowd" (or, to say the same thing, how these faces strike him at the moment). As a *metaphor,* "apparition" therefore defines the speaker's sudden initial perception of the crowd in a station of the Metro. It is a perception or mental impression which brings on somehow the next comparison to his mind: these faces like "petals, on a wet, black bough." This metaphor, then, further delineates the event, i.e., the speaker's impression of the same crowd of faces; an impression, moreover, that only someone in a certain frame of mind can receive.

off and are scattered on the bough, and they are not necessarily "white," "fresh," etc.; the main impression being rather of petals in disarray and stuck or clinging to a bough). The distinctness of the image ("petals on a wet, black bough")[6] also suggests the startling and ghostly character of "the apparition." Indeed, there is something ghastly about "these faces in the crowd."[7]

We have, perhaps, read the poem rather too closely; but, on the other hand, we cannot simply "drift" into the poem's "vein of thought." Moreover, we are trying to show a different sort of reaction to the poem that is perfectly legitimate since the poem supports it—even more, I think, than it supports Pound's expressed intention. And, perhaps, what Pound means by his poem's being "meaningless" is the probability of different, even contradictory, reactions to it, each in some way legitimate, though not equally satisfactory in terms of the poem itself.

But any poem is successful, not because the poet has accomplished what he says he had set out to do (after all, we are not always so fortunate as to know *the poet's own intention*), but because the poem has achieved a *distinctive effect* which the reader may always know by his own response to it. As regards Pound's "In a Station of the Metro," my own opinion is that it succeeds as a poem because it has a distinctive effect: not, however, what Pound had intended, but rather, a sense of *the speaker's dismal frame of mind*. Both "the

---

[6] Such distinctness is not due to the contrast between "petals" (*white?*) and "*black*" bough." It is due to the word *petals* occupying the first position in the last line of the poem, to the very sound (perhaps) of the word and the stress on its first syllable, to the suddenness or unexpectedness of the comparison, to the isolation of the object (only petals) on the bough, and to the vividness of the setting (they are clinging to a rain-stained bough).

[7] It is perhaps significant that Brooks and Warren suggest (though only to illustrate comparisons without "inner significance," or comparisons that involve "no leap of the poet's imagination") either of the following lines as an alternative to the last line in Pound's poem:
     Dead leaves caught in the gutter's stream.
   (or)
     Dry leaves blown down the dry gutter.
Significant, in that either line conveys a rather unpleasant impression about "these faces in the crowd." *Unpleasant*: Pound did *not* (as we may happen to know) *intend* it, and so, as it seems to me, Brooks and Warren try to make the poem *not* evoke it.

apparition" and "petals, on a wet, black bough" suggest a kind of prostration or dejection of spirit on his part since both comparisons (mental impressions) can occur only to someone in that frame of mind or disposition. We tend to feel similarly as the speaker since the poem allows us to see only what he sees. We cannot deny, of course, a certain ambiguity of poetic effect, but that is only, as it seems to me, an initial reaction that is clarified just as soon as one grasps the speaker's vein of thought and feeling or his mood.

A Few Poems on the Order of Issa's "Spring Day"

The formal critic of literature would do well, it seems, to begin with terse forms of the so-called "lyric poem"—the haiku, or rather, their translations considered as "lyric poems", and similar forms or structures. Since he does not commit himself at once to any assumption as to what a "poem" is, or ought to be, he simply examines what people in general have taken to be "poems," comparing these with other pieces of writing that people in general have never seriously considered as "poems". This seems reasonable enough if we consider an alternative procedure: to begin by defining in advance (or on the basis of a few "poems" we have already examined) what a "poem" or a "lyric poem" is. For what, then, would be the definition, for example, of a "lyric poem?" Is it (1) "A brief poem"? A matter, then, of *physical* length. But how brief? Epigrams, aphorisms, proverbs, are briefer still; and some, like Shelley's "Adonais," Tennyson's "In Memoriam" or T. S. Eliot's "The Waste Land," are very long. (2) "A poem of intense emotion"? Shall we say that the emotion in lyric poems is more intense than the emotion in such works as *King Lear* or *The Brothers Karamazov?* In any case, do *all* lyrics involve intense emotion? What is so intense about Browning's "Pippa's Song" or Emerson's "Fable" (of the mountain and the squirrel) or Herrick's "Upon Julia's Clothes"? (3) "A poem expressing the poet's innermost feelings"? How is it, then, we recognize *anonymous* poems as lyric poems? Conversely, what were Yeats' innermost feelings about old age? He has expressed incompatible feelings about old age in quite a number of poems on the subject. Does, in fact, our recognition of the lyric form, or the pleasure we derive from lyric poems, depend upon our reflection on the poet himself and his innermost feelings? (4) "A poem capable of being sung or set to music"? But any discourse, in verse or prose, can be sung, if you will, or set to music—even Aquinas' *Summa Theologicae* or Webster or a telephone directory. (5) "Well, then, a poem characterized by lyrical quality"? Alas, we have completed a vicious circle.[1] And thus, it seems best to begin, *for our purposes*, not with some grand or subtle conception of poetry in general, but with the poems themselves, — those, for instance, that people usually regard (on whatever ground) as "lyric poems"—and discover what we may about their structures or forms.

Here, then, are a few more poems on the order of Issa's "Spring Day" as regards the represented action; i.e., poems that imitate a single, indivisible human activity.[2]

Pure Sappho
(Alkaios)

I want to speak to you but shame
     disarms me—
Pure Sappho of the violet braids
    and tender smile.

Poems By Sappho
The Lyric Poem

Come, holy tortoise shell,
my lyre, and become a poem.

Dear Atthis, Did You Know?

In dream Love came out of heaven
and threw down his purple cloak.

Paralysis

Mother darling, I cannot work the loom
for the Cyprian has almost crushed me,
broken me with love for a slender boy.

---

[1] I derive this exercise on the definition of *the* lyric poem from a copy of Elder Olson's essay called *"The* Lyric*"* which he gave me; I have been unable to find its published form.

[2] The poems by Alkaios, Sappho, and Archilochos are taken from *Greek Lyric Poetry*, tr. Willis Barnstone (Bantam Books, 1962). A number of these poems may only be fragments, but as we have them, they may still be regarded as poetic wholes.

"Pure Sappho" imitates a sudden movement of "shame."
Someone calls Sappho to mind but is suddenly abashed or awed
by her as she appears in the full radiance of her character.
"The Lyric Poem" imitates a movement of desire. Someone
would sing, and sing beautifully, her lyre become a poem
(i.e., as instrument, partaking as it were of the character
or nature of her lyric poem). Or someone, desirous of singing,
perceives her tortoise shell as holy and wishes that it be-
come a poem in her song (i.e., even as the subject of her
song). "Dear Atthis" depicts a single act of recollection. Some-
one recalls how, in a dream, she saw her desire's fulfillment:
for even Love, the Divinity, came down from his height and
stood not on ceremony but mingled with mortals. She would
want Atthis to know her dream that he also (god-like in her
eyes) might do likewise.[3] "Paralysis" is a complaint: some-
one, distracted by her passion for a slender boy and unable
to work her loom, complains of her distraught condition to
her mother.[4]

[3] Cf. a similar poem by Sappho:

To Atthis

I loved you, Atthis, long ago,
when my girlhood was in full flower
and you were like a graceless child.

[4] Cf. Walter Savage Landor's imitation (in, of course, another sense
of the term):

Mother, I Cannot Mind My Wheel

Mother, I cannot mind my wheel;
  My fingers ache, my lips are dry;
O, if you felt the pain I feel!
  But, O, who ever felt as I?

No longer could I doubt him true —
  All other men may use deceit;
He always said my eyes were blue,
  And often swore my lips were sweet.

As in Sappho's poem, the speaker is bewailing her lovelorn condition.
But there is an obvious difference in the *dramatic situation*: Sappho's
speaker is pining for a young man who, as far as the depiction goes,
does not even know about her passion, whereas in Landor's version, she
has apparently lost her suitor. Clearly, the girl in Landor's poem is not
only complaining of her painful condition to her mother, but also ruing
a past mistake that brought her to her present state. Her action, there-
fore, is divisible into *two distinct activities*: she is performing more
than one action. For, reflecting on her present misery, she bewails it;

[142]

The specific action depicted in the following poems by Archilochos also varies, but in regard to it, all have likewise the same essential form: i.e., each poem imitates a single, indivisible human activity.

Paros Figs

Say goodbye to the island Paros,
farewell to its figs and the seafaring life.

Lament[5]

If only his head and handsome limbs
had been wrapped in white burial cloth
and touched by Hephaistos' hand of fire.

On the Daughter of Lykambes

I pray for one gift: that I might merely touch
Neoboule's hand.

On Pasiphale, A Friend to All

As the figtree on its rock feeds many crows,
so this simple girl sleeps with strangers.

In "Paros Figs," is someone himself bidding farewell to Paros or addressing someone else who is leaving? In either case, the poem depicts a leave-taking, full of regret over the things one would miss—Paros figs and the seafaring life. The next poem is a lament, quite touching for its simplicity. The speaker, dwelling on the person of the dead sailor with subdued tenderness, sadly notes what is no longer possible— the white burial shroud and the holy pyre. The poem on Neoboule simulates the activity of someone who, in a tender mood, desires the girl. He would already consider himself favored by the gods if he "might merely touch Neoboule's hand." The poem depicts a lover's shy and fearful approach, from a great imagined distance, to his beloved. It is to this quality of the lover's action that we respond. The poem on Pasiphale pays

but reflecting on her lover who, unlike other men, was true, she bewails her past misjudgment of him. Note, also, that in the first stanza, the girl's "pain" is ambiguous (a physical illness? a moral anguish of sort?); the second stanza leaves no doubt as to her true condition and determines our final response to the poem.
5 The title in Barnstone runs: "On the Lack of Proper Burning and Burial for his Brother-in-Law Who was Shipwrecked."

tribute to a simple girl who sleeps with strangers and is friend to all. The girl's character is described only in so far as such a description is required by the speaker's action. Hence, the subject of the poem is not, formally speaking, Pasiphale, but someone's tribute to her. We respond, not to Pasiphale (who exists in the poem only as the object of someone's thought), but rather, to the tribute being paid to her by someone who knows her well. The girl is directly described: she is simple and sleeps with strangers. The comparison with the fig tree is meant to point up the exact quality of her simplicity: the fig tree does not choose which crow to feed, but feeds all, since there is nothing else for crows on its rock. There is no further need, as it seems to me, to locate other implications of such words as "rock," "crows," "strangers," etc. We must not be deceived, for example, by unpleasant associations we may ourselves have about crows as carrion birds.

Consider also these poems:[6]

Return to the North
(Yü P'ing-Po)

The baked-bun peddler,
Midnight, in the biting wind,
Slowly calls.
I hear it, I know "I have come home."

From The Spring Waters
(Ping Hsin)

25

In shaping the snow into blossoms—
The north wind is tender after all.

43

Spring has no words
But her quiet latent power
Has already
Made the world tender for me.

28

All beings are deceived by light and shadow.
Beyond the horizon—
When did the moon ever wax and wane?

[6] From *Twentieth Century Chinese Poetry: an Anthology*, tr. and ed. Kai-Yu Hsu (Anchor Books, 1964).

60

The falling star—
Shines only when crossing the sky of man;
It darts out from darkness,
And flees into darkness again.
Is life also so unaccountable?[7]

The Dreamer
(Wen I-to)

If that blue ghost light
Is the sparkle bursting from the dream
Of the entombed,
What fear have I of death?!

P'ing-Po's poem depicts a momentary *feeling or sensation,* that of the speaker in the poem who, on hearing the peddler's call, suddenly feels a sense, a deep certitude, of his having "come home." The poem is mainly evocative; it requires the reader to imagine for himself the sensation of someone who, long gone from his native place, is suddenly, on his return, struck by some familiar scene that fills him with a sense of his having at last returned home.

The series of momentary poems in Hsin's *The Spring Waters* depict, in the main, particular impressions of the moment which are highly evocative of the speaker's mood or frame of mind: in (25) and (43), impressions of the north wind, or of the season of spring, render not so much a thought or idea as a particular *sensation* or mental impression which manifests the speaker's tender mood; and in (28) and (60),

---

[7] Cf. the speech of one of Edwin's nobles in Bede's celebrated account of the conversion of Northumbria to Christianity in 633: "So, O king, does the present life of man on earth seem to me, in comparison with the time which is unknown to us, as though a sparrow flew swiftly through the hall, coming in by one door and going out by the other, and you, the while, sat at meat with your captains and liegemen, in wintry weather, with a fire burning in your midst and heating the room, the storm raging out of doors and driving snow and rain before it. For the time for which he is within, the bird is sheltered from the storm, but after this short while of calm, he flies out again into the cold and is seen no more. Thus the life of man is visible for a moment, but we know not what comes before it or follows after it. If, then, this new doctrine brings something more of certainty, it deserves to be followed." (From Bede, *Ecclesiastical History*, Book II, chap. xiii, as quoted in Emile Legouis and Louis Cazamian, *A History of English Literature*, rev. edn. (MacMillan, 1935, p. 12.)

an observed event in nature evokes in the speaker a *sense* of the permanence of nature, or of the mystery of human life, which, again, shows her pensive frame of mind.

I-to's poem simulates the speaker's feeling of relief and assurance in regard to death on reflecting that the "blue ghost light" in the graveyard may be "the sparkle bursting from the dream Of the entombed." He has a sense that the dead are only asleep, that in fact they are as full of the mysterious life-force as the living in that one might see on wet nights flashes of the dream they dream. We respond to the speaker's action and emotion; we do not take his reflection as a form of self-deception, but rather, as a kind of glorious conviction or belief in some mysterious form of life for those who seem to have passed away.

The Japanese Haiku

The *haiku* commemorates an experience in a single moment of time. It requires us to dwell on the moment, without questioning what it "means," for "the only thing that matters is what effect it has."[8] The *effect* is a state of mind or of the feelings which the experience, as poetically rendered, evokes.

Haiku by Bashō
On a withered branch
a crow has settled—
    autumn nightfall.

Summer grass:
of stalwart warriors' splendid dreams
    the aftermath.[9]

[8] See Harold G. Henderson's *An Introduction to Haiku* (Doubleday Anchor Books, 1958), from which all the haiku I present here are derived. Henderson writes: "all haiku worthy of the name are records of high moments ... they usually gain their effect not only by suggesting a mood, but also by giving a clear-cut picture which serves as a starting point for trains of thought and emotion. But, ... owing to their shortness, haiku can seldom give the picture in detail. Only the outlines or important parts are drawn, and the rest the reader must fill in for himself." (pp. 2-3.) The haiku is a severely restricted form of expression, and one reason may be that the poet wishes to avoid the danger of what the Veda calls "putting words between the truth and ourselves." (p. 4.)
[9] The original Japanese runs:
Natsu-gusa ya

In the first haiku, the observed comparison evokes the speaker's emotion: a feeling of desolation and sadness. As in most haiku, it is difficult to define exactly the poetic mood; yet, it is by no means mysterious if we reflect on our own emotional experiences and consider how often we are unable to find the words for them. We must, therefore, contemplate the speaker's experience in Bashō's poem and not only apprehend his perception of a particular autumn nightfall but also enter, as it were, into his mood in which he sees an evening scene.[10]

The second haiku conveys a deep sense of the speaker's grief and regret. We are told by Bashō himself about the *genesis* of this poem:

It is here [at Hiraizumi] that the glory of the three generations of the Fujiwara family passed away like a snatch of empty dream. The ruins of the main gate greeted my eyes a mile before I came upon Lord Hidehira's mansion, which had been utterly reduced to rice-paddies. Mount Kinkei alone retained its original shape. As I climbed one of the foothills called Takadate, where Lord Yoshitsune met his death, I saw the river Kitakami running through the plains of Nambu in its full force, and its tributary, Koromogawa, winding along the site of the Izumi-ga-shiro castle and pouring into the big river directly below my

---

    tsuwamono-domo ga
     yume no ato
 "It is almost impossible [says Henderson] to reproduce this in English, because we have no proper words. *Natsu-gusa* stands for all the quick-growing plants of summer; *tsuwamono*, literally 'the strong ones', was a name for medieval warriors, somewhat archaic even in Basho's time; *domo* is a plural suffix; *yume*, 'dream', has overtones of 'splendor' and of 'lives like dreams'; and *ato*, a noun which basically means 'after', includes the ideas of relic, trace, aftermath, what is left behind, etc." (p. 27.)
 10 "There are at least two points of technique which made [this haiku] a model. First, the over-all mood or emotion is produced by a simple description, a *plain statement* of fact which makes a picture. Second, the two parts that make up the whole are compared to each other, not in simile or metaphor, but *as two phenomena* each of which exists in its own right. This may be called 'the principle of internal comparison' in which the differences are just as important as the likenesses. Here it is not simply that 'over the withered landscape the autumn nightfall settles like a crow.' It is also the contrast of the small black body of the crow with the vast amorphous darkness of the nightfall—*and whatever else the reader may find in it.* It is easy to see how the use of this technique helps to give depth to haiku, and to make them starting points for thought and imagination." (Henderson, pp. 18-19; underscoring mine.)

IN ANOTHER LIGHT

eyes. The ruined house of Lord Yasuhira was located to
the north of the barrier-gate of Koromo-ga-seki, thus
blocking the entrance from the Nambu area and forming
a protection against barbarous intruders from the north.
Indeed, many a feat of chivalrous valour was repeated
here during the short span of the three generations, but
both the actors and the deeds have long been dead and
passed into oblivion. When a country is defeated, there
remain only mountains and rivers, and on a ruined castle
in spring only grasses thrive. I sat down on my hat and
wept bitterly till I almost forgot time.[11]

Haiku by Issa

The place where I was born:
all I come to—all I touch—
blossoms of the thorn.

This Dewdrop World—
a dewdrop world it is, and still,
although it is . . .

The first haiku depicts the speaker's deep affection for
his native place. When we compare it with Buson's

Flowering thorn—
how like the roads about the place
where I was born!

we find that the difference lies in the feeling which each poem
conveys. Where "Issa is showing us the pain in his heart, Buson
is speaking as a man of the world."[12] Where Issa evokes a
deep, sad longing (all I come to—all I touch—remind me

---

[11] Bashō, *The Narrow Road to the Deep North and Other Travel
Sketches*, tr. with introduction by Nobuyuki Yuasa (Penguin Books, 1966),
p. 118. Compare Bashō's haiku with Shiki's:
Of those who pass
with spears erect, there are none.
Plumes of pampas grass.
The poem conveys a nostalgia for the glorious past, a regret that it is
no more. The pampas grass evokes in the speaker's mind a scene from
olden times: "the daimyo processions that in the days of the Tokugawa
Shogunate used to go regularly between Edo and the provinces. ... These
show a long cortege of retainers, not all spearmen, and among them a
number carrying long poles with colored tufts at the end, which acted
as identifying standards. It was probably such standards, rather than the
spears themselves, which the pampas plumes suggested to Shiki's mind."
(Henderson, pp. 166-67.)
[12] Henderson, p. 130.

[148]

of the place where I was born, bring to my mind's eye blossoms of the thorn), Buson simply presents a kind of homesickness that comes to him on a sudden but does not seem to leave any deep and painful feeling. Admittedly, the difference between these two poems is difficult to express exactly. What Stevens writes about "nobility" as "the peculiarity of the imagination" applies, as well, to the poetic mood which the haiku simulates:

> Nothing could be more evasive and inaccessible. Nothing distorts itself and seeks disguise more quickly. There is a shame of disclosing it and in its definite presentations a horror of it. But there it is. The fact that it is there is what makes it possible to invite to the reading and writing of poetry men of intelligence and desire for life. I am not thinking of the ethical or the sonorous or at all of the manner of it. The manner of it is, in fact, its difficulty, which each man must feel each day differently, for himself. I am not thinking of the solemn, the portentous or demoded. On the other hand, I am evading a definition. If it is defined, it will be fixed and it must not be fixed. As in the case of an external thing, nobility resolves itself into an enormous number of vibrations, movements, changes. To fix it is to put an end to it. Let me show it to you unfixed.[13]

Issa wrote the second haiku, his most famous "dew" poem, when he lost one of his children. It depicts a brooding grief which baffles any turn of the distressed mind that seeks solace, which frustrates any thought that seems to offer comfort. "The first line," says Henderson, "is taken from a scripture comparing the evanescence of life in the world with that of dew. But Issa is not thinking of generalities; he is suffering from the loss of his child... A 'Dew-World' though it is, it is no world for dewdrops. They will not stay in it—

---

13 Wallace Stevens, *The Necessary Angel* (Vintage Books, 1965), p. 34. Compare, for another instance, Buson's

> On the temple bell
>   has settled, and is fast asleep,
>   a butterfly.

with Shiki's

> On the temple bell
>   has settled, and is glittering,
>   a firefly.

and, much as he tries to, he can find no solace in the scrip-
ture."[14]

The reader should now try the haiku without the en-
cumbrance of commentary. For one need only bear in mind
that the poetic intention is to evoke a particular sensation,
feeling, or mood. The train of thought which each poem de-
picts expresses the speaker's emotion in a single moment of
experience. Needless to say, the emotion is not always serious
and grave; there are comic forms which depict a gay and
humorous mood. Compare, for example, Issa and Chisoku
on the dragonfly.

(by Issa)

In its eye
    are mirrored far-off mountains—
       dragonfly.

(by Chisoku)

The dragonfly:
    his face is very nearly
      only eye!

Or, again, compare Shiki and Issa on the fly:

(by Shiki)

At still-living eyes
    have they come here to prick?
      These ever-restless flies!

(by Issa)

Oh, don't mistreat
    the fly! He wrings his hands!
      He wrings his feet!

Here, then, are a few more haiku. "Let me show it to
you unfixed."

(by Buson)

There is no stir,
    not even a leaf: awesome
      is the summer grove.

[14] Henderson, p. 131. Without knowing the circumstances under which
the poet composed a particular haiku, it is still possible, of course, to
respond to it; for, otherwise, most poems would be unintelligible.

POEMS ON THE ORDER OF *SPRING DAY*

(by Ranko)

The grove in spring:
    even the birds that prey on birds
      are slumbering.

(by Kito)

Evening haze:
    when memories come, how distant
      are the bygone days.

(by Buson)

Morning haze:
    as in a painting of a dream,
      men go their ways.

(by Shiki)

Backward I gaze;
    one whom I had chanced to meet
      is lost in haze.

(by Buson)

The piercing chill I feel:
    my dead wife's comb, in our bedroom,
      under my heel.

(by Shiki)

The next room's light,
    that too goes out, and now—
      the chill of night.

(by Issa)

Lean frog,
    don't give up the fight!
      Issa is here!

(by Shiki)

On how to sing
    the frog school and the skylark school
      are arguing.

And here, if I may, are two *imitations* merely or *adaptations*
of the haiku in Tagalog:

Bago Tag-ulan

Sa kabilang pampang ng isip
Abut-abot ang tawag sa iyo;

Huwag kang paabot sa ulan:
Abang handog ang ulo-ulo lamang.

Tahan Na

Tahan na.
Tiisin ang hagupit ng panahon:
Ang atis ay nahihinog
Sa ulan.[15]

The chief point, in all our observations of possibilities in the *represented* action, is that all underlying forms or structures of any poem *that happens to be an imitation* are subsumed under its structure or form as *simulated action of a certain order,* i.e., as having a certain distinctive power to move us emotionally. The dramatic form or narrative structure of the poem, its structure of ideas or imagery, every element of the poem (thought, character, emotion, etc.) are all governed by the sort of action that the poem does in fact simulate or represent for the sake of the power that the poem in fact exerts.

---

[15] Translated into English:

Before the Rainy Season

On the other bank of thought
Follow one another the calls for you;
Do not be caught by the rain:
A lowly gift—tadpoles only.

Hush Now

Hush now.
Suffer the whips of time.
The *atis* fruit ripens
In the rain.

Perhaps, the beginning poet in English (or Filipino) would do well to exercise himself with such imitations or adaptations of the haiku format, either in the serious or comic vein. I remember a witty "activist" piece: "Pag di umalsa ang masa, Walang tinapay sa mesa." Its English version would probably ruin the double-entendre. One reason why the haiku format might serve our young poet well is that, since it is a severely restricted form of expression, it requires the utmost discipline of thought and feeling, whereas the young poet is usually over-emotional (even mawkish) and verbose.

The Serious and the Comic in Lyric Poetry *

Any literary work (a short-story, a lyric poem, etc.), which happens to be an imitation of a human action or experience, has an inherent and determinate emotional power. We are moved, when it engages our imagination, by a particular human experience which it represents to us—someone, for example, who after years of evasion and self-deception, finally accepts with great anguish of spirit the fact of "our naked frailty" (in Eberhart's "The Groundhog"), or someone who, thinking that the child Margaret is weeping over "Goldengrove unleaving," is moved to a pensive contemplation of "the blight man was born for" (in Hopkins' "Spring and Fall"). We always know at the end of the poetic representation how we feel and what in the representation has caused us to feel the way we do.

A given poem, then, when it happens to be an imitation, is *an imitation of a certain determinate kind* because it has been endowed with a certain *distinctive power* to evoke in its readers a certain emotion, to induce a certain attitude or disposition of soul. In other words, the emotional power of a given imitation finally determines its distinctive nature, form, or structure; it is, as Aristotle says, the *final cause* or *end* of the imitation *as imitation of a given kind*. Therefore, in defining a given form or species of the lyric poem, the critic must specify its distinctive power since that, precisely, is its "soul" or informing principle.

* The present essay is part of a monograph, *A Formal Approach to Lyric Poetry*, nearly finished, which the U.P. Social Sciences and Humanities Research Committee has, through a research grant, made it possible for me to undertake.

[153]

In general, lyric poems, like any other literary composite, are, in terms of their *power* or effect, either *serious* or *comic*.[1] After all, a given experience may always, in its representation, be either a serious or a comic version, depending only on how we propose to move our audience concerning it. The story of Pyramus and Thisbe as represented in Shakespeare's *A Midsummer Night's Dream* is, for example, a comic version of essentially the same experience which, as represented in *Romeo and Juliet,* is quite serious.

The distinction between the serious and the comic is, of course, a general one since it applies as well to various forms of drama, the novel, and the short-story as to various forms of the lyric poem. Nevertheless, like the distinction between *didactic* and *mimetic* works,[2] it is crucial to the discrimination of literary forms or structures.

Suffice it to say for our purposes that the serious and the comic are, essentially, different *attitudes* toward persons and events, attitudes which the writer has himself assumed toward his subject and built into his work in such wise that the work has now the power to evoke these in the reader. The distinction between these attitudes "is basically one of value;

---

[1] For a fuller discussion of the serious and the comic, see Elder Olson's *Tragedy and the Theory of Drama* (Wayne State University, 1961) and *The Theory of Comedy* (Indiana University, 1968).

[2] We must say something here about the distinction since it involves our concept of *imitation*. A lyric poem, like any other literary work, may be either *mimetic* or *didactic*. It is didactic when it inculcates an *idea* or *moral point*: Emerson's "Fable" or "Brahma," Emily Dickinson's "Much Madness is Divinest Sense," Blake's "The Sick Rose." It is mimetic when it represents or simulates *someone's action* or *experience*: Frost's "Stopping By Woods," Yeats' "Sailing to Byzantium," all the poems analyzed in this essay. When a poem is didactic, the poetic end or function is to win our intellectual assent. The capacity to convince or at least provoke us intellectually is, then, its distinctive power. When a poem is mimetic, the poetic end or function is to evoke our emotional response (based, of course, upon our intelligent apprehension of the whole experience as poetically rendered). The capacity to move or affect us emotionally in regard to a human experience which it has depicted is, then, its distinctive power. We are *not* saying that no emotion may be involved in a didactic poem or, conversely, that no idea may be involved in a mimetic poem; it is a matter of what is really the primary interest in the poem itself, whether it be the truth of a given *proposition* (either stated or implied) or the meaningfulness, *in itself*, of a given human *experience* considered as such. And neither, of course, is the distinction between mimetic and didactic works a question of literary merit. Dante's *Divine Comedy* and Shakespeare's *King Lear* are both literary masterpieces.

of value as reckoned in terms of benefit or harm."[3] When we take the fortunes and actions of others seriously, we regard these as importantly related to their happiness or misery. Another consideration is the degree of importance we assign to the persons involved, for we do not take seriously anything which happens to people for whom we feel no concern. Thus, the ground of the serious emotion is the importance of the character, action, and fortune represented to us; the ground of the comic emotion, their unimportance.

Compare, for example, T.S. Eliot's "Aunt Helen" with Emily Dickinson's "The Last Night That She Lived."

Aunt Helen

Miss Helen Slingsby was my maiden aunt,
And lived in a small house near a fashionable
    square
Cared for by servants to the number of four.
Now when she died there was silence in heaven
And silence at her end of the street.
The shutters were drawn and the undertaker
    wiped his feet—
He was aware that this sort of thing had occurred
    before.
The dogs were handsomely provided for,
But shortly afterwards the parrot died too.
The Dresden clock continued ticking on the
    mantelpiece,
And the footman sat upon the dining-table
Holding the second housemaid on his knees—
Who had always been so careful while her mistress
    lived.

The Last Night That She Lived

The last night that she lived,
It was a common night,
Except the dying; this to us
Made nature different.

3 Olson, *Tragedy*, p. 161.

We noticed smallest things —
Things overlooked before,
By this great light upon our minds
Italicized, as 'twere.

That others could exist
While she must finish quite,
A jealousy for her arose
So nearly infinite.

We waited while she passed;
It was a narrow time,
Too jostled were our souls to speak,
At length the notice came.

She mentioned, and forgot;
Then lightly as a reed
Bent to the water, shivered scarce,
Consented, and was dead.

And we, we placed the hair,
And drew the head erect;
And then an awful leisure was,
Our faith to regulate.

The narrator in Eliot's poem has, from the outset, so influenced our attitude toward Miss Helen Slingsby his aunt that, almost unawares, we soon find her a ridiculous person toward whom we can feel no particular concern or sympathy. The very name, *Slingsby,* like *Prufrock,* already tempts us to take her lightly, to expect some amusing incident or other touching this "maiden aunt." When, next, we are told that she lives "in a small house near a fashionable square," we have an impression of her gentility which, however, in the very next line, is ridiculed: she is probably an invalid (since she is "cared for" and, in the next line, she dies), and so, we ought probably to feel some pity toward her; but "servants *to the number of four*" has a humorous effect which not only fulfills our expectation from her odd cognomen but also undermines a possible ground (her being an invalid) for a serious concern over her. And thus, quite early in the poem, our attitude toward Miss Helen Slingsby is established.

Aware that there is, rather, a rejoicing in heaven when a just soul passes away, we sense something ominous in the heavenly silence at Aunt Helen's death. Yet, since the same silence reigns "at her end of the street," the celestial portent loses much of its force, and we feel that it may be gratuitous to suppose a spiritual disaster *as the chief point* in the poetic narrative. Indeed, we are at once assured that it is nothing of the sort:

> The shutters were drawn and the undertaker
>   wiped his feet—
> He was aware that this sort of thing had
>   occurred before.

There is nothing to be alarmed about *in Aunt Helen's case.* "This sort of thing" has occurred before; it is quite ordinary. It only means that one must observe decorum, as in the drawing of shutters and other signs of respect. The undertaker, for example, recognizing that he is in a respectable home, wipes his feet. As for "the silence in heaven," we take that as a sign, rather, of the narrator's derisive attitude toward his aunt; but since we tend to share his attitude, there being no ground on which to judge his aunt differently, we simply acquiesce in his humorous, if also sardonic, judgment of her.

Indeed, we find sufficient justification for the narrator's gibes in the ridiculous nature of what seems to be Aunt Helen's last will:

> The dogs were handsomely provided for,
> But shortly afterwards the parrot died too.

Her only beneficiaries, it appears, are her pets. But they also die "shortly afterwards," their end dramatizing not so much the servants' gross negligence as their mistress' fatuous character. At this point in the poetic account, it would be a serious distortion of its focus or thrust to conjecture that our narrator is an aggrieved heir; besides, such a conjecture would not even help us, really, to sympathize with Aunt Helen.

The disintegration that shortly afterwards sets in finally exposes the inanity of Aunt Helen's restrictive and perhaps puritanical gentility. The footman is not only sitting upon the dining-table (which would have been enough to shock Aunt Helen) but he is also

> Holding the second housemaid on his knees—
> Who had always been so careful while her
> mistress lived.

Only inanimate objects remain as they were while she lived; the Dresden clock, for example, which continues to tick on the mantelpiece. It also seems that Aunt Helen's spinsterhood is a sign of her moral or spiritual sterility.

In short, then, we are, rather than saddened, quite amused by Aunt Helen's death since the effect it has upon her own household shows her up to have been a rather shallow and ridiculous character. We do not feel pity for her nor, indeed, any kind of sympathy or concern. We are not alarmed by her probable condition in the other life: at the poem's close, we do not really concern ourselves with that; besides, if we did, we would probably feel that it is deserved. Nor are we seriously concerned over the harm that Aunt Helen's gentility does because of its warped moral sense: we do not, of course, condone her servant's loose behavior, and yet, we find it amusing, i.e., ridiculous, that somehow Aunt Helen (herself ridiculous), while she lived, had been, as it were, their conscience. The poem ends in a kind of *comus* which rejects Aunt Helen's values. We share the narrator's humorous, sardonic mood, and feel a kind of superiority to his maiden aunt's repressive gentility.

Evidently, Dickinson's poem is a *serious* version of essentially the same experience, i.e., someone's death and its effect on people around her. At the very outset, we are put into a solemn frame of mind by the narrator's attitude toward the same event:

> The last night that she lived,
> It was a common night,
> Except the dying; this to us
> Made nature different.

Of course, as we read on, we sense a difference in the poetic thrust: by fixing our attention on the effect that someone's death has on people around her, in "Aunt Helen," we are made to see and judge the character of the deceased, indeed, the moral tenor, as it were, of her whole life; but in "The Last Night," we are made to see, not so much the sort of person that the deceased must have been, as the emotional and spiritual condition of those who survive her so that, in the end, our sympathy is directed rather toward them than her.

The dying person's kin are keeping vigil at her deathbed. Watching her die, they become aware of a momentous change in their perception of reality.

> We noticed smallest things,—
> Things overlooked before,
> By this great light upon our minds
> Italicized, as 'twere.

Through our sympathy for the narrator who is their spokes-man, as it were, in the poem, we perceive how the presence of death can make their own sense of "nature" more acute, and thus, we apprehend their mental and emotional condition. Certainly, we do not find ourselves in the same mental and emotional state as the dying person's kin since we merely look on, as it were, and sympathize. At the poem's close, for example, there is for us none of that "awful leisure" in which "Our faith to regulate." Yet, through sympathy, we are quite affected by the narrator's mental or spiritual condition such that we find ourselves in a serious frame of mind, in a grave or solemn mood, at the end of the poetic representation.

> That others could exist
> While she must finish quite,
> A jealousy for her arose
> So nearly infinite.

We waited while she passed;
It was a narrow time,
Too jostled were our souls to speak,
At length the notice came.

Through a kind of fellow-feeling with the narrator, we apprehend in the poetic depiction (though we do not ourselves feel the *same* emotion) how her own kin, who now perceive the intense worth of reality (even "smallest things"), could feel a jealous concern for her "So nearly infinite," a kind of anguished protest "That others could exist While she must finish quite." And that inner condition has, of course, made them speechless, each one "jostled" by his anguish in that "narrow time" in which no one can hinder the onrushing event, in which they can only helplessly wait for the end.[4]

She mentioned, and forgot;
Then lightly as a reed
Bent to the water, shivered scarce,
Consented, and was dead.

Only in the penultimate stanza is our attention more closely fixed upon the dying person; yet, the poetic focus remains constant since we see her only through her kin's eyes. Her mind apparently wanders; nothing, at the last moment, seems to connect. And then, as death draws near, a hardly perceptible shiver passes through her, she consents, and quietly dies. The force of her consent derives from the narrator's new perception of the intense worth of the human reality which death ends.

And we, we placed the hair,
And drew the head erect;
And then an awful leisure was,
Our faith to regulate.

[4] Another interpretation of the third stanza makes her own kin jealous *of* her rather than *for* her. That is: they are jealous of her who, while they still must continue to exist, is about to cease from her labors and finally have her meed of peace. It is, then, a selfish emotion that moves them. We sense the intensity of their desire ("So nearly infinite") for their own death as a final rest and, thereby, we sense also a kind of intense weariness with mere existence.

But such an interpretation contradicts the new perception of reality in the preceding stanza. It also distorts the force of the dying person's "consent" in the penultimate stanza and the force of that spiritual crisis which the living face at the poem's close.

And so, finally, the last mournful gestures of respect and love for the dead woman. Death has taken her away from them; she is no longer there. It is not *her* strand of hair which they put in place, nor *her* head which they draw erect. And then, in contrast to that "narrow time" of helpless anguish over her coming death, her kin are suddenly faced with that "awful leisure" in which "Our faith to regulate." They suffer a crisis of the spirit in which they try to hold on to a faith shaken by death's terrible negation of life's intense worth; they try to recover a poise of mind or soul in which they may be renewed by their perception of that worth which "Made nature different."

In short, we take seriously the action or experience (essentially mental) of the dying woman's kin since we regard it as importantly related to their happiness; whereas, in Eliot's poem, we take a light-hearted view of the dead woman's entire life since we judge it as ridiculous. Through sympathy for their condition, we also feel a lively concern for the dead woman's kin and do in fact wish them well; whereas, in Eliot's poem, since we find Aunt Helen ridiculous, we feel rather a contempt for her than pity.

If, then, the distinction between the serious and the comic rests on the *attitude* which the representation of a given experience disposes us to take toward it, the same distinction may also be defined in terms of the *frame of mind* or *emotional disposition* which the poetic representation induces in us. Whenever it is serious, the poetic representation induces us to hold the opinion or belief that a matter of some consequence is at issue: an old man, confronting the problem of old age, is firming up his mind to a decision that he has made to enter into the realm of the spirit (Yeats' "Sailing to Byzantium") ; a traveler, stopping on impulse to enjoy the lovely woods, decides against the offered respite to keep those promises for which, apparently, he has made the journey (Frost's "Stopping By Woods"). Thus, the frame of mind conducive to the *serious emotion* is one in which we feel a certain uneasiness, agitation, tension, or at least some degree of solemnity. But the frame of mind conducive to the *comic emotion* is the reverse. We feel relaxed since the view we are induced to hold about the represented action or character makes us take it lightly, either with pleasure or amusement or with a certain feeling of superiority.

Compare, for example, in terms of the frame of mind which the poetic representation evokes in us, either Yeats' "Sailing to Byzantium" or Frost's "Stopping By Woods" with Robert Herrick's "Upon Julia's Clothes" or Edwin Arlington Robinson's "Miniver Cheevy."

Upon Julia's Clothes

Whenas in silks my Julia goes,
Then, then, methinks, how sweetly flows
The liquefaction of her clothes.

Next, when I cast mine eyes, and see
That brave vibration, each way free,
O, how that glittering taketh me!

Miniver Cheevy

Miniver Cheevy, child of scorn,
Grew lean while he assailed the seasons;
He wept that he was ever born,
And he had reasons.

Miniver loved the days of old
When swords were bright and steeds were prancing,
The vision of a warrior bold
Would set him dancing.

Miniver sighed for what was not,
And dreamed, and rested from his labors;
He dreamed of Thebes and Camelot,
And Priam's neighbors.

Miniver mourned the ripe renown
That made so many a name so fragrant;
He mourned Romance, now on the town,
And Art, a vagrant.

Miniver loved the Medici,
Albeit he had never seen one;
He would have sinned incessantly
Could he have been one.

Miniver cursed the commonplace
   And eyed a khaki suit with loathing;
He missed the medieval grace
   Of iron clothing.

Miniver scorned the gold he sought,
   But sore annoyed was he without it;
Miniver thought, and thought, and thought,
   And thought about it.

Miniver Cheevy, born too late,
   Scratched his head and kept on thinking:
Miniver coughed, and called it fate,
   And kept on drinking.

The principal part of the *object of imitation*[5] in Yeats' poem, as in Frost's, is a man's choice or moral action, but the mood or frame of mind which it evokes is in one, a noble exaltation, a deep rejoicing, as it were, of the spirit over a momentous choice that an old man has made, and in the other, a calm of mind through our sympathetic apprehension of the traveler's quiet moral triumph over an impulse or temptation. As we read Yeats' poem, we sympathize with the old man's profound agitation of spirit, we feel that a matter of tremendous consequence is at issue; as we read Frost's, we respond sympathetically to the traveler's uneasiness of mind, we feel that a matter of some concern is being resolved. But the speaker in Yeats' poem has been endowed by the representation of his mental experience with a certain nobility of stature (consider, for example, the "grand eloquence" of his "speech," the elevation of his thought and emotion, the spiritual magnificence of his choice), whereas Frost's traveler strikes us as simply a man of enough moral sensitivity to check an impulse of the moment and decide to keep certain promises he has made (note, for example, that we are not told about his promises and, hence, we have no ground to suppose that they are particularly momentous; note, also, the colloquial flavor of his "speech," the simplicity of his thought and feeling, the

---

[5] By *object of imitation*, we mean that which the poem simulates; e.g., in both Yeats' and Frost's poems, someone's mental experience or deliberative activity.

[163]

ordinary though also admirable character of his moral action).
Thus, we are more profoundly moved by the experience as
rendered in Yeats' poem, or, to say the same thing, the power
that inheres in Yeats' poem is on a higher or nobler plane
than that in Frost. But this, of course, is a formal or structural
difference in terms of the poetic effect or power, not a differ-
ence of literary merit. Both poems are excellent in that each
achieves its own proper end, i.e., the peculiar effect that each
poem does in fact evoke.

On the other hand, the principal part of the *object of
imitation* in Herrick's poem is a lover's fascination with his
beloved's attire and graceful movements, and in Robinson's,
the patently absurd character of Miniver Cheevy as a romantic
and effete daydreamer. The peculiar comic power in the one
representation is an *infectious gaiety* since the lover wins our
sympathy, his simple joy putting us in a lighthearted mood;
but in the other, the comic effect is chiefly owing to *the ridicu-
lous* since Miniver Cheevy cuts a rather absurd figure, putting
us in a scornful mood similar to that of the narrator. As we
read Herrick, we sympathize with the lover's simple delight
in his beloved and are disposed to be merry with him; we
feel no envy nor scorn, nor have we any doubt as to the
propriety, for example, of the lover's emotional behavior; in-
deed, we feel indulgent, granting the lover his ecstasy as we
grant Julia her charms. As we read Robinson, we share, from
the outset, the narrator's derisive attitude toward his subject;
we feel contempt for Miniver Cheevy, holding him inferior
to ourselves. The pleasure we feel at the poetic depiction in
Herrick is based on general human sympathy, the sort of sym-
pathy we feel toward any lover who is delighted with his be-
loved (granted, of course, that we know nothing more about
him or his beloved to qualify our sympathy); but the pleasure
we derive from the poetic narration in Robinson is of a moral
order since we are moved to disapprobation of Miniver on
moral grounds. We feel that he alone is to blame for his dismal
and hopeless condition: he spends his time dreaming of ro-
mantic exploits and even of sinful affairs; he only keeps on
thinking and drinking, without ever doing anything concrete
about his situation; he is probably ill from too much drinking

but when he coughs, he calls it fate; he never even sees that he is at fault, but puts the blame rather on his times. We feel no serious concern for him, but only a moral superiority over him and scorn since we think that his misery is well deserved.

To illustrate further: compare "Upon Julia's Clothes" with Charles Baudelaire's "A Celle Qui Est Trop Gaie" or "Miniver Cheevy" with Ezra Pound's "Ballad of the Goodly Fere."

A Girl Too Gay[6]

Your look, your movements take the eye
As landscapes do, lovely in space;
And laughter plays about your face
Like a fresh wind in a clear sky.

Brushing against you in the swarm
Of townsfolk, the glum stranger seems
Dazzled before the health that beams
From just your shoulder, just your arm.

Your loud dresses, where colour swirls
And scatters in a mode distraught,
Bring to the mind of poets the thought
Of flowers attempting ballet whirls.

These wild clothes are the emblem of
Your motley spirit, ungoverned child,
By whom I too am driven wild,
Whom equally I hate and love!

At times, when wandering listlessly
In a bright garden, I have felt
Horror for all I touched and smelt,
The sunlight was an irony

Slashing into my breast, the spring's
Raw verdure so rebuked my woes
That I have punished upon a rose
The insolence of flowering things.

So, too, if to your silent bed
And all its riches I could creep
When the voluptuous night is deep,
Like any coward with noiseless tread,

6 Tr. George Dillon. From Charles Baudelaire's *Les Fleurs du Mal*, tr. George Dillon and Edna St. Vincent Millay (Washington Square Press, 1962), pp. 119, 121.

[165]

To castigate, until you swooned,
The joyous, pardoned flesh you prize,
And in your stunned body incise,
With care, a large deep-throated wound —

And, solace heady and complete,
Through these more novel lips, through this
Brighter, more luring orifice,
Infuse you with my venom, sweet.

Ballad Of The Goodly Fere*
Simon Zelotes speaketh it somewhile after the Crucifixion

Ha' we lost the goodliest fere o' all
For the priests and the gallows tree?
Aye lover he was of brawny men,
O' ships and the open sea.

When they came wi' a host to take Our Man
His smile was good to see,
"First let these go!" quo' our Goodly Fere,
"Or I'll see ye damned," says he.

Aye he sent us out through the crossed high spears
And the scorn of his laugh rang free,
"Why took ye not me when I walked about
Alone in the town?" says he.

Oh we drank his "Hale" in the good red wine
When we last made company,
No capon priest was the Goodly Fere
But a man o' men was he.

I ha' seen him drive a hundred men
Wi' a bundle o' cords swung free,
That they took the high and holy house
For their pawn and treasury.

They'll no' get him a' in a book I think
Though they write it cunningly;
No mouse of the scrolls was the Goodly Fere
But aye loved the open sea.

* Vocabulary note: *fere*, comrade.

If they think they ha' snared our Goodly Fere
They are fools to the last degree.
"I'll go to the feast," quo' our Goodly Fere,
"Though I go to the gallows tree."

"Ye ha' seen me heal the lame and blind,
And wake the dead," says he,
"Ye shall see one thing to master all:
'Tis how a brave man dies on the tree."

A son of God was the Goodly Fere
That bade us his brothers be.
I ha' seen him cow a thousand men.
I have seen him upon the tree.

He cried no cry when they drave the nails
And the blood gushed hot and free,
The hounds of the crimson sky gave tongue
But never a cry cried he.

I ha' seen him cow a thousand men
On the hills o' Galilee,
They whined as he walked out calm between,
Wi' his eyes like the grey o' the sea,

Like the sea that brooks no voyaging
With the winds unleashed and free,
Like the sea that he cowed at Genseret
Wi' twey words spoke' suddenly.

A master of men was the Goodly Fere,
A mate of the wind and sea,
If they think they ha' slain our Goodly Fere
They are fools eternally.

I ha' seen him eat o' the honeycomb
Sin' they nailed him to the tree.

The principal part of the object of imitation in Baudelaire's poem is someone's strange and violent reaction to a beautiful girl whose "motley spirit" and gaiety fill him with both hatred and love:

> Ces robes folles sont l'emblème
> De ton esprit bariolé;
> Folle dont je suis affolé,
> Je te hais autant que je t'aime!

The frame of mind which the poetic representation of that condition evokes is an oppressiveness of spirit resulting from our moral repulsion or disgust over the speaker's morose and vindictive passion. As we read the poem, we begin awhile to sympathize with the speaker's fascination over the girl who strikes us as not only beautiful and lively but also young and innocent; but as we reach the fourth stanza, we are startled and not a little disaffected by the speaker's rather negative reaction toward someone whom we have found delightful. "O madcap for whom I am out of my wits! I hate you as much as I love you!"[7] In other words, we are quite ready by the fourth stanza to be as delighted with her as the speaker, and therefore, we did not expect his resentment. But since we began with sympathy toward him as toward the girl, we tend naturally to seek the reason or cause for such a reaction to a beautiful girl.

Indeed, we soon find that the cause is in the speaker himself. We need not psychologize Baudelaire the man to get at the speaker in the poem. For the speaker himself reflects on his own mental or spiritual disposition:

> Quelquefois dans un beau jardin
> Où je trainais mon atonie,
> J'ai senti, comme une ironie,
> Le soleil déchirer mon sein;
>
> Et le printemps et la verdure
> Ont tant humilié mon coeur,
> Que j'ai puni sur une fleur
> L'insolence de la nature.

His reactions do not strike us as normal; they shock us, rather, as signs of a strange and morbid condition of the soul. In the beautiful garden, he only drags his listlessness; the sunlight sears his breast like an offensive irony; springtime and all its greenery only humiliate his heart. He finds Nature in all her finery, not beautiful but insolent, so that he vents his anger upon a rose. And thus, he also finds a beautiful and lively girl an *object* not only of desire but also of revenge.

[7] Prose translation by Francis Scarfe in his *Baudelaire: Selected Verse* (Penguin Books, 1961), pp. 131-32.

Apparently, he is not her lover; he seems only to have met her somewhere in the manner of a "glum passer-by" brushing against her in the street.

We are shocked, then, by the speaker's pathological condition, by his berserk wish, "when the hour of sensuality strikes," to possess her, "to chastise your happy flesh, to bruise your pardoned breast . . . and—O blinding rapture!—through those new lips, more vivid and more beautiful, infuse my poison into you, my sister."[8] It is indicative of his morbid condition that he should wish to hurt her and find his rapture in the stifling of her gaiety which, striking him as a form of insolence, has put him beside himself with a vengeful ire. The feeling of self-contempt, or the judgment he casts upon himself, which is implicit in his thought that he would "slink noiselessly, like a coward, towards your body's riches,"[9] does nothing to excuse his morbid wish in our eyes; rather, it only increases our repulsion since he means nevertheless to carry out his wish. Indeed, at the poem's end, our repulsion is nothing less than complete: he not only imagines with delight "opening in your astonished side a wide, deep wound,"[10] but he also exults in his thought that, in their intimacy, she would become as a "sister" to him (or, infected by his sullen nature, a kindred spirit).

Clearly, Baudelaire's poem is *serious* since, if we are repelled by the speaker's mental action, it is because we take him seriously and cannot remain indifferent to the harm he intends to inflict upon an innocent victim; whereas Herrick's "Upon Julia's Clothes" is *comic* since, if we are delighted by the lover's behavior, it is because we feel indulgent toward him, his joy putting us in a lighthearted mood. In Baudelaire's poem, also, as in Robinson's "Miniver Cheevy," the pleasure we feel at the poetic depiction of someone's condition is of a moral order since we are moved to disapprobation of his character on moral grounds. But "Miniver Cheevy" has a comic effect which stems from the fact that we take Miniver lightly, that we feel contempt for him or feel superior to him, whereas Baudelaire's poem has a *serious* effect which stems from the

8 *Ibid.*
9 *Ibid.*
10 *Ibid.*

fact that, though we also morally disapprove of the speaker, we cannot take him lightly since we hold him capable of great harm. Such an effect bears comparison with the power of Browning's "My Last Duchess." For, as we read the poem, we are appalled by the proud and evil nature of the Duke of Ferrara who, like Baudelaire's speaker, speaks and acts in his own person; we wish him thwarted in his schemes; we are moved to sympathy for his last duchess and fear for the Count's daughter. We feel that the Duke's action (not simply a marriage proposal but a veiled threat) is importantly related to the happiness or misery of people toward whom (since no ground is offered for a contrary emotion) we feel some concern (based on general human sympathy for the innocent victim). We feel that the Duke himself (unlike the spiteful monk in Browning's "Soliloquy of the Spanish Cloister") is capable of doing great harm since he has already, in the past, coldheartedly put away his last duchess. Thus, we see that the persons who are the objects of the serious emotion are those whom we think liable to great good or harm, or capable of doing these; and that the persons who are the objects of the comic emotion are in some way opposite.

Again, Ezra Pound's "Goodly Fere" is *serious* while "Miniver Cheevy" is *comic*. And the reason is clear enough if we only examine and compare our own reaction to either poem.

In "Goodly Fere," as in "Miniver Cheevy," we are told about someone, our attention is fixed upon the sort of man he is which the whole course of his life manifests; but where, in one, the narrator is full of the highest praise for "the goodliest fere o' all," in the other, he is full of scorn. Now, in each case, we share the narrator's attitude toward his subject since no ground, in either poem, is given for a contrary attitude. Therefore, we take the Goodly Fere seriously, Simon the Zealot's recollections of him inducing in us an awe for this "man o' men" who knew how to die; whereas we take Miniver Cheevy lightly, someone's recollections of him inducing in us a contempt for this man who does not even know what to do with himself. We hold the Goodly Fere superior to ourselves, and hence, the emotion which the poetic narration evokes is that which we feel toward any great and noble man. We are not saddened by his death but rejuvenated in spirit since *Simon's account*[11] has led us also to his own belief, at the poem's close, that only fools can think he is no more:

> I ha' seen him eat o' the honeycomb
> Sin' they nailed him to the tree.

On the other hand, we hold Miniver Cheevy inferior to ourselves, and hence, the emotion which the poetic narration evokes is that which we feel toward any middling and ridiculous character. We do not feel pity for Miniver's lot since we think it is well deserved; rather, we dismiss *him* as unworthy of serious concern.

CONCLUSION

The Manner of Our Response

"Every emotion," says Olson, "is felt about some object, on some ground, in some frame of mind."[12] Consider, for example, the emotion of fear. We are, in the first place, more readily disposed to feel it when we are in a timorous or apprehensive mood. Next, we do not fear everyone or everything, for certainly we cannot feel it toward someone, for instance, who inspires our confidence in all he does. And finally, even if we are disposed to fear and there is someone of whom we may be fearful, even then we shall not feel afraid unless we are considering some aspect of his person or behavior which makes us afraid. Thus, three factors are involved in the emotion of fear: (1) a *frame of mind* disposing us to it; (2) an *object* at which we feel it; and (3) some *ground* on which we feel it. But since no emotion is produced without these factors, and since as these factors differ, the emotions that ensue also differ, they must be considered the *causes* of the different emotions.

11 The poem depends for its effect not so much on our religious faith or our knowledge of the Bible as on Simon's own personal account.
12 Elder Olson, "Introduction" to Lyric Poetry (MS.) which the author kindly lent me. Subsequent quotations, unless otherwise indicated, are from the same work.

"Emotions, as states of consciousness involving pleasure or pain, have as their *ground* either some sensation or memory or some image of imagination or some opinion." The sudden movement of a cockroach among our papers startles us; the solitary cry of a child at night fills us on a sudden with a feeling of great desolation. Our remembrance of things past brings a varied train of emotions. Our imagination of things possible and impossible arouse desire or aversion. The thought of a possible fire in the neighborhood makes us apprehensive; an opinion that someone intends to reward us for our pains gladdens our hearts.

In general, then, our response to the poem is either similar to or different from that of the speaker in the poem.[13] As Olson puts it,

> Where the *causes* of the speaker's emotion are *similar* to those which cause ours, *the emotions will be similar;* where they are *different, different.* Thus, where the causes of the emotion of the speaker have been adequately and fully rendered in the poem, and where we ourselves are subjected to these causes only, we shall respond in a manner similar to his; in all other cases, there must be some difference of response.

We shall feel *similarly* as the speaker in the poem when the experience as depicted (1) induces in us the speaker's *mood or frame of mind;* (2) sets before us, in its proper aspect, the *object* of his emotion; and (3) makes us react to that on the same *ground* on which he feels the emotion. In all other cases, we feel *differently* from the lyric speaker.

[13] When the experience is *dramatized* in a lyric poem, i.e., when the poet allows someone, the "speaker" in the poem, to speak and act in his own person, then we regard chiefly the speaker's action or experience: the lover in "Upon Julia's Clothes," the old man in "Sailing to Byzantium," the traveler in "Stopping By Woods." We *witness*, as it were, an *enactment*. When the experience is *narrated*, i.e., when the poet allows someone, the narrator in the poem, to tell us about someone else, then we regard chiefly someone else's action or experience: the narrator's maiden aunt, Helen Slingsby; the dying woman's kin in "The Last Night"; Simon Zelotes' "Goodly Fere." We *listen*, as it were, to an *account*. In short, when the *manner of imitation* is dramatic, we respond to the action or behavior of the speaker in the poem; when narrative, to that of the narrator's subject in the poem.

In Hopkins' "Spring and Fall," for example, the experience as poetically rendered (1) induces in us the speaker's pensive mood or frame of mind; (2) sets before us, in its proper aspect, the same object that he contemplates, i.e., "the blight man was born for"; and (3) makes us react to that object on the same ground on which he feels a sad, philosophic resignation of soul, i.e., we share his opinion that, though we grow insensitive to the sight, all things are mortal. Thus, we feel *similarly* as Hopkins' speaker. Likewise, in Arnold's "Dover Beach," the cause of the speaker's emotion as well as ours is the contemplation of "the turbid ebb and flow, Of human misery"; thus, also, we feel more or less as he does. But in Housman's "With Rue My Heart Is Laden," the cause of the speaker's ruefulness—the premature death of his friends —is *not* the cause of our own emotion; *we* only respond sympathetically to his sorrowful regret. In Wordsworth's "She Dwelt Among the Untrodden Ways," the manner of our response is also of the same nature, for we do not ourselves miss the speaker's beloved; we are only moved to sympathy for him.

The Serious and the Comic

The serious and the comic are contrasting attitudes toward life which the poet builds into his poem; one springs from earnestness and gravity, the other, from jesting and lightheartedness.

"All comic works depend upon *depreciation*: upon the depreciation, that is, of the importance of what is being depicted." The comic experience, as rendered, always lays "a claim to seriousness which is immediately or subsequently nullified." The comic effect is *not* laughter (though laughter may be a sign of the comic emotion) but rather, "one which has no name ... a pleasurable emotion produced by the relaxation of the mind from its concern with something as serious, through the evident absurdity of that thing's claim to seriousness."

Consider, for example, T.S. Eliot's "Aunt Helen." The experience it depicts is comic because its claim to seriousness is subverted by the narrator's mocking attitude toward his subject. We find his aunt ridiculous because the poem depreciates the importance of her action or character (her whole life as mere prudery). We feel a relaxation of concern toward her, viewing her misfortune with contemptuous amusement.

All serious works, on the other hand, "depend upon amplification, understood as the opposite of depreciation." The serious experience, as rendered, always evokes a concern on our part toward the protagonists which, as the representation progresses, is rather fortified than cancelled. See our discussion, for example, of Emily Dickinson's "The Last Night That She Lived."

There are kinds and degrees of the comic, as there are of the serious, effect or power. Among comic poems, "Upon Julia's Clothes" induces a gay and indulgent attitude toward the simple-hearted lover; "Miniver Cheevy" evokes contempt or a feeling of superiority toward the ridiculous daydreamer; Ogden Nash's limericks produce the kind of pleasure we derive from the witty or the humorous remark. Among serious poems, on the other hand, "Lord Randal" has the effect of pathos; "Edward" evokes moral disapprobation; "La Belle Dame Sans Merci" produces a horror of supernatural evil; "Sir Patrick Spens" has tragic, as Yeats' "Sailing to Byzantium" has heroic, power.

The Poet's Use of Language:
W. H. Auden's "Musée Des Beaux Arts"

"Poetic Diction"

Poetry, considered as an "art" of language, is chiefly concerned with it as a *medium of imitation,* i.e., as permitting the simulation of a human action or experience.[1] "Poetic diction," so-called, is therefore any particular use of language in any given imitation, be it a lyric poem, a short-story, a play, etc. It is not a special kind of diction set apart from the language, say, of conversation or scientific prose by some special quality. When one examines any considerable body of poetry (say, Oscar Williams' *Immortal Poems*), one finds diction of extraordinary heterogeneity, ranging, for instance, from comic nonsense (Carroll's "Jabberwocky") through language of childlike simplicity (Blake's "The Lamb") or colloquial naturalness (Frost's "Stopping By Woods") to diction of great elegance (Collins' "Ode to Evening") or complexity (Dylan Thomas' "Refusal to Mourn"). Thus, it is fruitless to look for a special "poetic quality" in language, such as "irony," "paradox," or "ambiguity," and then employ it either as a *principle of structure* by which we distinguish a literary composite called a "lyric poem" from another verbal construct called an "essay," or as a *criterion of excellence* by which we judge all literary wholes called "poems." A particular danger in such a procedure is that we inevitably require of *all* poems a given quality of their verbal medium which, though significant in one poem because

[1] By *poetry*, we mean all kinds of poetry, fiction, and drama except, of course, their *didactic* forms which, while employing language chiefly as a medium of persuasion, do also exhibit a complex variety of "styles."

of a particular function that it there serves, may not even be found in another poem in view of a different end that its own diction subserves.

"Poetic quality," then, is *any* quality or characteristic relevant to a particular use of language in a given poem, and "poetic diction" is *any* kind of diction required by a particular end or function governing the construction of the verbal composite called a "poem." Of course, it would not also be right to suppose that there is no difference whatsoever between the use of language for "poetic" ends (i.e., for constructing various kinds of wholes called "poems") and the use of language for any other purpose (e.g., for conversation or writing a "scientific report" or an "essay" in philosophy). Our chief point, precisely, is that the differences in use, due to different ends or purposes, make for differences in qualities of the language or the kind of diction employed in any given literary composite.

Moreover, "poetic diction" (or diction as employed in any given poem) is not a replica of actual speech but an *artificial language*. What the poet has done when he has achieved a "style" of his own is to have made *a* language out of the materials afforded by a natural language by turning it to purposes other than those of natural speech (i.e., to purposes of his own "poems"). Even when his diction in a given poem is most like natural speech, it is there serving a particular *artistic* end or purpose rather than the natural end of discourse or ordinary conversation (e.g., information).[2] Thus, when we regard the speaker in Hopkins' "Spring and Fall," we simply cannot assert that anyone would contemplate the human plight in just those words that the speaker uses; language is so employed and ordered in that poem for the sake alone of such a depiction (as we have) of a particular experience (the speaker's own pensive, "philosophic" meditation induced by Margaret's grief) with a certain power to move us (the way it does, in fact, move us). Again, Frost's "Stopping By Woods" approximates more closely to "natural speech" (or such words as anyone may well use when he is turning about in his mind some problem or other),

---

[2] I am hoping, of course, that I have made my point sufficiently clear without getting embroiled in controversies on "actual speech," "natural language," the "natural end" of discourse, etc.

but even then, its diction is yet artificial in that, to make it serve strictly the end of the poetic imitation (i.e., to evoke a particular response to someone's experience as simulated), it has been made more expressive, more concise, more characteristic of the lyric speaker, more strictly relevant to his circumstances (as rendered in the poem), than it might "naturally" have been.

When we examine any poet's use of language (his diction or "style"), we must also guard against the tendency to locate, as it were, his "poetry" in linguistic or rhetorical devices. The so-called "poem" is *not* merely a verbal composite made up of imagery, metaphor, symbol, paradox, irony, ambiguity, etc. by which some idea or other is enforced; it is rather, above all, when it is not didactic in nature (e.g., Emerson's "Fable" or "Brahma"), a *simulation* of an individual's experience by which such things as imagery and metaphor are strictly governed. The poet has to do only with such words and devices as may most effectively render such or such an experience with such or such a power to move us emotionally. He need not even resort to metaphor or paradox if the experience he seeks to depict or the power he seeks to evoke does not require it. Often, indeed, it is simply a matter of the *right* word or the *most effective* word; after all, even when he uses metaphor, employs irony, or evokes images, he still must needs choose the most effective word in view of the experience he seeks to represent or the power he seeks to endow it with.

Metaphor, Symbol, Image

It may be helpful, before we examine Auden's "Musée," to distinguish between metaphors, symbols, and images since, though they are in fact quite distinct, they are often confused.[3]

    1. Metaphor is always verbal; the name of one thing (say, *hooting* for the owl's characteristic cry) is transferred (*metapherein*) to another (say, the train's *whistling*) on the ground of a supposed likeness (say, the long-

---

[3] I take these distinctions from Elder Olson's "Introduction" to Lyric Poetry (MS.).

drawn hollow character of either sound).[4] A comparison, then, whether explicit or implicit, is always involved.

2. When something is a symbol, its name also takes on symbolic significance: in Yeats' "Sailing to Byzantium," the thing (the city called Byzantium) symbolically "becomes" something else (a particular state or condition of the soul) such that the name *Byzantium* can no longer be referred to the historical city (to repeat, the name *Byzantium* takes on symbolic significance, it now denotes a spiritual state rather than the city itself). But symbols may or may not be verbal: *Byzantium,* in Yeats' poem only, is a verbal symbol; but a flag (a physical object) may symbolize a nation, the color blue (a physical quality) the Virgin Mary, the cross (a particular shape), Jesus or Christianity, genuflection (a particular action), an act of worship, the Mass (a particular rite), the mystery of Redemption. "What constitutes something as a symbol is that the *idea of something else* is, for whatever reason, *substituted for the idea of itself.*"[5]

> Thus, a cloth on a stick, with a certain design on it, has as its proper concept a cloth on a stick, with a certain design on it, and nothing more; when it has been adopted as the flag of a nation, the idea of the nation supplants the idea of a mere cloth on a stick. Once something has become a symbol, it not only stands for the concept of what it symbolizes, but inherits the emotional associations, perhaps even the authority, of the symbolized, and may even represent the latter in action.[6]

Thus, in "metaphor, name replaces name, and the things remain distinct. In symbolism, concept replaces concept, the thing symbolically 'becomes' something else."[7] *Hooting,* for example, which denotes the owl's characteristic sound, replaces in Dickinson's poem the name or word for the train's sound (say, *whistling*); but the things denoted (owl's sound, train's sound) remain distinct since they are merely compared; indeed, if they were not distinct, no comparison would result, and the term *hooting* would not convey the figurative sense it does in fact convey *in the*

---

[4] See Emily Dickinson's "I Like To See It Lap the Miles."
[5] Olson, *op. cit.*
[6] *Ibid.* The flag at half-mast, for example, symbolizes the nation in mourning.
[7] *Ibid.*

poem. Again, the concept of a spiritual condition replaces the concept of a "holy city" in Yeats' poem; the thing denoted by *Byzantium* (i.e., the historical city) symbolically "becomes" something else (i.e., the highest spiritual state). What concept of a holy city?—in the poem, a city, for instance, of holy men, of "sages standing in God's holy fire." What concept of a spiritual condition?—in the poem, a condition in which the soul is, for instance, no longer "sick with desire" nor "caught in that sensual music" but, "studying Monuments of its own magnificence," is gathered, as it were, into eternity and sings "Of what is past, or passing, or to come." Thus, too, *sailing to Byzantium* is symbolic action: the concept of a sea voyage to a holy city called Byzantium is replaced by the concept of a spiritual process by which "the heart is consumed away" and the soul is reborn, "once out of nature," into an eternal form befitting her new state.[8]

3. An image is different from either a metaphor or a symbol, though metaphors and symbols may evoke (but not always) images. An image is "a construct of the imagination," i.e., the image-making faculty or power of the mind. It is "a phantasmal synthesis of remembered feelings or sensations produced by an act of the imagination of the reader as determined by the poem."[9] It is not very useful (sometimes, even misleading) to classify images, say, according to the five senses (visual, auditory, etc.) or the kinds of sensations evoked. "*Any* human experience may be *imagined as an experience;* and anything so imagined is an image."[10] One can imagine anything that one might perceive by the external senses (sight, hearing, etc.); e.g.,

> While barréd clouds bloom the soft-dying day,
> And touch the stubble-plains with rosy hue;
> Then in a wailful choir the small gnats mourn
>> Among the river sallows, borne aloft
>> Or sinking as the light wind lives or dies;
> And full-grown lambs loud bleat from hilly bourn;
> Hedge-crickets sing; and now with treble soft
> The red-breast whistles from a garden-croft;
> And gathering swallows twitter in the skies.

---

[8] I. A. Richards speaks of the *metaphor* as consisting of two parts, *tenor* and *vehicle*, the tenor being the idea with which another idea (the vehicle) is identified. Thus, when Macbeth says that "life is but a walking shadow," *life* is the tenor of the metaphor in which *walking shadow* is the vehicle. What happens, then, in a metaphor is *identification* (comparison) of tenor with vehicle, but in a symbol, a *supplanting* of tenor by vehicle.

[9] Olson, *op. cit.*

[10] *Ibid.*

One can also imagine or evoke an image of any bodily condition:

> My heart aches, and a drowsy numbness pains
> My sense, as though of hemlock I had drunk,
> Or emptied some dull opiate to the drains
> One minute past, and Lethe-wards had sunk:

Or any feeling at all or condition of mind or soul, such as that produced by a scientific discovery or a sudden and remarkable sight:

> Then felt I like some watcher of the skies
> When a new planet swims into his ken;
> Or like stout Cortez when with eagle eyes
> He stared at the Pacific—and all his men
> Looked at each other with a wild surmise—
> Silent, upon a peak in Darien.

"In short, any experience of man, real or imaginary, may be represented by an image; for the image is precisely whatever we may imagine."[11]

But let us consider more closely Olson's definition of the image. First, the image is "as determined by the poem." That is to say: the reader must not imagine anything that

[11] *Ibid.* Note in the passages from Keats that (1) the images evoked are *imagined experiences* — particular sights and sounds of an autumn dusk; a bodily condition of "drowsy numbness" and pain; a mental or spiritual state of awe; (2) in these images, as we produce them, we see, hear, etc. in our own imagination gnats wailing among the river sallows, someone drinking hemlock, Cortez and his men upon a peak staring at the Pacific, etc.; (3) strictly speaking, the image is not "someone drinking hemlock" or "Cortez and his men . . . staring at the Pacific," but rather the condition of "drowsy numbness" and pain as though you had drunk of hemlock, or a state of great awe like that of Cortez and his men when they first saw the Pacific; (4) the images or imagined experiences are evoked by the words of the poem; these words have depicted such or such experiences (e.g., "swallows twitter") and, therefore, are capable of evoking these in our own imagination; (5) the words include metaphors: *bloom, soft-dying, wailful choir*, etc.; even, I think, *touch* and *rosy*. "I felt as though I drunk hemlock" or "I felt like Cortez" are also metaphors: the name for one condition (say, numbness or awe) is transferred to another, thus effecting the comparison. Sometimes, there is no actual name or word for the *tenor*: for the particular sound of *gnats*, for instance; hence, the need for a metaphorical term (or, in Richards' terminology, the vehicle): *mourn*, for instance; (6) The specific *function* of the metaphors in Keats' poems is to evoke or project someone's mood or attitude at the moment of "speech" since the comparison which the metaphor effects is, after all, his own perception of *his* experience (this "someone" is the so-called "speaker" who exists only in the poem).

the poem does not warrant, nor must the poet expect his reader to imagine anything that his poem has not achieved. There is a discipline of reading, as there is of writing, poetry. As Wallace Stevens says of "The Snow Man," he "beholds Nothing that is not there and the nothing that is."

Next, the image is produced *only* by an act of the imagination on the reader's part (again, "as determined by the poem"). Unless the reader performs this act, no image (though achieved in the poem) will result.

Finally, an image is constructed out of the reader's remembered feelings or sensations which have been evoked by the verbal representation of such or similar experiences. When Keats, for example, represents the sights and sounds of an autumn dusk, but his reader has had no experience whatsoever of it (whether just such an autumn dusk or a similar experience), then either no image will result or only an inappropriate one. The reader must simply have had a similar experience of dusk since such an experience alone can supply the *materials* of the image that the poem has achieved; i.e., the materials of his own remembered sensations and feelings which the words of the poetic representation are intended to stimulate (precisely, in fact, what we mean by their being evocative).[12] "The image is synthesized out of these materials, . . . combined into a whole which is a *phantasm*—that is, a mental presentation of something, not as an idea merely conceived, but as experienced or felt. To grasp this distinction, notice the difference between having an idea of a triangle and actually visualizing one."[13]

W. H. Auden's *'Musée Des Beaux Arts'*

About suffering they were never wrong,
The Old Masters: how well they understood
Its human position; how it takes place
While someone else is eating or opening a window
    or just walking dully along;
How, when the aged are reverently, passionately
    waiting

[12] Again, when Keats represents the astronomer's awe "When a new planet swims into his ken," we simply must have had a *similar* experience if we are to be able to respond to the image achieved in the poem; not, indeed, very similar to the astronomer's experience necessarily (try hemlock!), but some sight or other that inspired us with a great awe.
[13] Olson, *op. cit.*

For the miraculous birth, there always must be
Children who did not specially want it to happen,
    skating
On a pond at the edge of the wood;
They never forgot
That even the dreadful martyrdom must run its
    course
Anyhow in a corner, some untidy spot
Where the dogs go on with their doggy life and the
    torturer's horse
Scratches its innocent behind on a tree.

In Brueghel's *Icarus*, for instance: how everything
    turns away
Quite leisurely from the disaster; the ploughman
    may
Have heard the splash, the forsaken cry,
But for him it was not an important failure;
    the sun shone
As it had to on the white legs disappearing
    into the green
Water; and the expensive delicate ship that
    must have seen
Something amazing, a boy falling out of the sky,
Had somewhere to get to and sailed calmly on.

Our chief point is that the poet's means or verbal medium is governed by everything else in the poem. Auden's words and devices, for example, are strictly controlled by every aspect of his poem as an *imitation of a given kind*—i.e., as a simulation of *someone's mental activity* by which we are chiefly moved. We said, "by *every aspect* of the imitation"; that is,

1. By its *power*: Auden intends us to be moved to sadness by a particular "truth" about human suffering—i.e., that suffering concerns only the sufferer or that the world is indifferent to his lot. Such being the power or effect of the poetic imitation, Auden's diction, for instance, must be quite plain and simple. The immediacy of the "truth," since we grasp it at once, moves us more powerfully (as this poem shows) than if it were somewhat concealed. The "truth" is also presented unemotionally by means of plain, even colloquial, language: if Auden's diction were elegant, florid, or "rhetorical," the speaker's thought might not have rung as true or we might even

have found the thought insincere or sentimental (and so, we might even have remained unmoved).

2. By its *object*: Auden is simulating *someone's private reflection* on suffering as he considers the Old Masters' understanding of it in their works. His "argument" (mental action) manifests his character: a mature and sensitive man, if also somewhat sardonic. For the action actualizes or instances his character: only such a man, for example, who is mature and sensitive, would consider seriously what the Old Masters have to say about suffering, and consider it in just that manner that he does. But such a character explains the thoughts that arise in the speaker as he views or recalls, for instance, Brueghel's *Icarus;* it explains his "argument" about suffering which, in turn, explains his emotion or mood at the moment of "speech" or reflection. The words, then, in the poem must be capable of depicting such thought and such emotion in a train of reflection as would depict such a character engaged in such an activity of contemplating the Old Masters' works. Though, for instance, the speaker is moved by his reflection to sadness, the words (which are his thoughts) must not give us the impression that he is merely sentimental (or, at another extreme, merely sardonic); though his subject is profoundly moral and disturbing, the words, again, must not give us the impression that he is "moralizing" or "preaching." Otherwise, the object of imitation (someone's action, character, thought, emotion) would change and, consequently, its power to move us; we would have quite a different poem.

3. By its *manner*: Auden permits the lyric speaker to speak and act in his own person since, if we witness directly, as it were, his own private mental activity, we would be more powerfully moved by it. If such an activity were narrated, we would be moved by a particular version or account of the mental event (mediated by a narrator) rather than by the event itself; our response to the event (as depicted or narrated) would also be influenced by the narrator's implied attitude toward his subject. But since such an event is to be represented dramatically, then the order, for instance, of the words, verses, and stanzas must depict the order and progress of the speaker's train of reflection.

In general, then, the poet's verbal medium is so constituted as to serve specific and concrete ends or purposes of the given imitation. Or, to say the same thing, what the poet does with his language depends on how he proposes to move us by such or such a simulation of a given experience. His metaphors, images, symbols, and other literary devices make up only a part of his verbal medium; in given instances, there may be little or none of such devices as metaphors or symbols, or, when employed, they may not be as original or startling or important as in other poems.

Take, for instance, the opening stanza of Auden's "Musée."[14] It is a plain statement "about suffering" which hardly uses metaphor and exhibits little imagery (which are neither vivid nor even too significant in themselves since they are easily replaceable); nothing in the poem or about the poem is symbolic by our definition.[15] As we read the poem, we briefly picture to ourselves "someone . . . eating or opening a window or just walking dully along" (while someone else is suffering) — not very sharp or vivid images (or imagined experiences) since, as we read the words, the images they evoke simply flash across our mind. Indeed, the poem does not invite us to dwell on any image that the words tend to make us produce since, after all, in the lyric speaker's reflection "about suffering," the words (which are his thoughts) or the images they provoke merely indicate instances of "how it takes place," i.e., quite unexpectedly and without causing concern on anyone else's part. The next line evokes, in a vague or general way, an image of "the aged . . . reverently, passionately waiting" for death—but, again, our imagination hardly forms a picture of such a death scene since what is more important for the poem (which depicts someone's reflection on suffering) is that we understand the sense of the speaker's line of thought or "argument." Thus, for example, we are supposed to understand that "the aged . . . reverently, passionately" hope for death since they regard it as "the miraculous birth," and that such "waiting" is the form of their agony. Thus, too, the next image is only a little more vivid (or only as concrete as "someone opening a window") since the poetic intention is not so much to evoke it fully (as

---

[14] To forestall the reader's weariness, I shall not discuss the second and final stanza.

[15] We are *not* saying that Auden's poem is somehow inferior to other poems. Precisely, a poem's merit as poem rests, not on *what* devices the poet employs, but rather, on *how* he employs them for particular ends.

in Keats' "To Autumn") as to enforce the meaning of some-
one's reflection: i.e., if old men desire death, the young do "not
specially want it to happen" (though, indeed, as in Icarus' case,
it may happen suddenly to them as they go "skating on a pond
at the edge of the wood"). The last image we form—hardly any
clearer—is that of "some untidy spot Where the dogs," etc.
The images evoked merely serve to underscore the "dreadful-
ness" of that "martyrdom must run its course Anyhow in a
corner"—a dreadfulness chiefly owing to the isolation of the
sufferer and the indifference of his environs. "Martyrdom"
is, of course, a metaphor for a severe trial or intense suffering,
even as "the miraculous birth" is a metaphor for death as pas-
sage to a new life.

Quite obviously, then, Auden's images and metaphors tell
less than half the story of how his stanza, considered as a ver-
bal composite, was put together. If we were to explain just
why the opening stanza of "Musée" is effective as "poetry,"
as a depiction of someone's private mental activity, we would
have to consider much more than such literary devices as images
and metaphors:

> 1. Auden's language (words and devices) is meant to
> help us appreciate the lyric speaker's "argument" since,
> the more we appreciate *his* understanding of suffering
> (which he gleans from the Old Masters), the more deeply
> we are troubled and saddened by it.[16] Such a power *in the
> poem* (the poem as imitation) is precisely what Auden's
> language seeks to establish through the capacity of this
> particular word or that particular device to represent now
> this aspect and now that element of the speaker's "argu-
> ment" or reflection.
>
> 2. *Reverently, passionately, miraculous, dreadful mar-
> tyrdom;* and perhaps, *always, never*: these are just about
> the only words that are "rhetorical" or showy, as it were,

[16] Of course, we cannot fully appreciate the speaker's "argument"
(which, in the poem, is someone's mental action of understanding the Old
Masters' lesson) without considering also the speaker's character and mood
or emotional condition at the moment of "speech": precisely, the speaker's
action (reflection), as rendered, manifests not only his "thesis" (the burden
of his meditation) but also other aspects of the represented experience—
his situation (viewing or recalling the Old Masters' works in a museum,
which accounts in part for his detachment), his character, his particular
thoughts, his mood at the moment, etc.

in eloquence.[17] The rest are quite simple and plain; indeed, there is an abhorrence of the gaudy and elaborate, a deliberate attempt to be quite casual and even flat: "just walking dully along" or "the dogs go on with their doggy life." Yet, it is important, *for purposes of this poem*, that its diction, *as diction*, be commonplace and even uninteresting in itself. It is not only because the lyric speaker refuses to be sentimental about his subject (indeed, he is a little sardonic, but not disdainfully or bitterly sneering), but also because, by undercutting the mystery and burden of human suffering, we are all the more powerfully affected by the unequivocal sense of the speaker's reflection. This rhetorical device called understatement also explains why Auden's images are quite plain (so that they hardly invite us to produce them), and why he hardly uses metaphors.

3. As we said earlier, the poet's skill in language is often a case of the right word or the most effective word for particular ends in the poetic imitation. There is, for instance, the matter of *word relation* (or "semantic parallelism"), i.e., how the words relate with one another in the context of verbal meanings *as determined by the poem*.

(a) Take the series, "they were *never wrong . . . how well* they *understood . . .* They *never forgot.*" It stresses the Old Masters' melancholy "wisdom" as they contemplate, through their works, the reality of human suffering; *never* and *how well* underscore their full understanding of it.[18]

(b) A similar series is "Its human *position . . .* how it takes *place . . .* Anyhow in a *corner,* some untidy *spot.*" The first word (or thought) is, of course, abstract; i.e., the Old Masters understand the "place" of suffering in human affairs, how, whenever "it takes place," you might "locate" it, as it were, in the context of other human activities.[19] An abstract notion, but since the Old Masters depict "its human position" in their works (which the lyric speaker is now contemplating), it is made concrete: first, by the series of insignificant actions (eating, opening a window,

[17] Add from the final stanza: *everything, disaster, forsaken, expensive, delicate, amazing.* Even the verbal ironies are subdued: "did not *especially* want it," "turns away quite *leisurely* from the disaster," "not an *important* failure," "sailed *calmly* on."
[18] Perhaps, a verbal pun is involved in the rhyme association of *understood* with *wood* (if we take the latter's archaic sense: insane, foolish); but I suspect this is an over-ingenious reading.
[19] Perhaps, another verbal pun: to take place is to happen; but when it happens, then you can place it. But the more obvious reason for the idiom is, of course, its colloquial flavor.

etc.) as one precise context of suffering[20]; next, by the contrast between "the aged" awaiting their death and the "children . . . skating" (obviously, another artistic depiction in the Musée Des Beaux Arts) ; and finally, by "the dreadful martydom" (which involves another contrast).

4. Indeed, the stanza is structured as a *series of contrasts,* from simple to more elaborate (depicted in the Old Masters' works), by which the "human position" of suffering is concretely specified so that the speaker apprehends it and is moved by it like the Old Masters—and we, in turn, following the speaker's line of reflection, are moved similarly as the speaker.[21] In general, the contrast is that between what is significant (or momentous) and insignificant when two events (say, suffering and eating) are viewed as taking place together. The contrast is, of course, a rhetorical device too by which we are made to so appreciate the "human position" of suffering that we are moved by the sufferer's solitariness and the world's indifference.

(a) The first contrast is simply that between any suffering and such inconsequential events as "eating or opening a window." Considering the total context of the speaker's thought, what is stressed is not so much that "it takes place" unexpectedly but that the sufferer suffers alone since his suffering does not excite the slightest concern in anyone else.[22] The same thought is enforced by the other sets of contrasts which, at the same time, carry the speaker's "argument" forward.

(b) If the first contrast has to do merely with events as such, the next has to do with *attitudes* toward suffering or death. Old men desire death—"passionately, reverently"—not only because they are "aged" and have little to do anymore with life but also because they think of their end as "the miraculous birth." "Children" or young people do "not specially want it to happen" not only because they are young and passionately attached, as it were, to the joy of living, but also because, presumably, they cannot regard

---

[20] *Insignificant*: that is to say, in contrast to the momentousness of any form of human suffering. Note also that "just" and "dully" (in "just walking dully along") ensure, as it were, that we do not take any event in the series as significant or momentous.

[21] The second stanza is similarly structured, the only difference being that, now, the speaker dwells at some length on the contrasts depicted in one specific work, Brueghel's *Icarus.*

[22] "In Brueghel's *Icarus*, for instance: how everything turns away Quite leisurely from the disaster." Thus, the second stanza opens—the final, most detailed, and specific illustration of the same theme.

death as "the aged" do. The contrast has the effect of heightening the aged's reverent and passionate wish for death (which ends their suffering) by isolating them from the children who, since they are having the time of their life, must be indifferent to the lot of the aged. What old men desire, the children do not want: this has also the effect of stressing the suddenness of "disaster" which makes it particularly grim. Since the children are "skating on a pond," what they do not want to happen may yet suddenly take place.[23] We have therefore an ironic possibility which the words *specially* (itself ironic) and *always* ("there always must be Children") enforce.

(c) The third contrast further develops the speaker's thought, the Old Masters' lesson. Even the most unbearable suffering ("the dreadful martyrdom") must needs be borne because it "must run its course Anyhow," it can neither be prevented nor stopped.[24] *Corner* and *spot* isolate the "martyr" (who then, if you will, becomes his own witness); *untidy* enhances our sense of his abandonment and the insufferableness of his lot. The unknown *torturer* and the *dogs* and the *horse* that go unscathed promote the insufferableness. "The dogs go on with their doggy life," as to say, *not* that they are indifferent to the sufferer's lot (since they cannot be expected to understand) but that they are better off than the sufferer (though theirs is only "doggy life"). The horse is "the torturer's horse": this adds a further grimness to the picture (or rather, the meaning of someone's reflection) since the torturer's victim is not his horse but his fellow human; like the dogs, even the horse (whose master is cruel) is much better off than the victim. *Innocent* has a similar effect since we cannot really attribute innocence to a mere animal (except metaphorically); but the victim's innocence is of no avail, his "martyrdom" must run its course. *Scratches* involves pleasure or relief: the horse has this distinct advantage over the "martyr." *Behind*, because it is colloquial (and perhaps, humorous), undercuts the seriousness of the event as depicted; yet, precisely because it is serious, our response to it is thereby all the more reinforced. If, moreover, our reading is correct, the sardonic note in "someone else is

---

[23] Note the semantic parallelisms, "Children . . . skating" / "*Icarus, . . .* a boy falling" and "pond" / "green Water" (deep sea), which insinuate at "disaster" in the merriment in the wood.

[24] Note, again, the parallelism, "skating on a pond" / "run its course in a corner," which, in contrasting moments of pleasure and pain, underscores "the dreadful martyrdom."

eating," etc. becomes a little stronger in the verses on "the dreadful martydom."[25]

5. There is also the matter of what we might call *poetic eutaxy*—the right order and arrangement in a given poem. For instance, the order of the words:

> About suffering, they were never wrong,
> The Old Masters:

To see why this is the most effective order, we need only consider the alternatives:

(a) The Old Masters were never wrong
    Abut suffering:
(b) About suffering the Old Masters
    Were never wrong:
(c) They were never wrong, the Old Masters,
    About suffering:

Why do Auden's verses have the right order, the right emphasis? Because, precisely, they best simulate the speaker's mental activity, the exact force and flow of his reflection, the subdued anger, frustration, sadness over the "human position" of suffering. First, as regards the first two verses, suffering is exactly the burden of the speaker's meditation; it does in fact initiate his mental activity. Next, what about suffering?—it must be that some people have thought rightly about it. Thus, the lyric speaker, himself beginning to think about it, *at once* considers "they were never wrong." He has identified who they are (the poem's title suggests it), but his mind has leaped to that

---

[25] If, on reading the poem, we saw all these elements of the speaker's thought, why may it not be said that we saw them precisely because we produced the images (that the words evoked) and dwelt on them; that, therefore, the images did not merely flash across our mind but were, in fact, vivid enough (as we produced them)? First, (a) the images and metaphors, such as they are, do help to enforce the speaker's "argument." Next, (b) our analysis is analysis of the speaker's thought, not of the images themselves; or, to say the same thing, analysis of verbal meanings as determined by the poetic experience. Therefore, we did not so much produce particular images (or imagined experiences) as apprehend, in the context of the speaker's reflection, the full sense of the words (which are his thoughts and which evoked images only in a vague or general way).

A similar question arises: Was Auden fully aware of all these elements of the speaker's thought that we saw? It seems fairer to assume that he was; after all, the act of composing the poem is not mechanical or automatic. Besides, in trying to appreciate fully the speaker's reflection on suffering (and therefore, Auden's skill in diction), we have refrained from mere cleverness or ingenuity at interpretation of meaning.

most remarkable fact about them: "they were never wrong."
The next line, of course, identifies them as a class; but
since they are remarkable thinkers, they begin the next
line, which is the emphatic position.[26]

Related to word order is the order of verses (lines)
and stanzas. The most obvious reason for a particular or-
der may be the prosodic requirement. Thus, for instance,
the first three lines in Auden's poem consist of ten syllables
each. From there on, however, the number varies without
any pattern. For the speaker's thought, at first tense and
concentrated as he begins to reflect, quickens after the
third verse and rushes freely along to the end, its swift
course suggesting a confident mastery of the burden of
his thought.

Auden's stanzas also follow a rhyme scheme, how-
ever loose, for the incidental pleasure of the sound and the
pleasure, perhaps, of the self-imposed discipline. But the
prosodic structure that Auden chose is itself strictly gov-
erned by the requirements of the speaker's "argument."
We need to remind ourselves constantly, when examining
the poet's verbal medium, that this private mental activity
is the object of imitation to which the power of the imitation
as a whole is chiefly owing. We explain the order of the
"parts" of the line or verse in terms of the required or-
der of "parts" of the speaker's thought or "argument"
which Auden, by means of this line or that verse, seeks
to represent as effectively as possible. *The required order*:
that is, we assume, from the "argument" as rendered, that
it required such or such an order or progression of the
thought. *As effectively as possible*: that is, we assume
that Auden wishes to affect or move us, by this line or
those verses, by exhibiting such or such a development or
unfolding of someone's thought.

Thus, the order of the words, verses, and stanzas has
a rhetorical dimension: i.e., it subserves the power of the
poetic imitation, in every part of it and as a whole, to
move us in some way. For instance, if my mind dwells (as
it is so made to dwell, briefly, in Auden's arrangement)
on the "significant units" or "parts" of the speaker's
line of thought, thus:

---

[26] There may, of course, be a "private reason" for the poet's order of
his words, verses, stanzas; e.g., Auden might simply have *felt* that the
order in any given instance was the most effective. But the poet's private
feeling or predilection is, of course, beyond the range of *formal* criticism.

> About suffering / they were never wrong, /
> The Old Masters: / how well they understood /
> Its human position; / how it takes place /

—then, at every such "mental pause," the sense of each
"unit" is "capsulated" momentarily and thereby receives
its proper stress (quite apart, of course, from the natural
stresses of the words and the natural rhythm of the lines).
Next, the poet can always reserve the first "part" of the
line for that "unit" of thought which, in that line, must
receive the greatest emphasis: e.g., "About suffering" or
"The Old Masters" or "Its human position." Such a "unit"
can be broken to achieve emphasis: "there always must be/
Children" or

> the sun shone /
> As it had to / on the white legs disappearing
> into the green /
> Water;/ . . .

(in which *green* is further stressed by rhyming it with
seen in the next verse). Quite obviously, of course, the
first position need not be the most emphatic in the line:
e.g., "While someone else is eating." After all, any "part"
may be the locus of some "force" of the meaning in the
line—if, that is to say, the line admits of a certain "alloca-
tion of force."

> While someone else is eating or opening a
> window or just walking dully along;

Here, strictly speaking, there is no "allocation of force";
the line has gone lax, as it were; it is a kind of "spill-over"
from the preceding three lines where most of the "force"
is, as it were, concentrated and evenly distributed. There
seems to be no special reason for the precise order of the
series (eating, opening a window, walking); relative one
to the other, each activity seems equal in importance (or
rather, inconsequence). Our "mental pauses" (eating /
or opening a window /") are merely convenient to make;
they do not seem to require that we appreciate (or dwell
on) each "unit" of thought; we read the line through rath-
er quickly, we grasp it mentally all at once. This is why
its "units" merely flash images to us; they are merely
instantial, illustrative of the thought that they underpin.
This is also why the line is not broken or divided into
two verses; it is, as a whole, one illustration of the speak-

er's thought (i.e., suffering concerns only the sufferer and no one else).

> skating /
> On a pond at the edge of the wood: /

The line, too, is "lax" (as compared, say, with "About suffering / they were never wrong," /) ; there is no special reason for breaking "skating / On a pond . . ." except that "skating" rhymes with "waiting" (which enforces the contrast), and that the preceding verse, if not broken, would be much too long. The line is a "spill-over": we take it as a whole "unit" of thought. (with "skating"); it does not "allocate the force" of its meaning. The last two verses (first stanza) are also "lax": as we said earlier, the speaker's reflection is rushing freely along to its end.

It is, of course, much easier to see why Auden's first stanza must come first, and his second, second; and why there need not be a third. In the first, the lyric speaker is just beginning to reflect how "About suffering they were never wrong, The Old Masters." It seems to be the greater probability that, in the beginning, he would (as indeed he does) regard now this, now that, work by the Old Masters which depicts "how well they understood Its human position." In the second stanza, he focuses on what to him is the most striking work in the Musée Des Beaux Arts: Brueghel's *Icarus,* which depicts "how everything turns away Quite leisurely from the disaster."[27] Our explanation, of course, is in terms of one aspect, but the principal part, of the object of imitation, i.e., the speaker's *action* (what he does) ; another aspect (which most readers of the poem would employ as the principle of explanation) is the speaker's *thought* (considered as an argument of sort). In the first approach, the order of the elements within the stanza simulates the order and progression of the speaker's thought considered as his mental activity; in the second, the order within the stanza is the required order of its thought (or substance) considered simply as an argu-

[27] Note that the probability is not natural but "poetic" probability, i.e., the probabilities set up in the poem itself. After all, in real life, one may just as probably begin with Brueghel's *Icarus* since it is a most remarkable instance. In the poem, however, the speaker begins with familiar scenes and simple contrasts (eating, *etc.*), then moves to more complex or evocative scenes (the aged, the martyrdom), and finally ponders a mythological scene which captures most fully and strikingly the universal "truth" about suffering (*Icarus*). By moving from reality to legend (both depicted on canvas), the speaker implies that Icarus (the only "martyr" named) is an archetype of human suffering.

ment of sort. The second approach is, of course, legitimate; its only danger is that we are likely to forget that the argument is *someone's* thought or mental activity. For the poem—Auden's "Musée"—is not a species of rhetoric (e.g., argument of a sort in verse). It is a species of imitation: the nature of someone's thought as argument of a sort is subsumed under its nature as *someone's action*—someone's own individual response to the Old Masters.

Conclusion

I must now confess that I chose Auden's "Musée" because the analysis of its diction would show quite clearly that (a) "poetic diction" is *any* kind of diction at all required by a given imitation; (b) the "poem" is not merely a verbal composite since, precisely, it renders someone's action or experience; and (c) "poetry" is a matter neither of certain devices nor of certain qualities of diction but, rather, a particular use of language for purposes of a given imitation. Note, again, that we are dealing only with the literary work (be it a lyric poem, a short-story, etc.) that *happens to be an imitation* of a given kind (e.g., a reflective lyric on the order of Auden's "Musée").

Let me elaborate a little:

1. Metaphor, irony, etc. have often been considered as essentially "poetic" devices or even as principles of "poetic" structure when, in fact, they are fundamentally linguistic or rhetorical devices which may or may not be necessary in a given "poem." It is perhaps true that they have more currency in poems; and yet the fact remains that they are controlled by everything else in the "poem."

2. From one point of view, the words in the poem are its most important part since they are the vehicle of someone's thoughts; one must apprehend these thoughts before one can apprehend anything of the poem at all. But someone's thoughts are not the *whole* poem; they imply those other things which are non-verbal (e.g., someone's *character* or the precise nature of his *action* as response to the Old Masters or his *emotion*) but which constitute the whole experience of which the poem is an imitation. No exact paraphrase, if that were possible, will do as well as the poem itself, not only because each word has somehow its own "integrity," but also because the poem is an imitation of a given order: i.e., no other word

but just this word or that word, in this poem, can more precisely or more forcefully render the speaker's thoughts, or invest him with a particular character, or define his action or situation, or limn his mood or emotion. All these elements of the poetic experience determine and control the words and devices in the poem; the complexity of such governance is indeed owing to the complexity of the experience which the poet, in employing particular words or deploying particular devices, seeks to render.

Two Poems by Carlos A. Angeles:
An Experiment in Poetics *

FROM THE ROOFTOP

From the rooftop now, the inward eye's
Concern, a sudden landscape and the green
Proximity confirm the space's, the sky's
Pleasure, and what could not be seen
Before, could be.

But for a time, it is window and door
Must shape the rectangular scene
By the neighbor's face, by the poor
And futile garden, by the focus thin
Upon a bee,

Or a bloom that, against the summer heat,
Is dazed by my city's rage and sun,
By the hostile space of a street
Where one by unsuccessful one
The eye must see

The human fable rise and swell and fall
And disappear beyond an actual wall.

THE SUMMER TREES

The copper sun that scalds the april boughs
Of summer, from the noon's burst cauldron, there,
In concentrates of fury, hardly knows
The pertinence of patience the trees bear,

Who, with their metal branches, scour the air
For rumors of impending May to flood
Their throbbing thirst, or, to defy despair
The stirring breeze makes vocable and loud.

* First published in *Asian Studies*, X, No. 3 (Dec. 1972), pp. 344-60; revised and enlarged.

All summer long the bare trees stand and wait
While roots probe deepest for a hoard of silt
And seepage—till, silver in the sky, the late
Rains pour at last, hard where the treetops tilt.

Principles of Formal Analysis[1]

Whenever a poem happens to be an *imitation* of a human action or experience,[2] the general principles of analysis that may be employed in a strictly formal approach are the object, the manner, the means, and the effect or power of the imitation since, collectively, they are capable of discriminating the kind of poem that a given lyric is.[3]

In terms, then, of the *object of imitation*, lyric poems may differ as they render different *objects*:[4]

1. Someone who is simply moved by an emotion, say, a passionate longing ("O Western Wind") or grief

[1] I gratefully acknowledge my indebtedness to Prof. Elder Olson and Prof. R.S. Crane for the critical method and concepts on which this experiment rests. See Elder Olson, "An Outline of Poetic Theory" in *Critics and Criticism,* ed. R.S. Crane (University of Chicago, 1952), pp. 45-82, and also his *Tragedy and the Theory of Drama* (Wayne State University, 1961); and R. S. Crane, *The Languages of Criticism and the Structure of Poetry* (University of Toronto, 1953).

[2] For the distinction between mimetic and didactic, see "The Poem Itself: A Concept of Form" and "Stopping By Woods: The Hermeneutics of a Lyric Poem."

[3] The definition of a given kind of lyric poem results, precisely, from "the formulation of the distinctive means, object, manner, and effect of the [poetic] synthesis [since it] gives all four of the causes which are collectively, but not singly, peculiar to it." (Olson, "Outline of Poetic Theory," *op. cit.,* p. 558.)

[4] Such a classification of the poetic object (or object of imitation) in relation to the lyric poem is found in Olson's "Outline," p. 560. He notes there that "these classifications must not be confused with species; they are not poetic species but lines of differentiation of the object of imitation." Indeed, the precise line of differentiation for *the object of imitation* that we have now from Olson has to do only with the *kind* of depicted action or behavior of the lyric speaker. There are other lines of differentiation; the speaker's *character,* for example, the sort of person he is that his action discloses or actualizes: whether he is morally undifferentiated (like the lover in "O Western Wind"), or his action or behavior enables us to judge him on some ethical or moral ground (we approve of Yeats' old man in "Sailing to Byzantium," but disapprove of Browning's old man in "The Bishop Orders His Tomb"). The various poetic objects admit also of a number of possible variations in terms of their specific organizing principle. Wallace Stevens' "Thirteen Ways of Looking at a Blackbird," for example, consists of a series of impressions or perceptions somehow unified in terms of the speaker, the object of the various perceptions, etc.

(Walter Savage Landor's "Mother, I Cannot Mind My Wheel"); or

2. Someone who is engaged in a solitary activity of thought, say, contemplating (Keats' "Ode on a Grecian Urn") or deliberating, making a choice (Frost's "Stopping by Woods on a Snowy Evening");[5] or

3. Someone who is committing a verbal act on someone else, say, persuading (Marvell's "To His Coy Mistress") or threatening (Browning's "My Last Duchess"); or

4. Two or more people interacting with each other as in "Edward" (where the dialogue between mother and son unfolds the real situation) or in Browning's "The Bishop Orders His Tomb" (where the dying bishop, as he perceives his children's reactions in the course of his plea, revises again and again his last wishes).

In terms of the *manner of imitation*, lyric poems may differ as they are (1) dramatic, i.e., the speaker acts in his own person, as in all the aforementioned poems; or (2) narrative, i.e., a narrator recounts the poetic experience, as in Edwin Arlington Robinson's "Richard Cory" or T.S. Eliot's "Aunt Helen"; or (3) a mixed mode, as in "Sir Patrick Spens" or "The Wife of Usher's Well."[6]

[5] Ordinarily, however, it does not seem necessary to decide whether the lyric speaker is *simply moved by an emotion* (Landor's poem, like "O Western Wind," is a clear instance) or *chiefly engaged in an activity of thought* (many poems by Wallace Stevens, like "Connoisseur of Chaos," "Anecdote of the Jar," and "The Idea of Order at Key West," are clear instances). Often, indeed, the speaker's activity is *both* mental and emotional since he is usually moved by the subject of his own reflection; see, for example, Hopkins' "Spring and Fall" and Wordsworth's "Composed Upon Westminster Bridge."

[6] I can only touch here on an interesting critical problem. Why is "Edward" a *lyric* poem, but a poem on the order of "Sir Patrick Spens" or "The Wife of Usher's Well" *non-lyric*, though a poem? *One* reason must be the *size or magnitude* of the depicted action. That is: the specific organizing principle of the depicted action in "Edward" is a single incident—the interaction between mother and son in a *single closed situation.* The given situation that their interaction (dialogue) unfolds does not constitute a *plot* or "story"; it merely explains, as we infer parts of it at each stage of the dialogue, the "real nature" of this present confrontation between mother and son in which the *chief interest* of the poetic depiction lies. The unfolding has finally the effect of shock since it changes completely our impression of the encounter which the poem *enacts* by means of the dialogue. The same thing can be said of "Lord Randal." On the other hand, the specific organizing principle of the depicted action in "Sir Patrick Spens" is plot or "story"—i.e., an interaction between several characters in a *series of situations* revolving about one dominant incident. You do not have only one particular action or

Again, in terms of the *effect or power of the imitation*, a lyric poem may in general be serious or comic. The distinction is, however, a thorny problem in criticism. Suffice it to say that the peculiar comic effect is "either infectious gaiety or the ridiculous."[7] Most lyric poetry today is perhaps serious since it is somewhat difficult to come upon specimens of the comic lyric poem: Marvell's "To His Coy Mistress," Herrick's "Upon Julia's Clothes" or "Upon the Nipples of Julia's Breast," and Suckling's "The Constant Lover" (all induce an infectious gaiety); Eliot's "Prufrock" and "Aunt Helen," Robinson's "Miniver Cheevy," and Browning's "Soliloquy of the Spanish Cloister" (all evoke the ridiculous).[8]

Finally, in terms of the *means of imitation* or the verbal medium itself, a poem may employ familiar or uncommon words, conventional or unusual imagery and other linguistic and rhetorical devices, ordinary or uncommon syntax, etc. Compare, for example, Burns' "A Red, Red Rose" or Leigh Hunt's "Jenny Kiss'd Me" with Donne's "A Valediction: Forbidding Mourning" or T.S. Eliot's "Sunday Morning Service."

But the object, manner, means, and effect or power of the imitation are, as we said, general formal principles since they apply equally well to other literary works—plays, novels, short-stories, etc.—which happen to *imitate* or simulate a human action or experience. We must, therefore, seek in the same principles a certain analytical refinement by which poems may

event which the poem isolates and renders; neither is the dramatic situation single and closed. Hence, both ballads, "Spens" and "Usher's Well," are *narrative poems*, i.e., poems whose organizing principle is plot. As we distinguish, in terms of the *manner* of imitation, between the *lyric enactment* or the lyric poem in the dramatic mode ("Edward") and the *lyric account* or the lyric poem in the narrative mode ("Richard Cory"), so also, in terms of their *organizing principle* in the depicted action, we distinguish between the *lyric poem* in either mode of representation and the *narrative poem* or "story poem." But the ballad is, of course, like the ode, the sonnet, the haiku, etc., a set of conventions. For purposes of discriminating *kinds* of lyric poems, we cannot use any given literary convention as a *formal* or *structural* principle of analysis though, certainly, in the appreciation of the *means* of imitation, a knowledge of literary conventions would be useful, if not strictly necessary.

[7] Olson, *Tragedy and the Theory of Drama*, p. 164.

[8] Note that we are not speaking of "the comic spirit" or "the comic vision," but rather, of something more specific, more concrete—that is, the immediate *effect* of the poem on the reader.

further be discriminated *inter se* as to their more specific kinds.

We have already seen how, in terms of the specific object, one could formally distinguish "O Western Wind" from "To His Coy Mistress" or Frost's "Stopping By Woods" from Hopkins' "Spring and Fall." For even when the object is the same in two given poems (e.g., an activity of thought), there may yet be found a specific formal difference in the same structural or organizing principle: thus, the speaker in Frost's poem is deliberating, making a choice, whereas in Hopkin's poem, he is simply meditating, brooding;[9] in one, the principal part of the poetic object is the choice or moral action, but in the other, simply the train of reflection; and obviously, the poetic power is different, for to the one imitation of action, we respond with a kind of relief, as over a temptation successfully resisted, but to the other, we respond with a kind of solemn and pensive mood.

Evidently, too, there are various dramatic and narrative devices and techniques by which one may differentiate among poems. A few obvious instances must here suffice. In "Richard Cory," the *narrator* is an "outsider," a somewhat unreliable spokesman, since we find him morally deficient; but in "Aunt Helen," an "insider" (a nephew) whose trustworthiness we do not doubt despite his sardonic humor. Such a difference significantly qualifies our response to the poetic experience in either poem.[10] Both poems, too, exemplify one kind of lyric poem in the narrative mode, what I may call the *lyric character sketch* or the *lyric portrait* since the delineation of character is the organizing principle. Yet another kind may be called the *lyric scene* since the description of a scene is the

---

[9] Simply, I say, because it is not, as in "Ode on a Grecian Urn," for example, a complex process of discovering a new "truth" or insight. The speaker has always known from experience "the blight man was born for," and is only responding, just now, to Margaret's situation. Margaret only confirms his knowledge of "sorrow's springs" and is, therefore, only the *occasion* for his pensive activity.

[10] A difference between the narrators in "Sir Patrick Spens" and "The Wife of Usher's Well" may also be remarked: in one, the narrator also comments at some length on the tragic action in order to enlist our pity, but in the other, he remains a detached and uninvolved reporter (except for his comment on the hats of "birk"). It is a formal difference since it is determinative of the effect or power of the poetic imitation.

structural principle; e.g., Shakespeare's "When Icicles Hang by the Wall" and Jonathan Swift's "A Description of the Morning."

In terms also of the effect or power of the imitation, a poem may induce in us an emotion or frame of mind similar to, or different from, that of the lyric speaker. In Hopkins' "Spring and Fall," we tend to share the speaker's grief or pensive mood; but in "O Western Wind," we do not ourselves long for the beloved though we feel a general sort of sympathy, as for any lover in distress. Or, again, the poem may move us with sympathy for the speaker or with antipathy toward him. In "Coy Mistress," we feel friendly toward the lover, we admire him as being clever and witty, and wish him well; but in "Last Duchess," we feel hostile toward the lover, we loathe him as a ruthless egomaniac, and wish him thwarted or punished.

And even in terms of the means of imitation, we can, if we like, distinguish between Hunt's "Jenny Kiss'd Me," for example, and Housman's "With Rue My Heart is Laden." Both employ conventional metaphors; but in Hunt, a single metaphor serves, in Housman, several, though both poems are of about the same length. It is a small point, of course, but indicative: in Hunt, a straight and almost literal statement of fact is sufficient to evoke the mood of celebration; but in Housman, the poetic statement is a little more elaborate and almost entirely metaphorical in order to induce the rueful mood.

Thus, it all depends how specific the critic wishes to be in any formal analysis of a given poem; but the more discriminating one is, the more one is able to appreciate and judge the peculiar excellence of a given poem in terms of determinate criteria relevant to one or another distinctive kind of lyric poem.[11]

---

[11] Note that what I have presented thus far is a mere *sketch* of the general critical framework. A fuller discussion is to be found in my forthcoming book, *A Formal Approach to Lyric Poetry*. My only intention now is to show how a critical study of the *forms* of the lyric poem may be most fruitfully undertaken. The basic assumption is that lyric poems should be appreciated and judged as poems of certain distinctive kinds such that criteria relevant to one form or species (e.g., a poem on the order of "O Western Wind") may not necessarily be relevant to another

AN EXPERIMENT IN POETICS

The Reflective Lyric

Most of the lyric poems in Carlos A. Angeles' *a stun of jewels*[12] belong to the same general class, i.e., serious lyric poetry in the dramatic mode, imitating a mental action or experience of a single character in a single closed situation,[13] through a verbal medium more or less remote from ordinary diction and construction. For the sake of convenience, I shall call this kind of lyric poem a reflective lyric.

The principal part of the reflective lyric is the activity of thought or reflection, whatever else is its more specific nature or character as someone's action. But the other parts of the object of imitation are, in the order of their importance, the lyric character, his situation, his thought and emotion, and his own idiom or diction. Character, thought and emotion, and sometimes a more or less specific situation,[14] are the causes of the lyric speaker's activity.

The lyric speaker must be one or another sort of character to act in just such a way and think just such thoughts and feel just such emotions; and sometimes, he must confront a particular situation in order that, given a certain character, he might react exactly as he does. But the lyric character is a potentiality in the sense that only a particular action in the poem actualizes and manifests it to us.[15] There is, for example, no villainous character as such; there must first be a villainous deed or a series of mean and cruel acts before the villainous character is established in the poem, to which you may then respond. You are not moved by character as such; you are moved by it only as a particular action ma-

form or species (e.g., a poem on the order of T. S. Eliot's "The Love Song of J. Alfred Prufrock").

[12] Manila: Alberto S. Florentino, 1963.

[13] That is: one which does not permit any interruption of the speaker's activity by another character. (Olson, "Outline," p. 560.)

[14] Strictly speaking, the situation is usually merely the occasion of the speaker's action in the poem.

[15] As noted earlier, when a poem is a lyric poem, such action may be an emotional movement or outcry, an activity of thought, a verbal act on someone, or an interaction between characters in a single closed situation; i.e., when an interaction is involved, a situation which does not permit any interruption of the activity by other than those originally present.

nifests it. Hence, in poetry, action is primary, and character, secondary.[16]

By *lyric thought* I mean not the "theme" or central idea of the poem but the speaker's own thoughts in the poem. We must of course distinguish thought from the activity itself of thought or reflection. As mental action or experience of one sort or another, someone's reflection is precisely, as we said, the principal part in the object of poetic imitation.

Diction is primarily the vehicle of the speaker's thoughts from which we infer what precisely he is doing, his character, his situation, and his mood or emotion.[17] In the analysis, therefore, of the words in the poem, we must keep aware of an important distinction: between their own distinctive character as thoughts, whosoever they are, or as a train of ideas signified by particular words such that their implications involve only other ideas; and their "dramatic" character as someone's own activity of musing, deliberating, etc. so that their implications involve such things as his character, his mood, his situation, etc.

The *lyric emotion* must, of course, be distinguished from our own emotional reaction to the poetic experience since, obviously, we may feel differently from the lyric speaker. We

[16] Given the size or magnitude of the action in lyric poems (i.e., a single character acting—but, sometimes, two or more characters interacting—in a single closed situation), we do not normally expect a highly individualized character in the lyric speaker. But the degree of individuality may yet vary from poem to poem, i.e., from a more or less universalized character, as in all of Angeles' poems, to a more or less remarkable fullness of identity, like Browning's Duke of Ferrara or Eliot's Prufrock. Of course, neither the Duke nor Prufrock can ever be as complex a character as, say, Hamlet or the Karamazovs, since these are involved in more actions and, consequently, we infer more about their character.

But the character of the lyric speaker is a formal element: however universalized his character is in a given poem, it remains an important part in the object of imitation, capable of affecting us in some way. If, for example, the lover in "O Western Wind" were less passionate, we should be a little less moved by his outcry of longing; the difference, also, in poetic power between "To His Coy Mistress" and "My Last Duchess" is due chiefly to the character of the lovers which their particular actions manifest. (But, strictly speaking, in "O Western Wind," being a lover and being passionate in a given instance are indications, not of *character* as such, but rather, of situation and emotional condition.)

[17] Diction as the lyric speaker's own peculiar idiom may be a sign of character; e.g., a shallow or conventional mind, a country bumpkin, etc.

do not quite identify with him since, otherwise, it would be difficult (and sometimes, impossible) to form an opinion upon which to react intelligently.

Our inferences from someone's "speech"[18] concerning his action, character, emotion, and situation lead to particular opinions and judgments[19] which form the basis of our emotional response to the whole poetic experience. Our response manifests the inherent power of the poem as an imitation.

"From the Rooftop" and "The Summer Trees"[20]

"From the Rooftop" and "The Summer Trees," to take two representative poems in Angeles, are *essentially* the same *kind* of lyric poem. For, in terms of the object of imitation, both imitate a mental experience involving a single character in a single closed situation. Again, in terms of the manner of imitation, both are dramatic since the lyric speaker acts in his own person. Also, in terms of the means of imitation, both employ diction more or less remote from ordinary words and ordinary construction, and embellished by rhythm and rhyme. And finally, in terms of the effect or power of the imitation, both are serious since, in responding to the poetic experience, we do not regard it as trivial, amusing, or ridiculous.

But we may discriminate among variant forms of the reflective lyric for purposes of a more specific formal criticism. We may, for example, discover in the object, the manner, the effect, and even the means of imitation, certain formal differences between "Rooftop" and "Summer Trees." Let us therefore examine these poems more closely in terms of our principles of analysis.

[18] Such "speech" is, of course, only the apparent form of the poetic imitation since the real nature or character of the speaker's activity remains to be inferred as an emotional outcry, etc.

[19] We must needs form an opinion concerning the poetic experience as warranted, of course, by the poetic data. Otherwise, we could not take the poetic experience either lightly or seriously, and we would not be moved by it in any way, since emotion proceeds from an opinion about something or about someone. We cannot feel the emotion of fear unless we have the opinion that something or someone is fearful; a confused emotion is owing to a confused opinion; etc.

[20] Angeles, *a stun of jewels*, pp. 9, 10.

The Object of Imitation: The Lyric Action

In "Rooftop," the experience is one of release from a mental or spiritual oppression. The lyric action therefore consists of two parts: someone makes a sudden discovery which brings about his release from a limiting outlook ("what could not be seen / Before, could be") ; and this, in turn, initiates a retrospective brooding on the oppressiveness of a dismal situation from which he has just now escaped. When one considers the speaker's present discovery and sense of freedom, there seems involved in his bitter cry of protest against "my city's rage and sun" a kind of plea for all frustrated lives which cannot share, as he does now, "the space's, the sky's/ Pleasure . . . the inward eye's/Concern." He realizes that those lives will remain a "fable" (i.e., "unsuccessful," uneventful, unreal) just so long as, given their particular situation, they are unable to scale, as it were, the imprisoning "actual wall" (i.e., the city as "hostile").

In "Summer Trees," on the other hand, the experience is essentially a joyful recollection, a celebration. The lyric action is from its inception to its end purely an activity of memory. There are no discrete parts: you have one and the same sort of mental action, and it is one straight or continuous train of reflection. What you have is a series of perceptions in someone's memory of summer trees by which he ever knows "The pertinence of patience the trees bear." It is a sort of habitual knowledge or permanent conviction.

Thus, it can be said that the lyric action in "Rooftop" is relatively complex, but in "Summer Trees," relatively simple. That is: in one, action consists of discrete parts since more things are involved; for example, the speaker's situation has undergone a sudden change and, hence, his own frame of mind and emotional condition have changed also.

In considering action as the principal part in the object of imitation, we also have to specify, in so far as that is possible, the character of the lyric speaker, his thought,[21] emo-

---

[21] The lyric thought, as the sole basis of inferences concerning all other parts of the object of imitation, is always involved in the analysis of those other parts as well as in the analysis of the manner, the means, and the effect of the poetic imitation.

tion, and situation. Only then shall we grasp *the whole poetic experience* which may be said to be the "soul" or form of the poem in more or less the same sense that Aristotle calls plot the "soul" of drama.[22] Then, also, shall we apprehend the unique power of a given poem as an imitation of action or experience.

The Lyric Character

The lyric speaker in any poem by Angeles is a perceptive and morally sensitive observer.[23] You do not have, as in Browning or Edwin Arlington Robinson, a complex variety of *dramatis personae*. It is clearly Angeles (or, if you will, the same mind or sensibility) who speaks through the lyric speaker in every poem. But in this, Angeles is like most other lyric poets.

Nevertheless, from poem to poem, we do respond in some way to the *character* of the lyric speaker. It is an aspect of the whole poetic experience and, therefore, part of its inherent power to move us. And thus, between two poems, it can sometimes happen that certain moral traits or qualities of the lyric speaker will make for a certain formal difference, i.e., a difference in their specific power.[24] It may of course be said that some sort of character is inevitably implied by the specific nature of the action in a given poem. True: but what I want to stress is that character, as a cause of the lyric action, is an aspect of the organizing principle in any poem which hap-

---

[22] In the *Poetics*, it is important to note that Aristotle considers only a particular kind or species of mimetic drama, i.e., tragedy on the order of, say, "Oedipus the King" or "Hamlet," but not tragedy on the order of, say, "Macbeth" or a "domestic tragedy" like "Death of a Salesman."

[23] Except in "Asylum Piece" (*a stun of jewels*, p. 18), which is a kind of lyric anecdote. It is the only instance in Angeles of the mixed mode in the manner of imitation, and the only instance of the comic lyric poem.

[24] In "The Invalid" (*a stun of jewels*, p. 11), for example, a certain habitual disposition of soul betrays an apparent moral deficiency of a sort in the lyric actor. Such a difference in character—quite apart from the specific nature of his action—establishes a formal difference between this poem and "Rooftop" or "Summer Trees." Generally speaking, one tends toward a kind of moral disapproval of the invalid, since one judges unfavorably of his disposition, and toward a kind of moral approbation for the speaker in "Rooftop" or "Summer Trees."

pens to be an imitation. The lyric action in such a poem always requires a given sort of character to carry it through and make it seem probable or necessary.

In "Rooftop," then, and "Summer Trees," the moral sensitivity and perceptiveness of the lyric speaker is more or less of the same cast. Again, it may be said that the similarity arises simply from the object, or subject, of the speaker's reflection: but this cannot be true. In one or the other poem, the sort of lyric action that you do have requires just that sort of moral sensitivity to render it probable or necessary. In "Rooftop," for example, someone does protest against "the poor/and futile garden" or lament "the focus thin/Upon a bee"; he is made unhappy by "a bloom that, against the summer heat,/Is dazed by my city's rage and sun"; he feels a compassion for "the human fable . . . (that) one by unsuccessful one (must) rise and swell and fall/And disappear beyond an actual wall." And of course, the speaker's "pleasure" is also a kind of moral triumph since his "inward eye's concern" is essentially a moral one, i.e., a concern for breadth of vision or perspective by which a certain freedom is secured and a richer or fuller life is made possible.

There is, too, in "Summer Trees," a similar moral sensitivity. The lyric speaker "knows / The pertinence of patience," and may also be said to feel a kind of moral triumph when,

> silver in the sky, the late
> Rains pour at last, hard where the treetops tilt.

As in "Rooftop," therefore, a moral interest may be said to underlie the speaker's perceptions and to be the cause of his pleasure when the trees seem to him to rejoice in the "late rains."

But when we say that the lyric speaker in "Summer Trees" is morally sensitive, we mean primarily that his impressions have a moral tenor: note, for example, "The pertinence of patience the trees bear" under the scalding sun, or their "metal branches" that seem in their sound "to defy despair." It may, therefore, be said that the moral concern is a more dominant element in "Rooftop" since there the speaker shows, for example, moral indignation and compassion for pent-up lives. The difference is of course a matter of degree, and yet, owing to it, the poetic imitation affects us somewhat differently.

The Lyric Emotion

In considering the lyric action and character, we have of course touched also on the emotion of the lyric speaker and his situation; but this is unavoidable since, after all, the poem is a certain interrelationship of such elements as action, character, etc. by which a unique and particular experience is constituted. The object of imitation is a whole unity to which we respond; its elements are more or less separable only in specific formal analysis.

Generally speaking, in both "Rooftop" and "Summer Trees," the central emotion is a kind of pleasure which we tend to share with the lyric speaker; but in "The Invalid" (to illustrate an obvious difference), a kind of pain, a resentment and uneasiness or perplexity which move us with pity toward the lyric actor.[25] More specifically, the speaker in "Rooftop" feels released from a past and dismal situation. Hence, the emotion is a certain buoyancy or exhiliration of spirit that the speaker's sudden discovery or insight brings on:

> From the rooftop now, the inward eye's
> Concern, a sudden landscape and the green
> Proximity confirms the space's, the sky's
> Pleasure, and what could not be seen
> Before, could be.

And yet, his present mood of joy is also tinged with gloom owing to his own compelling recognition of "the focus thin" and "hostile space" from which he is just now released. The manner of imitation enforces not only the sudden emotional

[25] We speak of a "lyric actor" because "The Invalid" (like "Bearded Lady," *a stun of jewels*, p. 21) is a reflective lyric in the narrative mode; i.e., you are told about someone, though the narrator, in both poems, enters fully into the lyric actor's consciousness. The pain, the resentment and perplexity—these indicate the invalid's emotional state, by which we are moved to pity; but, over and above that pity, we also disapprove of his attitude on moral grounds.

change from a past condition but also the exact character of the present mood. For, should one reverse the order of the speaker's thoughts, e.g., reserve the first stanza for the conclusion, the effect would be different: the gloom should be quite dispelled or mitigated, and the joy increased into a kind of exultation.

If "Rooftop" is a kind of affirmation of "the inward eye's concern," "Summer Trees" is a celebration of "the pertinence of patience." The speaker is vividly recollecting certain impressions which, from "copper sun that scalds" to "the late rains," progressively magnify the central insight. And therefore, his thoughts, unlike those of the speaker in "Rooftop," do not have a pensive cast but remain throughout a kind of joyful musing. The sombreness is entirely in the object of reflection ("the noon's burst cauldron," the trees' "throbbing thirst," etc.) ; the activity of recollection itself is one of celebration. Indeed, the speaker's thought and emotion even reach a kind of climax as he imaginatively shares in the trees' rejoicing when, released from summer oppression, they receive their patience's meed. There is no sudden discovery, no looking back from a changed perspective, no qualification of a present emotion or mood owing to any change in the speaker's situation. The speaker is only and simply recollecting and celebrating "The Summer Trees."[26]

The Manner of Imitation

Both "Rooftop" and "Summer Trees" are essentially dramatic. But each poem affects us differently, and part of the reason lies in the precise manner of imitation.

In "Rooftop," the manner has to do chiefly with the ordering of the parts of the lyric action itself and with the arrangement of the speaker's thoughts or perceptions. First, then, as regards the lyric action, you begin with the speaker's sudden

---

[26] He is not actually "there," watching "all summer long" and making his observations till "the late rains pour at last." This is patently absurd. It is only *as though* he were actually "there" as a witness, his memory being so vivid and perceptive that he could, for example, imaginatively feel, even now, "the noon's burst cauldron," or see what "roots probe deepest for," or even know the trees' motive, "to defy despair."

discovery of a new perspective which, though a mental event, is momentous since the speaker feels a certain exhiliration of spirit. You grasp the event and share the speaker's mood. But, next, you have the speaker's retrospection, an activity of thought initiated by his discovery; he looks back and considers what it was "before . . . for a time." And you realize, only then, that the speaker feels released just now from an oppressive outlook; you move from the present situation and mood of the speaker to his dismal past. Consequently, you feel at the end of the poem a certain admixture of gloom. The poem itself ends with the speaker's pensive consideration of "the human fable." As noted earlier, to reverse the order of the lyric action would change the peculiar effect or power of the poetic imitation.

The speaker's thoughts, on the other hand, are arranged in climactic and logical order: from the present view to a past "scene," and from each particular scene to its effect. Thus, you move from "a sudden landscape and the green proximity" to "the rectangular scene . . . the poor and futile garden . . . the hostile space of a street"; and from "the space's, the sky's pleasure" to the poverty and oppressiveness of the old "scene" and the futility of life under its narrow and limiting sponsorship. In the speaker's retrospection, particular stress is laid, from one object of perception to another, on the frustrating character of the "scene" as "the focus thin"; in fact, from "the rectangular scene" to "the human fable," there is a progression of oppressiveness. Logical order might also be seen in terms of the speaker's coign of vantage: he sees "from the rooftop now . . . a sudden landscape," but from "window and door" in the past, only "the poor and futile garden." Also, he shifts and adjusts his focus from larger to smaller "scene," and vice-versa: from garden to bee or bloom, and from "my city's rage and sun" to "the hostile space of a street." The effect of such shifts and adjustments is to make us see more vividly the objects of the speaker's perceptions, since a greater effort on our part is required than if the particular objects were observed from a more constant standpoint; and seeing more vividly what the speaker himself sees and judges reinforces the total effect of the poetic imitation.

In "Summer Trees," the manner has to do chiefly with the ordering of the speaker's impressions. You do not begin, as in "Rooftop," from a high point, so to speak, of the lyric action (such as a sudden discovery and release from oppression). What you have is something like a straight series of impressions in someone's recollection of trees in torrid summer. The speaker, who is only recalling a "scene," does shift his standpoint, but the object of perception ("The Summer Trees") remains constant. Such concentration has the effect of intensifying our own impressions of the "scene" (as of "concentrates of fury" in "copper sun" and "metal branches") toward the fullest apprehension of "the pertinence of patience the trees bear."[27]

The speaker's impressions are recalled in logical and climactic order: first, the occasion for the trees' "patience" in the punishing heat of summer; next, the defiant endurance of their "patience"; and finally, its fit requital in "the late rains." Or, you first have the hardship under "the noon's burst cauldron," the persevering toil for moisture, the long waiting—and then, the sudden succor when "the late rains pour at last." Or, again, you have first a statement of the speaker's central insight, "The pertinence of patience the trees bear"; and the rest of the poem demonstrates it in a kind of "dramatization" of the scene (trees versus sun, and then, the liberating rain).[28] Surely, then, however one views the order, it does serve to heighten the power of the poetic imitation, i.e., its capacity to make us rejoice with the speaker as he recalls his knowledge of summer trees.[29]

[27] Compare, again, with the various objects of perception and the marked shifts in standpoint and focus that they required in "Rooftop." The effect there is to deepen our sense of the speaker's moral agitation in the past.

[28] The speaker's thoughts in "Summer Trees" may thus be said to partake of the character of an argument. It constitutes a formal difference between this poem and "Rooftop" (where the speaker's thoughts may be said to be a kind of brooding)—a difference that pertains, of course, to the *object of imitation.*

[29] Note also that, at the outset of the poem, you are looking up with the speaker at "the copper sun"; next, you regard the trees' "metal branches," and then probe underneath where "roots probe deepest for a hoard of silt and seepage." And at the end of the poem, you are looking up again, but this time you see, not "the copper sun," but the "silver... rains"; not the "noon's burst cauldron.... In concentrates of fury,"

Thus, the manner of imitation, considered as a cause of the poetic power inherent in each poem, constitutes a formal difference between "Rooftop" and "Summer Trees"; i.e., the manner in each poem is directed toward a peculiar effect of the poem as an imitation of a mental experience. In one, the specific manner of imitation helps to qualify the effect of joy with a certain degree of gloom or pensiveness; in the other, it helps to intensify the mood of celebration.

The Means of Imitation[30]

The words in "Rooftop" are governed by two contrasting experiences of the speaker: the present satisfies, the past frustrates, his "inward eye's concern." The contrast is chiefly indicated by his particular coign of vantage: in one experience, "the rooftop," in the other, "window and door." The balance in the contrast is tilted toward his recollected past, and the effect is to make us perceive that the speaker's mood is yet alloyed with a certain oppressive gloom; he cannot yet enter fully into "the space's, the sky's pleasure." And thus, after the first stanza, the words serve to make the speaker's past loom into prominence and cast a pall over the moment's sudden triumph. The "landscape and the green / Proximity [which]

but the rains that "pour at last, hard." Where before you saw the "metal branches scour the air," now you see "the treetops tilt" as though fulfilled. Summer's trying regimen has ended in the joyful triumph of the trees' "patience."

[30] I only wish here to indicate the direction that an analysis of the specific *means of imitation* must take whereby we may apprehend any formal difference between "Rooftop" and "Summer Trees." We must note, however, that from another point of view, the words in the poem are its most important part since they are the vehicle of someone's thoughts; one must apprehend these thoughts before one can apprehend anything of the poem at all. But someone's thoughts are not the whole poem; they imply, as we said earlier, those other things which are non-verbal but which constitute the whole experience of which the poem is an imitation. And no exact paraphrase, if that were possible, will do as well as the poem itself, not only because each word has somehow its own integrity but also because, in a given poem, it is just this word or that word, and no other, which can more precisely or more forcefully render the speaker's thoughts, or invest him with a particular character, or define his action or situation, or limn his mood or emotion. All these elements of the poetic experience determine and control the words in the poem; the complexity of such governance is indeed owing to the complexity of the experience which the poet, in employing particular words or devices, seeks to render.

[211]

confirm the space's, the sky's / Pleasure" and fulfill his "inward eye's / Concern" are heavily counterbalanced by the rest of the poem—"the rectangular scene / By the neighbor's face," "the poor / And futile garden," "the focus thin / Upon a bee," etc. In contrast to his inward eye's "pleasure," all these recollections have, even now in his present mood, precisely that effect on the speaker on which the poem ends: "The eye must see"

> The human fable rise and swell and fall
> And disappear beyond an actual wall.

Take, for instance, the word "concern" or "proximity." Either word is meant to suggest all that is relevant to the speaker's experience, nothing more and nothing less. Of course, we would not know what exactly is relevant unless we have first grasped that experience. "The inward eye" is a metaphor for the mind or the imagination or, if you will, the spirit— not as an abstract entity, but the speaker's own faculty or spirit. Considering his experience, then, "concern" implies on his part an anxious moral care for and even preoccupation with breadth of vision. When he says, "it is window and door / Must shape the rectangular scene," he is saying that "for a time" there was no choice at all, and his spirit felt cramped and deprived. Note the full force of "rectangular scene." It derives not only from its juxtaposition with "the neighbor's face" (which has the painful effect of somehow demeaning the human or spiritual element in the "scene"), nor its connexion with such other words as "landscape" (in the sense of almost unlimited vista) and "wall" (which denotes a certain rectangularity). The full force of the description chiefly derives from its "dramatic" context, i.e., the experience of the speaker who feels released on "the rooftop now." The old "scene," to his "inward eye," is not only flat and uninteresting[31] since it confirms no pleasure in his particular "concern"; it is also oppressive, as though his mind or spirit were mured in a rectangle, or he himself were hemmed by "an actual wall." And

---

[31] "Scene" (as opposed to "landscape") adds to the speaker's sense of its dullness and spiritual aridity as he recollects it.

similarly, when he says, "The eye must see / The human fable rise and swell and fall," he is lamenting that "before" he was constrained to see the pitiful effect of that "hostile space" which gave his "inward eye" no pleasure; and so, his words imply, as we said, a protestation and a plea.

"Proximity," like "concern," is also governed by the poetic experience; we can claim that it is just the right word only in terms of the peculiar experience it bears on. "The green proximity" seems rather formal or stiff, for it really means the closeness of trees to the speaker or, at least, a clear prospect of greenery "from the rooftop now." But since it is a "sudden" view of "landscape" and the speaker "for a time" has had only "the rectangular scene," their closeness just now seems to him to have an alien or unfamiliar character; and that precisely is what the formality of the expression suggests in the speaker's own experience. As we said earlier, the speaker is not quite ready as yet to enter fully into "the space's, the sky's / Pleasure." This is why he can only say that the green vista "confirms" their "pleasure."[32]

Similarly, the words in "Summer Trees" serve to convey not only the speaker's insight but also his celebration of "the pertinence of patience the trees bear." The first stanza is governed by a vivid recollection of "the copper sun," but the recollection celebrates the speaker's central perception in the poem. Hence, the words must not only stress the intense heat (in such metaphors as "copper" and "metal") but also underscore the jubilant mood. This, in fact, is the peculiar effect of the ironic understatement in "The copper sun . . . hardly knows." The same effect is heightened in the second stanza which (even syntactically) flows directly from the central perception and demonstrates it, since there the speaker's thoughts bear directly on the persevering and defiant effort of trees

---

[32] The poet's *syntax* (an aspect of the *means* of imitation) is, of course, a clue to the meaning of his speaker's thoughts. "The inward eye's Concern" refers to "From the rooftop now"; that is, to a concern for vista, for breadth of vision (physical and spiritual). The "sudden landscape" and "green proximity" of it "confirm the space's, the sky's Pleasure"— a pleasure which is, in the first place, *of* the space and *of* the sky in themselves; but a pleasure which, because of the speaker's mood, also becomes an aspect of his "inward eye's Concern," a disclosure of its essentially joyful nature.

against summer. The first and second stanzas contrast two sets of perceptions: "the copper sun that scalds the april boughs" and the trees' "metal branches [that] scour the air [or] defy despair." The contrast not only accentuates the insight into the trees' "patience" by giving it body, as it were, but it also dramatizes the mood of celebration. Someone is not only recollecting sun versus trees: even as he seems to feel again "the noon's burst cauldron, there," so also he seems, even now, to participate in the trees' enduring toil against summer.

There is a sort of pause in the third stanza as the speaker recapitulates:

> All summer long the bare trees stand and wait
> While roots probe deepest for a hoard of silt
> And seepage—

Note that the pause, the recapitulation, is an aspect of the lyric action which the words are made to convey. But more than that, the words magnify the celebration. "All summer long" intensifies the speaker's impression of the punishing heat; and "the late rains [which] pour at last" underscore it further. The words ("All summer long") recapitulate the first stanza. But the speaker is also saying, "the bare trees stand and wait," etc. These words, recapitulating the second stanza, are ordered toward the speaker's final declaration of a deeply-felt admiration (or even reverence). "Bare" recalls the sun that "scalds the april boughs" and converts them into "metal branches"; but the roots that probe deep for moisture evoke those boughs that

> scour the air
> For rumors of impending May to flood
> Their throbbing thirst.

And finally, the advent of rain brings the celebration to its highest point:

> till, silver in the sky, the late
> Rains pour at last, hard where the treetops tilt.

[214]

Note that "silver" (as opposed to "copper sun" or "metal branches") at once sounds the triumphant note; that the rains "pour hard" even as the sun before poured "from the noon's burst cauldron . . . In concentrates of fury"; and that "the tree-tops tilt," rejoicing, even as before "their metal branches" could only sound in "the stirring breeze . . . to defy despair."[33]

If, then, there is any formal difference between "Rooftop" and "Summer Trees" in terms of the specific means of imitation, the difference is attributable to the particular ends for which the words are employed.[34] Generally speaking, "Rooftop" is more literal, and "Summer Trees," more metaphorical. A greater degree of literalness is effective in "Rooftop" toward a direct and unequivocal delineation of a past and oppressive situation of the speaker. The figurative statements (as in "a bloom . . . dazed by my city's rage") are quite simple in the sense that they do not really require any subtle interpretation; they translate more or less immediately into their literal purport. In comparison with the richly metaphorical language in "Summer Trees," they are intended primarily to assert a comparison, to describe a situation, at a certain level or depth of the sensibility. Neither poem is of course symbolic in the sense

---

[33] Incidentally, the striking shift in subject (since it is the breeze which "makes [the trees] vocable and loud") reinforces the speaker's impression of the breeze as an ally: it brings "rumors of impending May."

[34] We must note here that words may be deemed "dramatic" in another sense, i.e., when, considered as signs, they present whatever they signify so vividly or so cogently that we are struck by the expression and regard it as memorable. It is in this sense that metaphor, irony, etc. have sometimes been considered as essentially "poetic" devices, or even as principles of poetic structure, when in fact they are fundamentally verbal and rhetorical devices which may or may not be necessary in a given poem. It is perhaps true that they have more currency in poems; and yet, the fact remains that they are controlled by everything else in the poem itself. If there is ironic contrast, for example, between "rooftop" and "window and door," or between "human fable" and "actual wall," it cannot follow that, therefore, irony is the organizing principle of the poem itself (unless, of course, one considers the poem merely as a verbal composite). The irony is determined and controlled by the experience which the poem renders; and, certainly, the verbal irony is the least of it since the ironic effect results chiefly from our perception of the whole experience itself. For—to repeat—we are not chiefly responding to a linguistic structure (the poem as a verbal composition), but rather, to someone's experience (the poem as imitation).

that Blake's "The Sick Rose" is a symbolic lyric poem,[35] nor ironic in the sense of an "ironic" awareness in either poem of an opposite and complementary outlook or attitude.[36]

The Power or Effect of the Imitation

At this stage in our analysis, we need only recapitulate formal differences in terms of poetic effect.[37] Both "Rooftop"

[35] Here is the poem:

O Rose, thou art sick!
The invisible worm,
That flies in the night,
In the howling storm,

Has found out thy bed
Of crimson joy,
And his dark secret love
Does thy life destroy.

The poem compels us to interpret it symbolically because it insists on a further range of significance than a speaker's distress over the spectacle of a rose attacked by a worm on a stormy night. "The rose," says E.M.W. Tillyard, "is earthly love (with its potentialities of innocent fulfillment), the worm is the wicked instinct to be possessive and predatory that battens on and corrupts earthly love. . . . The first line violently personifies the flower, forces the mind to seek something more than the mere physical rose. . . .[Blake] expresses in 'thy bed of crimson joy' the shape and the feel and the glow of the physical flower with incomparable felicity. The same phrase helps out the symbolic meaning, for it . . . refers to the bed where the joys of love are experienced. The trend of the poem then is to make us dwell on the sick rose as the symbol of innocent love corrupted." Alex Hufana's interpretation is different, more specific, even blatant: "The particular sickness stands for love debased, the pleasure of a whore, only that it speaks here of all cheap human joy, the sanguine condition of life. It is because that it is cheap that the pleasure gets perverted. The 'invisible worm' needs no belaboring, except perhaps the view that it perverts the human condition with a 'dark secret love' that at its worst storms everyone else's privacy and, once there, destroys from within." C. M. Bowra allows the reader more leeway, which perhaps makes his interpretation more intellectually agreeable: "as in all symbolical poems, we can read other meanings into it. . . . We may say that it refers to the destruction of love by selfishness, of innocence by experience, of spiritual life by spiritual death. All these meanings it can bear, and it is legitimate to make it do so. But the actual poem presents something which is common and fundamental to all these themes, something which Blake . . . sees with so piercing and so concentrated a vision that the poem has its own independent life and needs nothing to supplement it." (For Tillyard and Bowra, see *The Case For Poetry*, p. 25; for Hufana, see his *Notes on Poetry* in *The Diliman Review*, XX (April-October, 1972), Nos. 2-4, p. 403.)

In Angeles' "Rooftop" or "Summer Trees," however, there is no compelling necessity to scour the air, as it were, for rumors of a hidden or more profound meaning than the speaker's experience itself as ren-

and "Summer Trees" put us in a frame of mind more or less similar to that of the lyric speaker. This happens naturally, so to speak, since we are made to reflect on the same object that the speaker muses on, in more or less the same manner that he does; and we are not given any ground for disagreement with his thoughts or disapproval of his action or charac-

dered. Alex Hufana (p. 430) considers "Rooftop" a symbolic poem in terms of its *verbal device* ("This poem has the 'inward eye' for a symbol") and its *subject* (i.e., "the 'human fable' seen from a vantage that drops 'beyond an actual wall'.") But such a classification (in terms of the verbal device and the subject of the poem *as interpreted*) would make any poem a symbolic poem whenever we are interested in "meaning" (other than the speaker's experience which the poem depicts for its own sake or for the sake of the power that, as a human experience, it evokes), and are enabled, by such an interest, to ferret out the symbolic machinery. The symbolic lyric, properly so called, is to my mind one species of *didactic* lyric poetry (of which "The Sick Rose" is an instance) which concerns itself primarily, not with an individual speaker's *experience* (meaningful in itself as a human experience), but rather, with a particular *idea* or *truth* (a theme in universal human experience). In "The Sick Rose," we do have someone's experience, the speaker in the poem seems distressed by the sight of a rose being eaten by a worm; but this experience, as depicted, compels us to seek a further meaning than that which the experience as rendered already conveys. But Blake's "Ah, Sunflower" is not, I think, a symbolic lyric poem since we can already respond to the speaker's experience in the poem (though indeed the verbal machinery is symbolic); i.e., we do respond immediately to the speaker who projects in the sunflower's action his own weariness of spirit, his sense of frustration and the incompleteness of human relationships in this world, his aspiration for "that sweet golden clime" after this mortal life where the youth and the virgin, where all frustrated lives, find their deepest fulfillment. We are not saying, of course, that we may not respond to this poem on a higher, i.e., symbolic, plane of meaning; we are only stressing the fact that, since we can respond to it on its own terms (i.e., respond to an individual human experience, the lyric speaker's private mental action, mood, situation at the moment of "speech"), the poem is not primarily a symbolic lyric. Of course, too, the symbolic lyric admits of various modes of representation; e.g., a direct statement (Blake's "Eternity"), an account of sort (Housman's "Infant Innocence," Blake's "I Saw A Chapel All of Gold," T. S. Eliot's "The Hippopotamus"). an enactment of sort or pseudo-drama (the distressed observer in "The Sick Rose" or the imaginary or pseudo-dialogue in Richard Wilbur's "Two Voices in a Meadow,"), etc.

36 Again, there is clearly no need to unravel an "ironic" tension between an implied attitude and an obvious or literally expressed evaluation. The speaker's attitude in either poem is unequivocally rendered.

37 I am unhappily aware that in what may be called "atomic analysis," the elements assume, after a time, a character of unrelieved monotony against which the mind rebels. There is perhaps a point in criticism at which the mind rests content with a kind of "negative capability." Any irritable reaching after fact or explanation ceases, and "the immovable critic," as Marianne Moore puts it, no longer "twitches his skin like a horse that feels a flea."

ter. In "Rooftop," the experience is one of sudden release from a mental or spiritual oppression, and hence, we feel a certain exhiliration or buoyancy of spirit with the speaker. But the greater part of the poetic experience consists of a brooding on a dismal and oppressive "scene" which reduces life into "the human fable," and hence, our exhiliration is depressed somewhat by a certain gloom. In "Summer Trees," on the other hand, the experience is essentially a joyful recollection, a celebration; and we share the speaker's jubilant mood, accepting without question "The pertinence of patience the trees bear" against summer. Such a difference in poetic power between the two poems is indicative of each their peculiar nature or kind as a reflective lyric.

Conclusion

Only a specific formal analysis of lyric poems can distinguish their various forms or distinctive kinds for purposes of evaluating their excellence as products of the poetic art in terms of their own peculiar standards or criteria. While such analysis is necessarily laborious and cannot give comfort or inspiration through grand insights into the nature of poetry or literature as a whole, it alone can judge individual poems according to their own nature as poetic wholes of a given kind.

We have discriminated at least two distinctive forms of the reflective lyric by specifying the object, the manner, the means, and the effect or power of the poetic imitation in each case. There may be other forms, but we cannot say what these are before we have specified their structures.

A Formal Analysis of Richard Eberhart's "The Groundhog": Towards a Theory of Lyric Forms *

THE GROUNDHOG

Part I, Sec. 1 In June, amid the golden fields,
            I saw a groundhog lying dead.
            Dead lay he; my senses shook,
            And mind outshot our naked frailty.
            There lowly in the vigorous summer   5
            His form began its senseless change,
            And made my senses waver dim
            Seeing nature ferocious in him.
      2 Inspecting close his maggots' might
            And seething cauldron of his being,
            Half with loathing, half with a strange   10
               love,
            I poked him with an angry stick.
            The fever arose, became a flame
            And Vigour circumscribed the skies,
            Immense energy in the sun,   15
            And through my frame a sunless trembling.
            My stick had done nor good nor harm.
      3 Then stood I silent in the day
            Watching the object, as before;
            And kept my reverence for knowledge   20
            Trying for control, to be still,
            To quell the passion of the blood;
            Until I had bent down on my knees
            Praying for joy in the sight of decay.
Part II, Sec. 1 And so I left; and I returned   25
            In Autumn strict of eye, to see

* First published in *The Diliman Review*, XXIII, No. 4 (October, 1975), 375-408; revised.

The sap gone out of the groundhog,
But the bony sodden hulk remained.
But the year had lost its meaning,
And in intellectual chains   30
I lost both love and loathing,
Mured up in the wall of wisdom.
2 Another summer took the fields again
Massive and burning, full of life,
But when I chanced upon the spot   35
There was only a little hair left,
And bones bleaching in the sunlight
Beautiful as architecture;
I watched them like a geometer,
And cut a walking stick from a birch.   40
3 It has been three years, now.
There is no sign of the groundhog.
I stood there in the whirling summer,
My hand capped a withered heart,
And thought of China and of Greece,   45
Of Alexander in his tent,
Of Montaigne in his tower,
Of Saint Theresa in her wild lament.

A verbal composite (short-story, play, lyric poem) may
happen to be an *imitation,* i.e., a simulation, likeness, or repre-
sentation of a human action or experience, artistically rendered,
not to enforce an abstraction, but to evoke the experience for
the sake of its emotional power. *As imitation,* the literary com-
position has necessarily the following parts in this order of
importance: (1) the *working power* (*dynamis*) or *effect* of
the imitation which determines its inner form or structure as
a whole of a certain kind; (2) the *object* of imitation (what is
depicted) to which is due, primarily, that power or effect;
(3) the *manner* of imitation (technique of representation) by
which that object has been rendered; and (4) the means of
imitation or the verbal medium in which that object has been
imitated in some manner. But, further, a given work is not
merely imitation, but *an imitation of a certain determinate
nature* as having a certain *distinctive power* or capacity to
evoke an essentially emotional but disinterested reaction to the

artistic simulation or representation.[1] When, therefore, a given literary composite happens to be an imitation of a certain kind, its parts are necessarily ordered in relation to its distinctive power (which is its essential form or structure), thus: first in importance are the various elements of the *object* of imitation (the represented action, character, thought, and emotion); next, the specific *manner* of imitation required by the represented object and the power it exerts; and last, the specific *means* of imitation (certain linguistic and rhetorical devices) required by all the other parts of the imitation.

Poetic Power

The distinction between the serious and the comic is, of course, a general distinction that applies to the various forms of drama, fiction, and poetry.[2] Eberhart's poem, for instance, is an imitation of a certain determinate *kind* because it has been endowed with a certain distinctive *power* to evoke in its readers a *serious* emotion. We are shown, in the poetic simulation of someone's mental struggle with himself, at least its most important stages from his physical and mental revulsion over the fact of death through his intellectual evasions and self-deception ("intellectual chains") to his pained realization and acceptance of our mortal condition. We feel differently from the speaker since, obviously, what moves the speaker is different, in every instance, from what moves us as we follow imaginatively the phases of his inner conflict. He is moved by the reality of death as his own "naked frailty"; we are, in turn, moved by his situation. He feels a profound agitation of spirit and mental distress, he moves from a kind of restless and inner discontent to a mood of anguished resignation at the end of the poetic depiction; and by all these we are affected, such that, for example, we feel tense and uneasy, since we think a matter of great consequence hangs in the balance. We do not ourselves share his evasions and self-deception ("And

[1] Needless to say, our emotional response to a literary work is based upon an intelligent apprehension of the whole human action or experience as represented.

[2] See our "The Serious and the Comic in Lyric Poetry."

mind outshot our naked frailty") for, indeed, he himself is not wholly taken in; yet, apprehending his rationalizations, we sympathize. We understand why he feels the way he does, without judging unfavorably of him since, as far as the poetic imitation goes, we see that there is sufficient and reasonable ground for his violent emotional reaction to death. That is: we see, not only the object of the speaker's "loathing" ("the sight of decay," "the senseless change"), but also his own character which his own action or behavior manifests. We feel, from the outset, a serious concern for him based on general human sympathy for anyone in distress; indeed, his action manifests a moral integrity of a high order since his intellectual evasions leave an inner, ineradicable discontent, and this, of course, wins him our sympathy all the more. We do, in fact, wish him well all the while so that, at the end, we can even feel a kind of relief that he no longer deceives himself or that he has achieved self-knowledge and self-control to the extent that he can already accept unreservedly the fact of "our naked frailty," at the same time that the anguish of his resignation puts us in a solemn and sombre mood:

> My hand capped a withered heart,
> And [I] thought of China and of Greece,
> Of Alexander in his tent,
> Of Montaigne in his tower,
> Of Saint Theresa in her wild lament.

This is the most remarkable fact about the power of Eberhart's "The Groundhog": that, at the very end, we are not quite released from the tension.[3] I said, just now, that we can feel "a kind of relief"; this may be true, but it is well to note that we *finally* respond, *not* to the speaker's *present* probable condition (say, one of calm, even peaceful, resignation to his own inevitable death), but rather, to a *past* event and condition in the speaker's life—the climactic point in his mind's long struggle with "the passion of the blood," the instinct, you might say, of self-preservation. At the poem's end, we tend to asso-

---

[3] Compare with our reaction to Frost's "Stopping By Woods" at its close, pp. 110-12.

ciate St. Theresa's great sorrow[4] with the emotional condition of the speaker *at the time when*, again, "I stood there in the whirling summer," near the same spot where once the groundhog lay decaying, and his "hand capped a withered heart" as a sign of his anguished resignation to "our naked frailty." Thus, the whole poetic imitation puts us in a sombre mood, evokes in us a painful emotion, a deep mental or spiritual sadness arising from our sympathetic reaction to the struggle and spiritual anguish of someone whom we judge to be a morally admirable character.[5]

---

[4] Needless to say, St. Theresa exists in the poem only *as the speaker's own thought in the past.*

[5] Brewster Ghiselin reads "The Groundhog" as "the drama of what is done with [the fact of death]. It is a drama of transmutation—of thought, of attitude, and, most of all, of belief. The poem represents in several stages a man's struggle to accept in joy, as he feels he must accept it, that idea of the fundamental process of reality which has predominated in our time." At the poem's close, "It is clear enough that peoples and individuals have vanished in physical death. Yet their spiritual energies, different from the maggots' might and of another process more essential, have continued to act, in a change that is not senseless, through transmission of vital form and quality from culture to culture and from individual life to life. The poet contemplating in joy those three, Alexander, Montaigne, and Saint Theresa, who stood at the peak of vision, and his reader sharing with him the stir and culminant power of the human spirit are assured of the reality of another energy than that of physical process in the universe: the energy of the spiritual process, traditionally imaged as that light of which the physical sun is no more than a sign." (See Ghiselin's interpretation of "The Groundhog" in Oscar Williams (ed.), *Master Poems*, pp. 1024-26.)

My own difficulty with such an interpretation of the poem's "drama" is that it seems to over-read the last few lines. I do not think we are prepared to accept the joyful assurance that Ghiselin sees at the poem's close simply because, in the poem's mental "drama," we have not been allowed to enter, as it were, into that mental process by which the speaker may be said to have perceived finally that "spiritual process" which has "continued to act, in a change that is not senseless, through transmission of vital form and quality from culture to culture and from individual life to life." Such a perception seems merely to have been read into the last few lines of the poem. Thus, for example, we are told that Alexander, Montaigne, and St. Theresa "stood at the peak of vision," implying that, to this day, their spiritual energies continue to act "from culture to culture and from individual life to life." Yet, we do not sense that the speaker is "contemplating *in joy* those three," for he says, "My hand capped a withered heart." Indeed, Ghiselin himself remarks that the "stony beauty" of the groundhog's remains "do not stir the passions of the man, whose 'withered heart,' though freed of fear, *remains depleted of the sap of joy.*" (The speaker, of course, does take an intellectual pleasure in those remains since he perceives them to be "Beautiful as architecture"; however, he had that pleasure the summer *before* he again "stood there... My hand capped a withered heart.") And if we do not sense the speaker's joy—excepting that "event," three years ago, when he "kept my reverence

The Object of Imitation

The specific *power* or *effect* of a given imitation determines its essential form or structure as a literary composite of a certain kind since it is precisely the effect that the work exerts which governs all its parts in relation one to the other and to the whole. The precise nature or *form of the object of imitation* in a lyric poem is determined, for example, by the sort of emotional power that the poem is to be capable of evoking (and does in fact evoke).[6] The object of imitation comprises such elements of any human experience as the action and character of the agent, his thought and emotion, etc.; but the poet need represent only whatever circumstances of a particular experience are required for the peculiar effect of the poetic imitation in a given instance.

"The Groundhog," then, in terms of the object of imitation, is a lyric of *expression* depicting *complex sequential action* of the *first magnitude*.[7]

By *expression* is here meant, "whatever form it takes, the *external* manifestation of activities and events in the mind that would otherwise remain private."[8] The *lyric of expression* is, then, the lyric of the private or internal sphere since what the poet depicts, *as the whole action*, is someone's mental and

for knowledge"—neither do we sense, "now," in his own thought of those three, a perception of their spiritual energies; rather, we sense only a mournful solitariness about those three. The speaker in the poem, we must note, thinks of Alexander *in his tent*, of Montaigne *in his tower*, and of St. Theresa (by implication) *in her cell* or cubicle. Significantly, too, Ghiselin is silent on St. Theresa's "wild lament" *which ends the poem* (or the speaker's protracted mental struggle with the fact of "our naked frailty").

Ghiselin chooses to belittle and deny what he suspects: "the poem... *may* appear to end in *romantic* suspiration of regret for all the transitory greatness of man, whose highest representatives in action, thought, and ecstasy have vanished like the corpse of the groundhog, of which 'no sign' remains. Indeed, with an *inconsiderable* part of its concluding breath, the poem does so end." (Underscoring mine.) Ironically, then, Ghiselin succeeds in transmuting "our naked frailty" where the speaker in the poem does not.

[6] We are, of course, as Kenneth Burke would say, "prophesying after the fact."

[7] See Elder Olson, "An Outline of Poetic Theory," *Critics and Criticism*, ed. R.S. Crane, pp. 546-66; also, his "Introduction" to his theory of lyric poetry and his "The Lyric" (both are still, as far as I know, in manuscript form; but Prof. Olson had kindly shared them with me in 1968 and, since then, I have found them invaluable in teaching and criticism).

[8] "The Lyric" (MS)

emotional activity in a single closed situation.[9] We are here regarding, of course, the private thoughts and feelings of *the speaker in the poem* which, unless expressed, we would not be moved by. Note, therefore, that in the lyric of expression, the external events (someone, for example, chancing upon a dead groundhog "In June amid the golden fields") "are simply the circumstances of the internal or private events," i.e., the speaker's mental and emotional behavior. In so far, also, as the continuity of the action is concerned, its depiction only "involves the continuity of expression."[10]

More specifically, the essential form or structure of the experience which "The Groundhog" imitates is that of a mental activity on the part of someone who, unwilling to accept the fact of "our naked frailty," struggles inwardly for three years with that fact. What is important for the total effect of the poetic imitation is that we are shown at least the most important stages in the lyric speaker's *mental struggle* from his revulsion over the fact of death through his intellectual evasions and self-deception to his sorrowful realization and acceptance of his own mortal condition.

Thus, the depicted action is what Olson calls *complex sequential action*: *sequential* in that the poet represents, with respect to the speaker's activity, a *process*, over a period of

---

[9] By *closed situation* is meant one which does not permit intervention or complication, at any point in the course of the individual's activity, by some other agent or force not originally present in his situation. The lyric speaker "is as it were hermetically sealed off from the rest of the world so that his action, thought, or emotion runs its uninterrupted course from beginning to end." (Olson, *Tragedy and the Theory of Drama*, p. 41.)

[10] Note that the principle of classification is the *kind of action* which the poet represents. A poem on the order of "To His Coy Mistress" or "My Last Duchess" may be called a *lyric of address*, or a *lyric of verbal action*, since what the poet represents, as the whole action, is some form of verbal act (of persuading, threatening, etc.) performed upon another person (who, in the poem, does not in any way respond) in a single closed situation; and this, of course, only "involves the continuity of address." A poem on the order of "Edward" or "The Bishop Orders His Tomb" may be called a *lyric colloquy* or *dialogue*, or a *lyric of verbal interaction*, since what the poet depicts, as the whole action, is some form of verbal interaction between two or more characters in a single closed situation; and this, of course, only "involves the continuity of interchange or interaction." (I am quoting from Olson's "The Lyric.")

time, rather than a *single moment;*[11] and *complex* in that the
process involves a *reversal* or *turning-point.*[12] Indeed, there
are two reversals in "The Groundhog." First, the emotional
denial ("the passion of the blood") which initiates the speak-
er's mental struggle with himself: for, after his recognition of
death's objective reality ("Dead lay he"), we are shown his
"intellectual" evasion ("And mind outshot our naked frailty")
on account of an intense revulsion ("my senses shook"). His
self-deception progressively grows worse until he can even
watch the groundhog's bones "like a geometer" under a de-
lusion ("Beautiful as architecture"). And then, the final cli-
mactic reversal—the speaker's grieving avowal of his own
"naked frailty" ("My hand capped a withered heart").

But the depicted action is of the *first magnitude.* That is:
what Eberhart represents is the *uninterrupted* activity of a
single individual in a single closed situation. We may, then,
call the poem a *lyric speech* since the action it simulates has
the size or magnitude of a single uninterrupted speech.[13] You

---

[11] In "Western Wind" or Pound's "In a Station of the Metro," for
example, the speaker's action is *momentary* rather than sequential. Most
haiku, I believe, depict a single indivisible human activity evocative of
a mood or state of mind.

[12] Otherwise, it is *simple* sequential action. In Yeats' "Sailing to
Byzantium," for example, there is no reversal; the depicted action is like
a straight line in that it moves in only one direction: the old man is
simply clarifying to himself a momentous choice that he has already made
("And therefore I have sailed the seas and come To the holy city of
Byzantium"), firming up his mind to it by considering its significance and
consequences. But in Frost's "Stopping By Woods," there is one reversal;
the depicted action is like a bent line: it moves first in one direction—the
traveler stops by some villager's woods to watch them fill up with snow;
and then, it changes course, and there is a reversal—for the traveler, made
uneasy by his tarrying there, examines the impulse to enjoy the lovely
sight and finally decides against it to keep certain promises for which he
has made the journey.

[13] Note that someone's "speech," in a lyric poem like "The Ground-
hog" or "Sailing to Byzantium," is merely a *device* to represent his
thoughts (mental activity); but in a poem like "To His Coy Mistress" or
"My Last Duchess," someone's speech constitutes a verbal *act.* It is *only*
with regard to the *magnitude* of the depicted action that we call any one
of these poems a *lyric speech.*
When a lyric poem simulates action of the *second magnitude,* i.e.,
an interaction between two or more characters in a single closed situation,
we may call the poem a *lyric 'scene.'* For such interaction "parallels the
notion of 'scene' in French classical drama." Examples: "Lord Randal,"
"Edward," Browning's "The Bishop Orders His Tomb," etc. In each case,
the depicted action consists of actions of several agents upon each other

do not have a series of scenes, situations, or events; the stages in the *narrated* action are really stages in the speaker's continuous, uninterrupted activity of reflection. What is represented, or narrated, at each stage (the speaker returning, at various times, to the same spot where he found the dead groundhog, and inspecting it in various stages of decomposition), is merely an *occasion* for the same activity, and so, what you have is essentially a single, continuous mental activity by a single individual in a single closed situation (i.e., the situation of someone who, from beginning to end, is inwardly distressed by "our naked frailty").

There are, of course, other things that may be remarked about the depicted *action* in "The Groundhog."

In each section of the poem, it is the speaker's "watching" which initiates the action (a mental struggle). He seeks the same object—the dead groundhog; and consequent upon his finding it is his *reaction* to it as a sign of death: he is repelled, he misinterprets the sign, evades it, loses "its mean-

---

in a single closed situation (though, in Browning, we get only one end of the interchange).

There are, of course, poems that simulate action of the *third magnitude* ("Sir Patrick Spens," Keats' *The Eve of St. Agnes*, Arnold's *Sohrab and Rustum*) where the poet represents the interaction of two or more characters in a *series of situations* centering on a *single dominant event;* and poems that imitate action of the *fourth magnitude* (the *Iliad* and the *Odyssey*) where the poet represents the interaction of several agents in a series of situations involving *more than one principal event*. The third magnitude parallels the notion of an "episode," the fourth, that of a "grand plot." But we no longer regard such poems as *lyric*.

When, therefore, we classify lyric poems according to the magnitude of the depicted action, we can speak only of the *lyric speech* and the *lyric 'scene.'* But when we say that the same poem by Eberhart is a *narrative* lyric poem, our principle of classification is entirely different; that is, we are now regarding the *mode of representing* the lyric action. "Sailing to Byzantium" and "Stopping by Woods" are both *dramatic* in terms of the manner of imitation: i.e., the action or experience to which we respond is not mediated by a narrator; rather, the agent or agents enact it directly, and we witness it (imaginatively) like an audience at a play.

NOTE: In our essay on Angeles, we referred to Shakespeare's "When Icicles Hang by the Wall" as an instance of the *descriptive lyric* or *lyric scene*. There we are *not* classifying Shakespeare's poem according to the magnitude of the action depicted (since, indeed, the poem does not focus on any individual's action *as the whole poem*), but according to the organizing principle of the narration or account (i.e., the description of a winter scene).

ing," and finally accepts it (the very absence of the object, as a sign, reinforcing the "meaning" of the sign).

The persistence of the groundhog as the speaker's object through each section of the poem signifies its persistence *in the speaker's mind* as a sign of death's objective reality, as a cause of his mental distress. His return, time and again, to the same spot where his groundhog lay dead, his constant scrutiny of the same object, manifest his attempt to evacuate the sign of "its meaning," his unwillingness to accept "our naked frailty."

The groundhog undergoes two kinds of transformation: a purely natural transformation (the various stages of its decomposition) and a transformation in the speaker's mind under the force of his evasions and self-deception. There also exists a kind of correspondence between the state of the object and the state of the speaker's mind. In Part I, sec. 1, of the poem, the speaker's illusion (death as "nature ferocious") is based on the objective reality of decaying matter; in sec. 2, the maggoty object becomes in the speaker's mind the sign of "Vigour," of life itself as "immense energy"; in sec. 3, the delusion has collapsed, and we have again "the object, as before," merely a "sight of decay," since the speaker has ignored his realization of death as personally relevant fact. In Part II, sec. 1, the groundhog's "bony sodden hulk" makes the speaker aware of what has "gone out" within himself; in sec. 2, its "bones bleaching in the sunlight" induces the speaker to fall under another delusion ("Beautiful as architecture"); in sec. 3, the groundhog has finally become nothing, but this only intensifies the speaker's realization of "our naked frailty."

In Part I, the speaker also regards the groundhog as a kind of happening, a spectacle; i.e., it occurs before his own eyes in such a manner as to force itself violently upon him. In fact, he perceives it as "active," in the sense implied by "*his* maggots' might," and even deludes himself farther about it, since the "seething cauldron of his being" cancels his sense of death and makes him associate the "fever" of its stench with "Vigour." But in Part II, the object is no longer "active" (either as a kind of spectacle or in the illusory sense); "sodden," for instance, is in direct opposition to "see-thing," and similarly, it is Autumn rather than summer. The speaker is no longer emotionally affected by it: "in intellectual chains I lost both love and loathing." He can watch it "like a geometer" and then walk away from it complacently. His mind has, indeed, "outshot our naked frailty." But, of course, until the final resignation, the object continues to act upon his mind as the sign of death.

The *character* of the lyric speaker is precisely that which his action requires (or, to put it another way, that precisely which we should expect). The principle involved here is of this sort: The human experience which a given work seeks to imitate requires such or such a form of the particular action (say, the form of Hamlet's action) *if* it is to evoke such or such an effect (the tragic effect of *Hamlet*); but such an action of such a form necessarily requires such or such a character in the agent (the character of Hamlet) since, otherwise, such an action, with such an effect, cannot take place.

So, then, in Eberhart's poem, the speaker is endowed with a very fine sensibility such that, for example, he is shocked ("my senses waver dim") and filled with "loathing" by the sight of a decaying groundhog; and with a kind of moral integrity such that, for example, his intellectual evasions and self-deception leave an ineradicable, inner discontent (since he returns, time and again, to the scene of death). Obviously, we can only *infer* someone's character from his action or behavior since we cannot, for example, judge someone to be a coward unless we have first seen him do a cowardly deed; and thus, in the object of imitation, someone's action is the primary element, and his character, secondary.

As character is determined by the requirements of the depicted action, so, likewise, the speaker's *thought* and *emotion* (as elements of the object of imitation) are governed by the requirements of his character as represented. Someone's *thought*, as depicted in the poem, can proceed only from the sort of character that the represented action has made him out to be, in precisely that sense in which noble thoughts, for example, can arise only from a noble character; similar-

[229]

ly, someone's *emotion* can proceed only from the thought or opinion that his character permits in the poetic imitation, since no emotion can be felt except upon some opinion or belief, in precisely that sense in which we feel fear, for example, because we hold the opinion that something is fearful.

So, then, in Eberhart's poem, because the speaker's character is such as his action or behavior manifests—i.e., one endowed with a very fine mind and sensibility and a moral integrity of no mean order—we find what we should really expect: a certain elevation, even grandeur, of thought, and an intensity and poignancy of emotion. A loftiness of spirit is manifest in the restlessness of the speaker's mind "Trying for control, to be still, To quell the passion of the blood." Thus, when the speaker finally accepts the fact of "our naked frailty," we sense a grandeur in the sweep of his "thought of China and of Greece, . . . Of Saint Theresa in her wild lament," even as we are also moved by the anguish of spirit that his resignation implies: "My hand capped a withered heart." The same quality of splendor in the thought, the same poignancy of feeling, in-here even in the speaker's intellectual evasions, as when he perceives the decaying mass of the groundhog to be "his maggots' might And seething cauldron of his being," or the "fever" of his stench to be "a flame," an element of the "Vigour circumscribed the skies, Immense energy of the sun."

The Manner of Imitation

The specific *manner of imitation* is determined by the experience to be depicted (the *object of imitation*) and the power that the depicted experience as a whole is to evoke. It seems best, for example, to depict the experience in "My Last Duchess" *dramatically,* i.e., to allow the Duke to act and speak in his own person since, first of all, the precise form of the depicted action is to be that of a veiled threat from a proud and cruel lover, and since, if we should witness directly, as it were, his own present action, we would be more powerfully moved by his evil nature (his own speech being a most telling conviction). It seems best, on the other hand, to depict the experience in Robinson's "Richard Cory" *narrative-*

ly, i.e., to permit someone else to recount what he knows about Richard Cory since, first of all, the precise form of the depicted action or experience is to be that of Cory's public life over a period of time, as seen by outsiders who envy him, in contrast to his own troubled and unhappy inner life, which no one sees; and since, if we should only indirectly know about Cory from someone's account, we would be more powerfully moved by the sudden discovery of our ignorance. Finally, it seems best to depict the experience in the anonymous "Sir Patrick Spens" in the *mixed mode* of representation (i.e., both dramatic and narrative) for similar reasons: e.g., the depicted experience involves the interaction of several niscient narrator; we would be more powerfully moved by the characters in a series of situations which require an omhero if we should witness directly, as it were, his own action, as when he grieves over the king's letter but decides, nevertheless, to set sail.

So, then, the narrative mode is used in "The Groundhog" since both the *object* and the *power* of the imitation as a whole require it. To prophesy after the fact, the object has to have only such a form as may best evoke the intended effect. Now, the *form of the object of imitation* is, as we said, that of someone's mental struggle for three years, and we are to be shown those phases of his struggle with himself by which, at every stage, we may feel an uneasiness and tension of mind until the final resolution. Since, therefore, we must be shown those various phases, it seems best to have the action narrated, and narrated only by someone who knows it best (therefore, the speaker himself who endured that struggle).

Eberhart's poem is, therefore, a *narrative* lyric poem. The narrator is himself the "protagonist" in the action that he recounts, i.e., a protracted mental struggle *in the past.* It may, of course, be pointed out that the narrator is *now recollecting* past events. Nevertheless, we do respond, not to a present *activity* of recollection (as in George Barker's "Sonnet to My Mother") nor to the speaker's *present reaction to what he narrates* (as in Hopkins' "The Wreck of the Deutschland"), but rather, to certain past "events" (chiefly mental) which are presently recollected, that is, narrated. We respond to an *account* of a mental experience rather than to a *direct enactment* of it (as in Frost's "Stopping By Woods").

The shift to the *present time,* toward the end of the poetic narration, serves to emphasize the final resolution of the speaker's problem.

> It has been three years, now.
> There is no sign of the groundhog.

The lines introduce the last section of the poem. We infer that, since the speaker has struggled with his problem for three years, it must have been particularly distressing to him. Since, also, at the end of the poem, we tend to associate St. Theresa's "wild lament" with the speaker's emotional condition *at the time when* he finally accepted the fact of death as personally relevant, we infer, on retrospect, that "now," after that anguished resignation, he may have won "control" over himself and gained at least a measure of peace.[14] But the poem, of course, does not end with the "now" (11. 41-42); it ends, rather, with that moment when the speaker again "stood there in the whirling summer," and his "hand capped a withered heart." It is, as we said, to this *past event* in the speaker's life that we *finally* respond, rather than to his present probable condition. Indeed, we are *not* at all affected by his present condition, but only by his past, since as we read the poem, we do not really concern ourselves with *how the speaker is presently reacting to what he narrates (or recollects)*. Nothing in the poem indicates how, at every stage, the speaker is affected by his recollection; to that, therefore, as the speaker's present action or experience, we cannot (and do not, in fact) respond.

Let us now examine the *narrative form or structure* of the depicted experience.

The narrative, essentially chronological, has two main divisions. Part I (the first 24 lines) shows the speaker's ini-

---

[14] The speaker's self-complacency, which is a specious form of mental calm, in the last summer of his self-deception ("I watched" the groundhog's bones "like a geometer, And cut a walking stick from a birch"), seems "now" (*after* the "wild lament") to have been replaced by a calmness of self-control underlying the matter-of-fact tone in which he observes, for example, that "It has been three years, now," or that there is, of course, "no sign of the groundhog."

tial reaction to the fact of death and the early stages of his self-deception. All these take place when, one summer day, he sees "a groundhog lying dead." Part II (the next 24 lines) represents the later stages of his self-deception and the resolution, after three years, of his problem. The "events" here (chiefly mental) occur at various times after that summer day in Part I.

We can distinguish three sections in each part. To show how a cause-and-effect relationship[15] obtains between these sections and how each stage in the speaker's self-deception becomes progressively worse, we may schematize these sections, thus:

I, *sec. 1* (11. 1-8): The speaker's realization of death as an objective reality affects him with a physical and mental revulsion (2-4) which leads to intellectual evasion (4): a rationalization (5-7) resulting in an *illusion* (8);

sec. 2 (9-17): The illusion, under the force of his "loathing" and "strange love," becomes a *delusion*[16] (9-15), but it collapses (16-7) when his realization of "our naked frailty" returns: "a sunless trembling" (16);

sec. 3 (18-24): Having failed to convince himself of his own delusion, he ignores the fact of death. His evasion, which takes the form of a "reverence for knowledge" (20), is apparently successful, for he is seized with a specious ecstasy even "in the sight of decay" (24).

II, *sec. 1* (25-32): Part II (secs. 1 and 2) shows the results of the speaker's unwillingness in Part I to accept the fact of death. Sec. 1, in particular, is the direct result of his apparently successful attempt to ignore

---

15 Of course, strictly speaking, the relationship of "events" is not *consequential* (as in the *plot* of *Hamlet* or *Macbeth*); what we have, in the poem, is something like a series of "episodes" *in someone's mental experience*, each serving to show a particular phase in his long and lonely struggle with death as a personally relevant fact.

16 Webster's distinction is useful. An *illusion* "suggests the false perception or interpretation of something that has objective existence." A *delusion* "implies belief in something that is contrary to fact or reality, resulting from deception, a misconception, or a mental disorder." (Webster's *New World Dictionary of the American Language*, 1964).

death's "meaning" ("our naked frailty") in Part I, sec. 3. The result is an "intellectual" detachment in which "the year had lost its meaning," since his mind has indeed "outshot our naked frailty," since his evasions have released him from the emotional tension of "both love and loathing." He is, ironically, "mured up in the wall of wisdom" (32).

sec. 2 (33-40) : A direct consequence of the preceding "event," it represents the worst stage in the speaker's self-deception: an intellectual detachment so complete (39) that he takes an aesthetic pleasure in the contemplation of death's bones (37-8) and, self-satisfied, walks away from the objective fact of death.

sec. 3 (41-8) : This section is the climactic consequence of everything that preceded it. It is the final outcome of the persistence of the sign of death in the speaker's mind: a persistence of his inner struggle, the conflict between his perception of death as an objective fact and his unwillingness to accept it. But this summer, he accepts unreservedly, though with great sorrow, the truth of "our naked frailty."[17]

Let us also examine the second reversal in "The Groundhog" to illustrate a principle of construction in representing *complex, sequential action,* to wit, that

the reversal must be unexpected if it is to be effective [i.e., capable of moving us emotionally] ; but, also, it must be probable; the complex activity must therefore always contain an *apparent* or on-the-surface probability, which

[17] The tight narrative structure of the poetic experience may also be seen in the fact that each section in one Part serves as a kind of foil for its parallel in the other Part, thus:

    I, sec. 1: The speaker's recognition of death as a fact, his physical and mental revulsion, and his "intellectual" escape;

    II, sec. 1: His loss of death's "meaning" and "both love and loathing" in his "intellectual chains."

    I, sec. 2: His delusion concerning death (as "Vigour") which, however, does him "nor good nor harm";

    II, sec. 2: Yet another delusion (death as "beautiful architecture") which, apparently, satisfies him.

    I, sec. 3: He evades, successfully, the fact of death: his "reverence for knowledge" (ironically, a self-deception) makes him "pray for joy in the sight of decay";

    II, sec. 3: Confronted with that vacuity which death brings, he does not evade the fact of "our naked frailty," but thinks of China and Greece, and joins (through a kind of fellow-feeling) "Saint Theresa in her wild lament."

founds our expectation, and the *real* probability, which defeats it. The real probability must be more probable than the apparent, for otherwise we should not accept it; and it must be hidden (that is, concealed by the poet), for otherwise we should expect *it,* as the more probable.[18]

In the final section of the poem, the speaker, having lived with his problem for three years, implies that "now" he can no longer evade the sign of death. Indeed, since there is now no *external* sign, what he recognizes is a reversal of its referent: the groundhog is nowhere (suggesting that death is, in fact, a kind of absence from our time and space), and therefore, death as an objective reality has no longer any external sign other than the speaker's own self, his "withered heart." "Summer" is not "vigorous" (or "full of life") but "whirling," hinting at the speaker's sense of being overwhelmed, not by "immense energy" but by a vacuity—the presence of death even in the fullness of life. His "hand capped a withered heart" as though he feels again "a sunless trembling"—but this time, with a kind of emotional vengeance, as his original realization of "our naked frailty" returns.

But the speaker finds the sign of death not only in himself but also in the history, as it were, of that "frailty" over which, apparently, he has been brooding for three years: ancient China and ancient Greece, dead civilizations; the soldier Alexander, the thinker Montaigne, the religious mystic, St. Theresa[19]—they show that death is the common lot. The body cannot conquer death, the mind cannot evade it, the soul can only mourn the body's fate. "Tent" and "tower" (and perhaps, St. Theresa's cell) not only suggest the speaker's physical and mental solitude throughout his struggle, but also, that one is most alone when one meets his death. In fact, the speaker and his problem now become universalized. This seems to be the point for the rather abrupt, if brief, procession of historical figures through his mind, for what underlies his struggle is precisely his relation to "our naked frailty."

---

[18] From Olson's "Introduction" (MS.). Comment on *effective* supplied.
[19] They may be said to be conquerors in their own right: Alexander, of the physical realm; Montaigne, of the world of mind; St. Theresa, of the spirit.

The poem ends on "Saint Theresa in her wild lament." It ends then on a note of intense sorrow which determines our final response to the poetic depiction. Perhaps, the speaker identifies himself with the saint "in her wild lament" over our common fate; in any case, his mood marks a kind of distance that he has travelled from "Praying for joy in the sight of decay." Perhaps, too, he recognizes that to accept death is a deeply spiritual or religious act; in any case, the significant "event" is that finally he has accepted the fact of death.

Thus, the climactic reversal in "The Groundhog" is both unexpected and probable. For the *apparent probability* is that the speaker would continue to deny the personal relevance of death. We expect a final rejection since "There is no sign of the groundhog," no disturbing sign, finally, of death's reality. The *real probability*, however, turns out to be more probable than the apparent: if the speaker has struggled for three years with his problem, then certainly he has not yet reached a satisfactory resolution; that he keeps returning to inspect the groundhog's remains signifies that he is haunted by it as the sign of death; for that length of time, three years, all that he can finally show is "a withered heart"; the thought of China and of Greece, of Alexander, Montaigne, and St. Theresa, seems also to be a summary of his years of meditation on "our naked frailty." But all these things, of course, are hid or underplayed in the poetic narration since what we have, until the final section, is chiefly the speaker's "intellectual" evasion progressively growing worse.

The Means of Imitation

The *means of imitation* are governed by everything else in the poem: by the *power* it is to have, by the *object* it seeks to depict, and by the *manner* that object is to be represented. The analysis of the means chiefly involves, therefore, the analysis of verbal meanings and linguistic and rhetorical devices *in relation to* the experience that a given poem has rendered; i.e., an experience of a certain order as having a certain distinctive power. Thus, since at the root of the speaker's mental distress in "The Groundhog" is his perception of the antithesis between "lowly" (death or decay as the ultimate humiliation) and "vigorous" (life as fullness and pride of "energy"), the basic poetic means is what we may call "ironic contrast."

> In June, amid the golden fields,
> I saw a groundhog lying dead.

The very first verses of the poetic imitation establish the underlying contrast, and thus, the speaker's *mental struggle* is developed in terms of parallel variations upon that ironic contrast since those variations show the various phases of the speaker's unwillingness to accept "our naked frailty." As regards the structure of the poetic narration, for example, we have already shown how every section in Part I serves as a foil to its parallel section in Part II. Eberhart also employs contrastive pairs of words and phrases throughout the poem: "senses" / "senseless"; "loathing" / "love"; "sun" / "sunless"; "summer" / "Autumn"; "angry stick" / "walking stick"; "praying for joy" / "wild lament"; "reverence for knowledge" / "passion of the blood"; "I returned . . . strict of eye" / "I chanced upon the spot"; etc.

It has not really been possible, of course, to speak about the distinctive *power or effect* of the imitation ("The Groundhog") without somehow speaking about the depicted experience in which that power inheres, nor to speak about the *manner* of imitation (how the poet has represented something) without somehow speaking also about the *object* of imitation (what in fact the poet has represented) ; so, likewise, we have somehow been discussing the *means* of imitation or the verbal medium since, indeed, we had first to apprehend the words in the poem before we could apprehend anything at all of the poem. Therefore, at this point in our essay, the analysis of the poetic means, though chiefly grammatical and rhetorical in nature, would really involve an elaboration on how the poetic effect was achieved by the poetic object as depicted in some manner by some means.[20]

20 Indeed, I feel that this part of the analysis had better be left to the sensitive reader of the poem. But since my intention is to construct a model of "formal analysis" (as I understand the term), it seems I must still proceed (my patient etherised upon the table) at the risk of being tedious and redundant.

Part I, Sec. 1 (lines 1-8)

Time ("the vigorous summer") and place ("amid the golden fields") intensify the shock of the speaker's recognition of "our naked frailty" since, under those circumstances, one would expect life to flourish in all its splendor. The setting and the decomposing groundhog provide him a basis for his delusion: death as "Vigour." Indeed, it is always summer when he returns to his groundhog, implying that what is particularly distressing to him is the presence of death at the very center, as it were, of life's exuberance. But there is, of course, one significant exception: when he realizes that "the year had lost its meaning," it is Autumn; ironic, since we associate autumn with age, and age, with wisdom.

Note also the ironic antithesis between the first two verses: we pass abruptly from life to that which ends it suddenly. We may regard those verses as consisting of two propositions: "In June . . . (There is) a groundhog lying dead"—an assertion of a fact which exists independently of an observer; and "In June . . . *I* saw a groundhog lying dead"—an assertion by someone who perceives the objective fact. This, of course, may sound over-subtle, but it is a useful distinction, for each time that the speaker perceives the objective fact, his unwillingness to accept it as the sign of death has the effect of negating the perception. In 11. 7-8, for example, he ceases to see "the object, as before," i.e., as simply a *dead* groundhog, since to his mind it has become "nature ferocious"; in 1. 38, similarly, the object is lost to the speaker since the bones become "Beautiful as architecture."

In line 2, the speaker perceives at first only the bare physical fact, and the poetic statement ends there, suggesting that when one is confronted with death, one cannot at once grasp its relevance to one's own self. And then, the shock of recognition in the emphatic verbal repetition: "Dead lay he." It pulls the rhythmic beat of the first two verses to an abrupt halt, suggesting that the object forces, as it were, the fact of death upon the speaker as relevant to his own self. And the force of his perception is equalled by the violence of his reaction—a physical and mental revulsion—which, in turn, turns his mind

[238]

against its own perception, against his inner realization of death's "meaning": "our naked frailty." The phrase, in fact, discloses the "soul" of the poem since it underlies his distress: *he* participates in the groundhog's "frailty," *will* also die; and "naked" stresses the essential helplessness of man and beast. This is death's "meaning"—not that it is "senseless change" nor "nature ferocious," but that it is simply *our* lot.

We see, indeed, in sec. 1 a pattern of action which repeats itself in every other section of the poem. In line 2, the speaker sees the object ("a groundhog lying dead") and, immediately, he perceives the fact of death ("Dead lay he") and reacts ("my senses shook And mind outshot our naked frailty"). This original perception and reaction in fact provide the motive force in the poem. Again, he sees the object "there" and perceives that it is "lowly"; watching it intently ("His form began . . ."), he perceives its "senseless change" and reacts: his "senses waver dim" and he falls under an illusion ("nature ferocious in him"). The speaker's mind, compelled to accept what *appears* to be an abhorrent fact, and repelled by the antithesis it perceives between "lowly" and "vigorous summer," reacts instantly against its own dismay, would see farther, and will not acquiesce, brooking no "senselessness"; it begins to rationalize, to reinterpret the sign, to see it *not* as the sign of death but as the sign of "nature ferocious" (i.e., as sign, rather, of "Vigour"). And thus, as in every other section of the poem (but the last), his mind does indeed "outshoot our naked frailty."

I, Sec. 2 (9-17)

"Inspecting close": the speaker now seeks an explanation for the "senseless" fact, as though he would accept it if only it made sense. But this, of course, is an act of self-deception by which his illusion ("nature ferocious in him" rather than "our naked frailty") only becomes a compelling delusion. We see how the mind tricks itself, how its own subtlety insures its success at self-deception—at least, for a time. Thus, "his" should have been "*the* maggots' might," but the speaker's subtle phrasing (or thought) implies, for him, both the "mystery" ("senseless change") and the "insight" into it; similarly, "being" should have been "carrion," but again, his thought conveys both the "mystery" and its own "revelation." He perceives not so much the decay and rout of matter as (because of the stress on "his might" and "his being") the power, heat, and combustion of life consuming itself with its own "Vigour."

His delusion, then, converts "our naked frailty" to "his maggots' might And seething cauldron of his being" in which there is neither "lowliness" nor "senseless change." The sign of death is now sign of "the vigorous summer." Where before senses and mind reacted with unqualified revulsion, now it is only "half with loathing, half with a strange love." "Loathing" and "angry," because the speaker's realization of death remains; but "strange love," because he has conceived, in spite of himself, a fascination with death as "nature ferocious." This "strange love" is, therefore, a part of his delusion, an aspect of its emotional grounding.

Lines 13-5 affirm the force of the delusion. Having "poked" the groundhog "with an angry stick, The fever arose," the reek and heat of him "in the vigorous summer." But

> The fever ..., became a flame
> And Vigour circumscribed the skies,
> Immense energy in the sun,
> ....

These are *triumphant* lines. The "fever" becomes "a flame," and death, "Vigour," and decay, "immense energy." It is as though with the "angry stick" of his mind, the speaker had stirred up, or poked up, not so much stench as flame, not death but life. Again, to circumscribe is "to draw a figure around (another figure) so as to touch it at as many points as possible." Thus, it is as if the world were girded with fire, as though life's "immense energy" encompassed death and touched it at all points, so that death itself is charged with such energy, becomes a "seething cauldron" and bursts into "flame." In short, the delusion is "revelation" of life-in-death: a reversal of the original perception of death-in-life. The mind has converted the sign of death to a sign of life!

And yet, the mind is not completely routed by its delusion. The speaker himself implies a doubting of the object of his "love": he calls it "strange" since its object is not the *dead* groundhog but the groundhog under an illusional aspect. Indeed, the very force of the delusion negates it, for it returns the original perception: "And through my frame a sunless trembling." "Sun" is negated by "sunless" in the very next verse;[21] and "trembling" returns "my senses shook," but now, not simply a physical revulsion but an inner realization of death.

Line 17 is anti-climactic. The speaker's delusion "had done nor good nor harm." His original perception has only returned with greater force. The verse also implies "our naked frailty" for it suggests that death is unalterable fact, that it is vain to distort its sign. It explains the speaker's silence with which sec. 3 begins, and thus, it is a perfect transitional line.

I, Sec 3 (18-24)

The speaker's silence manifests his failure to invest the sign with some other meaning which would enable his mind to accept it. His only recourse, then, since he is unwilling, is to evade it.

Let us inspect this "intellectual" evasion. "Reverence" suggests his respectful detachment as he views the effort of his mind "Trying for control." He sees his own violent reaction (sec. 1) as a conflict between the senses, "the passion of the blood," and the mind, the passion for knowledge, when both are confronted with a "senseless" fact. The senses, by themselves, are incapable of any rational grasp; they can, as it were, reach no farther out than such feelings as stir them in the presence of an external stimulus; and, when confronted with "the sight of decay," they only recoil in disgust and confusion. But the mind has farther reach, it "outshoots" them, transcends their limitations, "our naked frailty"; through its effort to understand and possess its own knowledge, it "quells the passion

---

[21] A similar device is the verbal pun in "senses" and "senseless."

of the blood" and maintains a calm control over the senses
Thus the speaker occupies himself with rationalizing

> Until I had bent down on my knees
> Praying for joy in the sight of decay.

He cannot, of course, rejoice *over* "the sight of decay," for
he has lost his almost ecstatic delusion (sec. 2). His "praying
for joy" *in* the presence of death simply manifests his "rever
ence for knowledge." What in fact has brought his feelings
and thoughts to a state of equilibrium is but the effort of his
own mind "trying for control, to be still." The passion for
knowledge has indeed led his mind to delude itself, but *that*
does not now concern him. He distracts himself and ignores
death. That it still remains a "senseless change" he has for
gotten in his "joy." And thus, at the end of Part I, he has
only evaded his problem, and quite successfully, too: "And
so I left."

Only a few more observations about the poetic *means* in
Part II must here suffice.

II, Sec. 1 (25-32)

The abruptness and casual tone of line 25 suggest the
ease with which our speaker has ignored death; but the leap
in time between "I left" and "I returned" and his "strict
ness of eye" accentuate his agitation. The time is, ironically,
Autumn. He has lost, not his perception of death as an ob
jective reality (for this, precisely, is why he returns), but
his inner realization of death's relevance to himself, which is
a part of "wisdom." He inspects without conviction since he
has "lost both love and loathing," that capacity for shock
which brings conviction. He has lost both the emotion and
the inner realization because, as he admits, he is "in intel
lectual chains"; he has, in fact, that summer day (Part 1) be
gan at once to insulate himself from death's reality. "Chains"
and "mured" signify a prison—Montaigne's "tower"; i.e., the
speaker's own mind has immured him and dried up a certain
sensibility necessary for "wisdom."

II, Sec. 2 (33-40)

The persistence of "summer" in the poem suggests that the speaker's perception of the antithesis between "decay" and "Vigour" has also persisted as a rationalization of his unwillingness to accept death as a fact. That now he only "chanced upon the spot" implies that he lacks the *conscious* motivation he had that Autumn, and that he is now secure in his "tower" or "intellectual" detachment. The chance rediscovery is, as a matter of fact, a form of self-deception. And thus, his "inspecting close" is not so much "strict" as cold of eye: "I watched them like a geometer"; and perceiving the groundhog's remains as "Beautiful as architecture," he is completely unaware of this new "intellectual chain," since he "cuts a walking stick from a birch" (in direct contrast with his "angry stick"). He is completely "mured up in the wall of wisdom" for he takes a purely "intellectual" or aesthetic pleasure in "the sight of decay" (less ecstatic than his "praying for joy," but certainly a worse state than before), and then walks away unperturbed.

II, Sec. 3 (41-48)

We have, in fact, discussed this section twice or thrice over. But repetition has been unavoidable because all our evidence, so to speak, exist within such a small circle of interrelated *causes* (causes why the poem is such or such a kind of lyric poem: namely, the power, the object, the manner, and the means of imitation).[22]

The means of imitation, or the verbal medium, while the least important as a differentia, does yet constitute a formal difference among lyric poems. It is the least important because, as we said, it is governed by everything else in the poem; yet, certainly, there are obvious differences, even only in terms of the poetic medium, between poems on the order of Leigh

[22] As Aristotle would say, the *final,* the *formal,* the *efficient,* and the *material* causes of the poem *considered as an imitation.*

Hunt's "Jenny Kiss'd Me" or Robert Burns' "A Red, Red Rose" and poems on the order of Wallace Stevens' "Sunday Morning" or Dylan Thomas' "Altarwise By Owl-light."[23] It is easy enough to see that, generally speaking, lyric poems are similar or different as they employ familiar or unfamiliar words, ordinary or uncommon syntax, conventional or unusual imagery and other rhetorical devices, traditional or novel metrical patterns, etc.; that, in short, the difference lies chiefly in the kind of diction and the degree of elevation of style required by the power, the object, and the manner of the poetic imitation in any given case. However, since not even the object of imitation, as such, can *finally* determine the specific nature or kind of a given lyric poem (after all, "My Last Duchess," for example, is only a *serious,* and "Soliloquy of the Spanish Cloister," a *comic* version of villainous behavior) *a fortiori,* the poetic means cannot by itself be used as a principle of differentiation among lyric *kinds* of poetry. The chief point is that it is only *collectively* that the power, the object, the manner, and the means of imitation are capable of discriminating the specific *form* or *structure* of a given lyric poem. The *definition* of a given kind of lyric poem or *poetic species* results, precisely, from "the formulation of the *distinctive* means, object, manner, and effect of the [*poetic*] synthesis [since this] gives all four of the causes which are collectively, but not singly, peculiar to it."[24]

Conclusion

Having examined the power, the object, the manner, and the means of imitation in Eberhart's "The Groundhog," we are now in a position to define the *kind* of lyric poem that it is, or, to say the same thing, to describe its *essential form* or *inner structure* as a poetic imitation, thus: It is a lyric poem of expression in the narrative mode, depicting serious, com-

---

[23] Compare also the difference between Marlowe's "The Passionate Shepherd to His Love" and Marvell's "The Garden," or that between Browning's "Pippa's Song" and Shakespeare's "Full fathom five thy father lies," or that between even Blake's "The Lamb" and "The Tiger."
[24] Olson, "Outline of Poetic Theory," p. 558. Underscoring mine.

plex, sequential action whose agent is morally differentiated as a "noble" character; employing verse in a style some degree removed from ordinary speech or conversation; the whole poetic imitation evoking a sombre mood, a great sadness of spirit arising from our sympathetic reaction to the inner struggle and anguish of soul of a "noble" character.

A few terms in such a definition need to be clarified:

1. We have not, as a matter of fact, determined the precise meaning of "poem" or "lyric" in order to avoid fruitless controversy. It seems best, for our purposes in this essay, to consider whatever can be generally agreed upon as a "lyric poem" (whatever the grounds of general agreement) and proceed without further ado to examine its *peculiar nature as a verbal composite that happens to be an imitation*. Besides, "lyric poetry" is a heterogeneous class; i.e., there are various kinds or forms of the so-called "lyric poem."

2. By *verse*, we mean simply a sequence of words arranged metrically according to some rule or design; the line, for example, in Eberhart's poem is basically iambic tetrameter (in classical prosody). By *diction* or *style*, we mean the linguistic and rhetorical means which the poet has employed to endow his poem, *considered as a meaningful verbal composite*, with a certain dynamic quality of its own. Verse and especially diction or style have been unduly stressed in literary criticism but, as aspects merely of the poetic or verbal medium, they are the least important insofar as the discrimination of literary *kinds* or *species* is concerned.

3. By "agent morally differentiated as a 'noble' character," we mean that someone's action or behavior, as depicted in the poem, exhibits his character as "noble"—not, of course, in that sense in which Oedipus or Hamlet is noble, but only in the sense that we find Eberhart's speaker, as he struggles with himself, morally admirable.

As regards the power or effect of the poetic imitation *in such poems as* "The Groundhog," we must also note the following:

1. Our response to the poetic simulation is not based only on *general human sympathy*, i.e., on a kind of fellow-feeling, on a general sort of perception that the lyric speaker is more or less like ourselves *in that respect which*

moves us most about him. In "The Groundhog," for exam-
ple, we perceive that the speaker is like ourselves in that
respect which disposes us sympathetically toward him
i.e., that we too, though to a lesser degree, are distressed
by our inescapable mortality. But, over and above our
sympathy for the speaker, we perceive that he is "noble"
and, therefore, better than ourselves. Hence, since he has
won not only our sympathy but our admiration as well, we
are more profoundly moved by his distress. The power
of Yeats' "Sailing to Byzantium" is based, similarly, upon
our impression of the speaker as a noble character (but
here, certainly, his nobility is on the same order as Oedi-
pus' or Hamlet's own).

2. The emotion or frame of mind that the poetic re-
presentation evokes in us is *different* from that of the ly-
ric speaker since the cause of his own emotional condi-
tion is different from what moves us. In "The Ground-
hog," for instance, we feel differently from the speaker
he is moved to great anguish of soul, perceiving that he
too is subject to death; we are moved to admiration for
his "noble" character and, touched by his distress, we feel
a great sadness of spirit, perceiving as he does the truth
of "our naked frailty." These are different emotional states
or dispositions of the soul. Certainly, for example, we do
not ourselves undergo, for years, the speaker's spiritual
anguish; besides, as we already said, it is not merely sym-
pathy that we feel; if we are moved by the speaker's an-
guished resignation to death, it is also because we ad-
mire his "noble" character.

3. The emotion evoked by such poems as "The
Groundhog" is *serious* since the depicted action is serious
in nature. Of course, it is of a lesser degree than the
tragic emotion for, obviously, we do not have to do in such
poems with *tragic action,* i.e., serious action that arouses
pity and fear and catharts them.[25] Since we are here re-
garding the *degree* of seriousness, it seems best to take, as
the standard, the extremely serious emotion: therefore
the emotion of pity and fear (which is, following Aris-
totle, the tragic emotion) aroused by that *form* of drama
called "tragedy" (like Sophocles' *Oedipus Rex* or Shake-
speare's *Hamlet*).

There is one further thing to observe as regards our de-
finition of that *form* of "lyric poetry" of which "The Ground-

[25] See Olson, *Theory of Comedy,* esp. pp. 34-41.

hog" is a concrete instance. It is a definition of a certain determinate kind or species of "lyric poem" and, therefore, what is important is the *essential* form or structure. We must not be misled by more specific differences among lyric poems in the same class—differences, for example, in terms of the kind of metre employed. And we must not confuse poetic species with literary conventions. The *sonnet*, for example, is not an essential structure (form or species) of the "lyric poem" since, like the *haiku*, it is essentially a prosodic convention; indeed, sonnets differ in kind as lyric poems, i.e., as to the nature of the poetic composite in given instances. The same thing may be said of the *ballad*, the *elegy*, the *ode*, etc. which are all literary conventions in terms of metrical structure or subject matter or diction, etc. or any combination of these elements. Since they are governed by incommensurate principles of classification, they do not exist, as it were, on the same plane of definition and, hence, the terminology they afford us is misleading in the criticism of forms.

When we say that a given lyric poem is *essentially* the same *kind* of poem as "The Groundhog," we mean that, as regards *all four causes of a poetic imitation,* both poems have essentially the same *form* or *structure.* That is: when we examine, in both poems, the *object* of imitation, we find that: (1) it is someone's inner struggle and anguish of soul that the whole poem represents to us; and (2) the whole action, as depicted, is serious, complex, sequential action whose agent is morally differentiated as a "noble" character. And when we examine the *manner* of imitation in both poems, we find that: (1) the poet employs the narrative mode of representation; (2) the narrator is himself the agent in the action that he narrates; and (3) the narrator is reliable, i.e., we have no reason to doubt his account nor do we need to interpret it differently. And when we examine the *means* of imitation or the poetic *medium,* we find that: (1) the poet employs a style some degree removed from ordinary speech or conversation; and (2) the style effects in the poetic representation a certain elevation of action, character, thought, and emotion. And, finally, when we examine the *power* of the poetic imitation, we find that: (1) the whole experience, as rendered, evokes a

[247]

mood of anguish; (2) the poem puts us in a frame of mind which, though different in kind from the speaker's own, is yet a painful condition; and (3) more precisely, the poem induces in us a deep sadness of spirit arising from our sympathetic reaction to a "noble" character's inner struggle and anguish of soul.

Is, then, Gerard Manley Hopkins' "Spring and Fall" or A. E. Housman's "With Rue My Heart Is Laden" the same *kind* of lyric poem as "The Groundhog"? Do they have, essentially, the same form or structure; i.e., do they have, above all, essentially the same power or effect?

Spring and Fall: To a Young Child

Márgarét, are you grieving
Over Goldengrove unleaving?
Leaves, líke the things of man, you
With your fresh thoughts care for, can you?
Ah! ás the heart grows colder
It will come to such sights colder
By and by, nor spare a sigh
Though worlds of wanwood leafmeal lie;
And yet you wíll weep and know why.
Now no matter, child, the name:
Sórrow's spríngs áre the same.
Nor mouth had, no nor mind, expressed
What heart heard of, ghost guessed:
It ís the blight man was born for,
It is Margaret you mourn for.

With Rue My Heart Is Laden

With rue my heart is laden
    For golden friends I had,
For many a rose-lipt maiden
    And many a lightfoot lad.

By brooks too broad for leaping
    The lightfoot boys are laid;
The rose-lipt girls are sleeping
    In fields where roses fade.

Both poems are lyrics of expression in the *dramatic* mode, depicting serious, *simple*, sequential action whose agent is morally *undifferentiated,* and employing rhymed verse in a style some degree removed from ordinary speech. But since they differ in their distinctive powers, they are essentially different *forms* of the lyric poem—different from "The Groundhog" and different one from the other. Certainly, like "The Groundhog," both poems induce a serious frame of mind, but in either poem, our reaction is based simply upon general human sympathy for the speaker. Moreover, as we said, it is the precise emotional power of a given imitation that finally determines its distinctive nature or form; it is the *final cause* or *end* of the imitation as imitation of a given kind. We can describe this power within a very limited range of possible emotional reactions to the experience as depicted in a given poetic imitation; i.e., from reader to reader, given a certain range of sensitivity to poems *as poems,* there may be certain variations, but certainly, not very wide of the mark one from the other.

Thus, Hopkins' "Spring and Fall" is the kind of lyric poem which evokes a pensive mood, a sad and philosophic calm of mind or soul, arising from our sympathetic apprehension of *someone's meditation* on some truth about the human condition. We do not question this truth since what gives it validity in the poem is simply its dramatic context; i.e., we understand perfectly, from the outset, that the meditation as depicted in the poem is the form that someone's reaction takes toward a given human situation which he faces (the child Margaret weeping, perhaps "over Goldengrove unleaving"). Similarly, we do not question the truth of Hamlet's observations on woman's frailty since what gives them validity is simply the situation which he faces (his mother's infidelity). Neither Hamlet nor the speaker in Hopkins' poem is proposing a truth about some aspect of the human reality for philosophical consideration; they are merely reacting mentally at the moment to their own individual situation, and with that we have chiefly to do.

We feel similarly as the speaker in "Spring and Fall" since what causes his emotion is also what causes our own. The poem puts us in a pensive frame of mind much like that of the speaker since it makes us contemplate the same object that the speaker contemplates (i.e., the human condition which Margaret exemplifies) in that manner by which we perceive, as he does, "the blight man was born for." Though we are aware that the speaker is reacting to a given human situation in the poem, his reaction takes the form of a meditation; hence, we have to do chiefly with the subject or theme of his meditation and, thus, perceiving his subject as he does, we feel the way he does.

Matthew Arnold's "Dover Beach" has, to my mind, essentially the same *form* as Hopkins' "Spring and Fall."

Dover Beach

The sea is calm to-night.
The tide is full, the moon lies fair
Upon the straits;—on the French coast the light
Gleams and is gone; the cliffs of England stand
Glimmering and vast, out in the tranquil bay.

Come to the window, sweet is the night-air!
Only, from the long line of spray
Where the sea meets the moon-blanch'd land,
Listen! you hear the grating roar
Of pebbles which the waves draw back, and fling,
At their return, up the high strand,
Begin, and cease, and then again begin,
With tremulous cadence slow, and bring
The eternal note of sadness in.

Sophocles long ago
Heard it on the Aegean, and it brought
Into his mind the turbid ebb and flow,
Of human misery; we
Find also in the sound a thought,
Hearing it by this distant northern sea.

The Sea of Faith
Was once, too, at the full, and round earth's shore
Lay like the folds of a bright girdle furl'd.
But now I only hear
Its melancholy, long, withdrawing roar,
Retreating, to the breath
Of the night-wind, down the vast edges drear
And naked shingles of the world.

Ah, love, let us be true
To one another! for the world, which seems
To lie before us like a land of dreams,
So various, so beautiful, so new,
Hath really neither joy, nor love, nor light,
Nor certitude, nor peace, nor help for pain;
And we are here as on a darkling plain
Swept with confused alarms of struggle and flight,
Where ignorant armies clash by night.

Arnold's poem, like Hopkins', evokes a pensive mood, a sad and philosophic calm of mind or soul, arising from our sympathetic apprehension of the speaker's own understanding of the human reality ("we are here as on a darkling plain"). Though we are not in the same situation as the speaker, we are moved by his dismal attitude and, consequently, are brought into a similar emotional state. For we are made, from the outset, to contemplate a seascape[26] in that manner by which we also perceive, as he does, "the turbid ebb and flow, Of human misery." He is, of course, reacting to his own individual situation: he is with his beloved[27] and,

26 The seascape in Arnold's poem not only projects the lover's mood but also kindles his thought ("we Find also in the sound a thought"). Compare with Tennyson's "Break, Break, Break" in which, however, the speaker's *action* is clearly different; i.e., Tennyson's speaker is mourning the loss of someone very dear to him. As in Housman's "With Rue My Heart Is Laden," we feel *differently* from the speaker in Tennyson's poem.

27 It can be said that, while Hopkins' poem is a lyric of *expression* (as we have defined the term), Arnold's is a lyric of *address* (as Marvell's "To His Coy Mistress" is); i.e., Arnold's lover is *actually* addressing his beloved (who, as in Marvell's poem, remains passive throughout as the object merely of the lover's action or address). If this is true, then Arnold's poem is, on that ground alone, *formally different* from Hopkins'. Yet, it can also be said, contrariwise, that Arnold's lover is addressing his beloved *only in his thoughts*; i.e. like Margaret, she is merely the *occasion* of the speaker's *meditation*. If this is true, then the speaker's action is not that of persuading his beloved to his own point of view (as in Marvell's poem), but only that of meditating on the human condition (as in Hopkins' poem). Which seems the more probable as the *dramatic situation*? The critic, as "literalist of the imagination," would put more weight on the first hypothesis since, after all, we cannot ignore the lover's invitation to his beloved ("Come to the window . . . Listen"!) nor his touching plea ("Ah, love, let us be true To one another!"). Nevertheless, Hopkins' and Arnold's poems strike me as *essentially* the same *kind* of lyric poem since, above all, they have essentially the same *power*. The lover's *action* (the primary part of the *object* of imitation), though an *actual* address, has yet, as poetically rendered, the character of a meditation. He is not so much talking to his beloved as talking in her presence. The very opening stanza of the poem underscores this characteristic of his address. If this is true, then he is not

[251]

reflecting that "the world ... Hath really neither joy, nor love .. nor help for pain," he falls back on the possibility or, rather, the illusion that he and his beloved may still "be true To one another." Though necessarily an illusion if his own perception of the world were true, love or fidelity to one another is yet the only thing that may give solace to his troubled soul. Our sympathetic apprehension of such a reflection (which does not require our intellectual assent to such a dismal outlook any more than *Hamlet* requires us to believe that womankind is essentially weak in their moral being) affects us with a kind of sad and philosophic resignation to the solitariness of the human condition in which love itself, though it gives spiritual solace, is yet finally a mere illusion.[28]

But Housman's "With Rue My Heart Is Laden" is a different *form or species* of the lyric poem from either Hopkins' or Arnold's poem. It is the *kind* of lyric which evokes a grave or solemn frame of mind arising from our sympathetic reaction to *someone's emotional condition*. In this particular instance, we feel differently from the lyric speaker since what moves him is different from what moves us; i.e., he is moved by the premature death of his friends, but we are moved by his rueful mood. The effect, therefore, is a solemn but not sorrowful state of mind; we do not grieve with the speaker, yet we are affected through sympathy by his grief.

William Wordsworth's "She Dwelt Among the Untrodden Ways" is essentially the same *kind* of lyric poem as Housman's.[29]

so much persuading his beloved nor pleading with her, but brooding in her presence on the human condition ("the world...Hath really neither joy, nor love," etc.). When, therefore, he invites her to "Come to the window" or appeals to her to "be true" to him, as he to her, such action or behavior, as it seems to me, is chiefly a device by which the lover underscores the burden of his reflection. We respond, then, primarily to his meditation (or, his action is chiefly meditation).

[28] It would be interesting, I think, to compare the "theme" of Arnold's poem (i.e., the speaker's thought in that poem) with the "theme" of Sherwood Anderson's "Seeds" (i.e., the narrator's thought in that story). Incidentally, "Seeds" is a *didactic* short story.

[29] But not Wordsworth's "A Slumber Did My Spirit Seal" since it has a different power.

She Dwelt Among the Untrodden Ways

She dwelt among the untrodden ways
   Beside the springs of Dove,
A maid whom there were none to praise
   And very few to love:

A violet by a mossy stone
   Half hidden from the eye!
—Fair as a star, when only one
   Is shining in the sky.

She lived unknown, and few could know
   When Lucy ceased to be;
But she is in her grave, and, oh,
   The difference to me!

As in Housman's poem, someone's "speech" assumes the form of a recollection that at last breaks forth into a cry of deep inner distress. It evokes in us a solemn frame of mind arising from our sympathetic reaction to the speaker's emotional state. It is he who grieves the loss of his beloved, he who feels the exact difference that her absence makes in his own life. We feel his grief but do not ourselves grieve; we are merely put into a solemn frame of mind through our sympathy for the speaker.[30]

In such poems, then, as "Spring and Fall" and "Dover Beach,"[31] we feel similarly as the speaker since what moves

---

[30] Incidentally, as to whether the speaker's description of Lucy is "unflattering" (since the searcher of "poetic" irony would be quick to ferret this out), it may be observed that (1) his intention is not to praise Lucy ("A maid whom there were none to praise") but to lament his loss; (2) he is recalling with rueful affection how "she lived unknown," a maid whom there were "very few to love"; (3) the violet and the star put the stress not upon any "praise" of Lucy so much as upon her obscurity and the charm, for the speaker, of her plainness and simple ways; and (4) above all, his recollection of Lucy is meant to evoke, not so much any particular emotion toward her (say, our admiration or pity) as his own pain and distress over her death. Indeed, if the speaker had made her out to be a startling beauty or a magnetic personality, like Walter Savage Landor's Dirce or Lucretia Borgia, we would probably not be as profoundly touched by "the difference" that her death has made to the speaker.

[31] Yet another instance is W. H. Auden's "Musée Des Beaux Arts." But there is at least one crucial difference which affects our response to it: where both Hopkins and Arnold use a more or less elevated style, Auden is content with a plain, even colloquial, style. One may also note the somewhat sardonic irony of Auden's lyric speaker.

us in the poetic simulation is a *perception* about the human reality similar to that of the speaker—a perception which, though it does not require our intellectual assent, yet affects us emotionally since we apprehend its validity through our sympathy for the speaker in his own individual situation. But in such poems as "With Rue My Heart is Laden" or "She Dwelt Among the Untrodden Ways,"[32] we feel differently from the speaker since what moves us in the poetic imitation is someone's *emotional condition*—we apprehend its cause but, though we sympathize with the speaker in his own situation, it obviously cannot produce in us the same emotion. In such poems also as "The Groundhog,"[33] we feel differently from the speaker since what moves us in the poetic representation is someone's *inner struggle* or conflict with himself *which exhibits his "noble" character.*

In an important sense, of course—and, perhaps, in the final analysis,—all great art is ultimately *sui generis*. No other work, for example, is quite like *The Divine Comedy* or *Paradise Lost*; by the same token, no other lyric poem is quite like "The Groundhog" or "Stopping By Woods on a Snowy Evening." But we are interested primarily in *essential forms or structures,* not in the unique and individual character of particular poems. In general, then, it is safe to assume that, though indeed we may discover lyric forms of the *sui generis* type, poems with essentially similar forms or structures have been written; that, considering the long history of lyric poetry, most lyric forms have probably given rise to a considerable number of poems which are essentially similar in kind.

[32] Tennyson's "Break, Break, Break" is, of course, essentially the same *kind* of poem as either one.
[33] We have not, till now, come upon another lyric poem that is similar in *kind* to Eberhart's "The Groundhog." Yeats' "Sailing to Byzantium" does *not* show the old man's conflict with himself; his *action*, as the poem renders it, is that of firming up his mind to a choice that he has already made (or that of clarifying to himself the exact nature of his choice). Besides, the *character* that his action manifests is far nobler than that of our speaker in "The Groundhog." Then, too (and above all), the *power* of Yeats' poem is quite different: *not* a great sadness of spirit but rather, a kind of noble exaltation.

Bibliography

Angeles, Carlos A. *a stun of jewels*. Alberto S. Florentino, 1963. (For two poems, "From the Rooftop" and "The Summer Trees," pp. 9, 10.)

Arcellana, Francisco. *Storymasters V: 15 Stories*. Alberto S. Florentino, 1973. (For "Trilogy of the Turtles," pp. 8-13.)

Barnstone, Willis (tr.). *Greek Lyric Poetry*. Bantam Books, 1962. (For poems by Alkaios, Sappho, and Archilochos.)

Basho. *The Narrow Road to the Deep North and Other Travel Sketches*. Tr. with intro. by Nobuyuki Yuasa. Penguin Books, 1966. (For Basho's own account of the genesis of one of his own haiku.)

Bateson, F. W. [Comments on "O Western Wind"] in Frederick L. Gwynn *et al.* (eds.), *The Case For Poetry*, p. 13.

Baudelaire, Charles. *Les Fleurs du Mal*. Tr. into English by George Dillon and Edna St. Vincent Millay. Washington Square, 1962. (For Baudelaire's "A celle qui est trop gaie.") See also Baudelaire's *Selected Verse;* ed. with prose translations by Francis Scarfe (Penguin Books, 1961).

Brooks, Cleanth. "Irony as a Principle of Structure" in Morton Dauwen Zabel (ed.), *Literary Opinion in America*, II, 729-41.

──────────. *The Well Wrought Urn. Studies in the Structure of Poetry*. Harcourt, Brace, Harvest Books, 1947. Especially "The Language of Paradox," pp. 3-21; and "Keats' Sylvan Historian: History Without Footnotes," pp. 151-66.

──────────, John Thibaut Purser, and Robert Penn Warren (eds.). *An Approach to Literature;* alternate fourth edn.

Appleton-Century-Crofts, 1967. (For the interpretation of "Edward," pp. 289-92.)

———————— and Robert Penn Warren (eds.). *Understanding Poetry;* third edn. Holt, Rinehart, and Winston, 1960. (For the interpretation of Pound's "In a Station of the Metro," pp. 88-91.)

Burke, Kenneth. "Symbolic Action in a Poem By Keats" in *A Grammar of Motives* and *A Rhetoric of Motives* (World Publishing Co., Meridian Books, 1962), pp. 447-63. See also his "The Problem of the Intrinsic (as reflected in the Neo-Aristotelian School)," pp. 465-84, a critique of the "Neo-Aristotelian School" of critics (*i.e.*, Crane, Olson, *et al.*) from Burke's own "dramatistic perspective."

Crane, R. S. (ed.). *Critics and Criticism Ancient and Modern.* University of Chicago, 1952. Especially his "Introduction," pp. 1-24. But see also his "I. A. Richards on the Art of Interpretation," pp. 27-44; "The Critical Monism of Cleanth Brooks," pp. 83-107; and "The Concept of Plot and the Plot of *Tom Jones*," pp. 616-47.

———————. *The Idea of the Humanities and Other Essays Critical and Historical;* 2 vols. University of Chicago, 1967. Especially "Questions and Answers in the Teaching of Literary Texts," II, 176-93. But see also his "Philosophy, Literature, and the History of Ideas," I, 173-87; "History versus Criticism in the Study of Literature," II, 3-24; "Criticism as Inquiry; or, The Perils of the 'High Priori Road'," II, 25-44; "Every Man His Own Critic," II, 194-214; and "Varieties of Dramatic Criticism," II, 215-35.

———————. *The Languages of Criticism and the Structure of Poetry.* University of Toronto, 1953.

Dickinson, Emily. *Selected Poems and Letters.* Ed. Robert N. Linscott. Doubleday Anchor Books, 1959. (For Dickinson's "The Last Night That She Lived.")

Eliot, T. S. *The Complete Poems and Plays, 1909-1950.* Harcourt, Brace and World, 1952. (For Eliot's "Aunt Helen.")

Empson, William. *Seven Types of Ambiguity.* World Publishing Co., Meridian Books, 1955.

BIBLIOGRAPHY

Ghiselin, Brewster. [An interpretation of Eberhart's "The Groundhog"] in Oscar Williams (ed.), *Master Poems*, pp. 1022-26.

Gwynn, Frederick L., Ralph W. Condee, and Arthur O. Lewis (eds.). *The Case For Poetry.* Prentice-Hall, 1954. (For "Critique" of "O Western Wind," p. 13; see also symbolic interpretations of Blake's "The Sick Rose" by E. M. W. Tillyard and C. M. Bowra, p. 25.)

Hanzo, Thomas A. [Comments on Pound's "In a Station of the Metro"] in *The Case For Poetry*, p. 287.

Henderson, Harold G. *An Introduction to Haiku.* Doubleday Anchor Books, 1958. (For the haiku in our text and critical commentary on them.)

Hsu, Kai-yu (tr.). *Twentieth Century Chinese Poetry: an Anthology.* Doubleday Anchor Books, 1964. (For poems by Yü P'ing-Po, Ping Hsin, and Wen I-to.)

McKeon, Richard. "Imitation and Poetry" in his *Thought Action and Passion* (University of Chicago, 1954), pp. 102-221.

——————. "Literary Criticism and the Concept of Imitation in Antiquity" in R. S. Crane (ed.), *Critics and Criticism*, pp. 147-75. See also his "Aristotle's Conception of Language and the Arts of Language," pp. 176-231; and "The Philosophic Bases of Art and Criticism," pp. 463-545.

Olson, Elder. "Hamlet and the Hermeneutics of Drama," *Modern Philology* (Feb. 1964), pp. 225-37.

——————. "Introduction" [to Lyric Poetry] and "*The* Lyric" (both MSS.).

——————. "An Outline of Poetic Theory" in *Critics and Criticism*, pp. 546-66. See also his "William Empson, Contemporary Criticism, and Poetic Diction," pp. 45-82; "The Argument of Longinus' *On the Sublime*," pp. 232-59; and "A Dialogue on Symbolism," pp. 567-94.

——————. "The Poetic Method of Aristotle: Its Powers and Limitations" in *Aristotle's Poetics and English Literature*, ed. Elder Olson (University of Chicago, 1965), pp. 175-91. See also his "Introduction," pp. ix-xxviii.

——————. *The Poetry of Dylan Thomas.* University of Chicago, Phoenix Books, 1961. Especially his analysis of Thomas' "Altarwise By Owl-Light," pp. 63-89.

[257]

————————. *The Theory of Comedy*. Indiana University, 1968.

————————. *Tragedy and the Theory of Drama*. Wayne State University, 1961.

Pound, Ezra. [His own account of the genesis of "In a Station of the Metro"] in *The Case For Poetry*, p. 287; also in Brooks and Warren (eds.), *Understanding Poetry*, p. 90.

Quiller-Couch, Sir Arthur (ed.). *The New Oxford Book of English Verse;* new edn. Oxford University Press, 1939, (For Walter Savage Landor's "Mother, I Cannot Mind My Wheel.")

Ransom, John Crowe. "Criticism as Pure Speculation" in Morton Dauwen Zabel (ed.), *Literary Opinion in America*, II, 639-54.

————————. "Poetry: A Note in Ontology" in James Harry Smith and Edd Winfield Parks (eds.). *The Great Critics*, pp. 769-87.

Richards, I. A. "Science and Poetry" in Mark Schorer *et al.* (eds.), *Criticism: The Foundations of Modern Literary Judgment*, pp. 505-23; the essay is also found in Smith and Parks (eds.), *The Great Critics*, pp. 732-66.

Schorer, Mark, Josephine Miles, and Gordon McKenzie (eds.). *Criticism: The Foundations of Modern Literary Judgment*. Harcourt, Brace, 1958.

Smith, James Harry, and Edd Winfield Parks (eds.). *The Great Critics;* third edn. W. W. Norton, 1951.

Stauffer, Donald A. [Comments on "O Western Wind"] in *The Case For Poetry*, p. 13.

Stevens, Wallace. *The Necessary Angel. Essays on Reality and the Imagination*. Vintage Books, 1965. (The best introduction to Stevens' poetry; a major instance in the "criticism of qualities.")

Sutton, Walter, and Richard Foster (eds.). *Modern Criticism Theory and Practice*. Odyssey Press, 1963. (For Kenneth Burke's "Symbolic Action in a Poem By Keats," pp. 571-80; and Cleanth Brooks' "Keats' Sylvan Historian: History Without Footnotes," pp. 580-87.)

Tindall, William York. *A Reader's Guide to Dylan Thomas*. Noonday Press, 1962. Especially his analysis of Thomas' "Altarwise By Owl-Light," pp. 126-43.

Warren, Robert Penn. "Pure and Impure Poetry" in his *Selected Essays* (Vintage Books, 1966), pp. 3-31. See also his "The Themes of Robert Frost," pp. 118-36; and "A Poem of Pure Imagination: An Experiment in Reading," pp. 198-305.

Williams, Oscar (ed.). *Immortal Poems*. Washington Square, 1952. (For most of the poems in our text.)

——————. *Master Poems*. Washington Square, 1967. (For James Wright's comments on Frost's "Stopping By Woods," pp. 920-25; Brewster Ghiselin's comments on Eberhart's "The Groundhog," pp. 1022-26; and William York Tindall's comments on Thomas' "Altarwise By Owl-Light," pp. 1063-72.)

Untermeyer, Louis (ed.). *Great Poems*. Simon and Schuster, Permabooks, 1953. (For e.e. cummings' "somewhere i have never traveled.")

Zabel, Morton Dauwen (ed.). *Literary Opinion in America;* third edn., rev.; 2 vols. Harper Torchbooks, 1962.

Index